Gender in the Middle Ages

Volume 16

TREASON AND MASCULINITY IN MEDIEVAL ENGLAND

Gender in the Middle Ages

ISSN 1742-870X

This series investigates the representation and construction of masculinity and femininity in the Middle Ages from a variety of disciplinary and interdisciplinary perspectives. It aims in particular to explore the diversity of medieval genders, and such interrelated contexts and issues as sexuality, social class, race and ethnicity, and orthodoxy and heterodoxy.

Proposals or queries should be sent in the first instance to the editors or to the publisher, at the addresses given below; all submissions will receive prompt and informed consideration.

Professor Jacqueline Murray, Department of History, University of Guelph, Guelph, Ontario, N1G 2W1, Canada

Professor Diane Watt, School of Literature and Languages, University of Surrey, Guildford, Surrey GU2 7XH, UK

Boydell & Brewer Limited, PO Box 9, Woodbridge, Suffolk IP12 3DF, UK

Previously published volumes in the series are listed at the end of this book.

CONTENTS

PREFACE AND ACKNOWLEDGEMENTS

I have long been interested in political dissent: how people position themselves in opposition to the political authority embodied in individuals or in institutions; the language they use to articulate their demands and justify their resistance; and the strategies they deploy when protest 'within the system' fails to achieve change. As I was writing this book, I found myself equal parts heartened by and fearful for Hong Kong's pro-democracy protestors, and disturbed by the discourses of treason that became so prominent in both UK and US politics in the febrile climate of Brexit and Donald Trump's presidency, with combatants on all sides terming each other traitors and enemies of the nation. While resisting the temptation to make ahistorical comparisons, I am nevertheless struck by certain echoes of the medieval past in our current political moment, not least in the distinctively gendered terms in which battle lines over loyalty, treason and claims to power are so often drawn. Watching the rise of authoritarian 'strong men' across the globe and the parallel demeaning treatment of women politicians reinforced my own conviction (if such reinforcement were even necessary) that we cannot write comprehensive political histories, whether of the recent or distant past, without fully incorporating gender into the analysis. This book focuses on the history of treason, a phenomenon that I argue was inherently gendered by its utter entanglement in conflicts over manly honour and claims to political agency in an overtly masculine body politic. I have been intellectually inspired and practically guided by the rich body of research on queenship and, more recently, on kingship that puts questions of gender and political authority firmly at the centre of historical inquiry. I hope my own contribution to the field of gender and medieval politics might in turn inspire others to travel further along the same path.

I am indebted to the many generous scholars who have helped me along the way. Andrew Brown, Christopher Fletcher, Kim Phillips, Karen Jillings, Clare Monagle, Katie Barclay, Mark Ormrod, Sally Fisher and Christopher van der Krogt read and critiqued work in progress, discussed ideas, challenged my thinking and asked probing questions. I have likewise been fortunate to enjoy the support of my colleagues in History at Massey University, who have proved an ever-reliable source of practical advice and scholarly wisdom. I also owe my thanks to the staff of The National Archives, Kew and the British Library for their invaluable expertise and guidance.

I was able to pursue research on medieval England from Aotearoa New Zealand thanks to the financial support of a number of organisations. Funding to attend international conferences and to conduct archival research was gratefully received from the Massey University Travel Abroad Bursary, the Australian and New Zealand Association for Medieval and Early Modern Studies (ANZAMEMS), the International Medieval Congress (IMC Leeds), the Society for the Study of Medieval Languages and Literature and Monash University. I also benefited from a grant from the Institute of English Studies (University of London) that enabled me to attend the London International Palaeography Summer School, a vital step in learning to decipher medieval legal records.

Finally, on a personal note, I wish to thank my family and friends for their curiosity and sustained encouragement. I am particularly grateful to my partner Andrew, who patiently listened to many hours of research-related monologue while keeping me well supplied with wine and snacks, and to my ginger cats, Tweak and Jones. The latter were not at all helpful but as my daily companions throughout the writing process, they provided much-needed periodic comic relief.

A NOTE ON TRANSLATIONS

Translations from manuscript Latin and French sources are the author's own unless noted. Scribal abbreviations have been expanded. To address constraints of space, words or phrases in the original language are only included where this is important to the argument or where there may be debate over translation. Middle English is quoted in the original, with any obscure or difficult words translated into modern English in brackets. Some of the manuscript legal records used here appear in print as partial transcriptions or translations. Where published versions exist, they are included in the footnotes and have been consulted in conjunction with the original records. Latin spelling has been modernised by substituting 'v' for 'u' and 'j' for 'i'.

ABBREVIATIONS

Adam Usk	*The Chronicle of Adam Usk, 1377–1421*, ed. and trans. C. Given-Wilson (Oxford, 1997).
AND	*Anglo-Norman Dictionary*, 7 vols., ed. Louise W. Stone, T. B. W. Reid and William Rothwell (London, 1977–92).
'Appendix II'	'Appendix II: The Confessions of Sir Thomas Gray of Heton, Richard, Earl of Cambridge and Henry, Lord Scrope of Masham', trans. T. B. Pugh, *Henry V and the Southampton Plot of 1415* (Gloucester, 1988), pp. 160–77.
BL	British Library
CCR	*Calendar of the Close Rolls*, 47 vols. (London, 1900–63).
Chronicle of John Hardyng	*The Chronicle of John Hardyng*, ed. Henry Ellis (London, 1812).
Chronicle of London	*A Chronicle of London from 1089 to 1483; Written in the Fifteenth Century and for the First Time Printed from Mss. In the British Museum*, ed. N. H. Nicolas and E. Tyrell (Felinfach, 1995).
Chronicles of the Revolution	*Chronicles of the Revolution, 1397–1400: The Reign of Richard II*, ed. and trans. Chris Given-Wilson (Manchester, 1993).
CPR	*Calendar of the Patent Rolls*, 53 vols. (London, 1891–1916).
An English Chronicle	*An English Chronicle 1377–1461: Edited from Aberystwyth, National Library of Wales Ms 21068 and Oxford Bodleian Library Ms Lyell 34*, ed. William Marx (Woodbridge, 2003).
Continuatio Eulogii	*Eulogium Historiarum sive Temporis*, III, ed. F. S. Haydon (London, 1863).
Foedera	*Rymer's Foedera*, 9 vols., ed. Thomas Rymer (London, 1739–1745).

Gesta Henrici Quinti	*Gesta Henrici Quinti. The Deeds of Henry the Fifth*, trans. Frank Taylor and John S. Roskell (Oxford, 1975).
Great Chronicle	Robert Fabyan, *The Great Chronicle of London*, ed. A. H. Thomas and I. D. Thornley (London, 1938).
HVRS	*Historia Vitae et Regni Ricardi Secundi*, ed. George B. Stow (Philadelphia, 1977).
MED	H. Kurath et al., *Middle English Dictionary* (Ann Arbor, 1954–2001).
Morley v. Salisbury	'A True Copy of the Roll of Proceeding in an Appeale of Treason before the Conestable and Marshall between Thomas Lord Morley, Appellant, and John De Montague, Earle of Salisbury, Defendant, Anno Primi Henrici Quarti', ed. M. H. Keen and M. Warner, in *Chronology, Conquest and Conflict in Medieval England. Camden Miscellany XXXIV* (London, 1997), pp. 169–95.
PPC	*Proceedings and Ordinances of the Privy Council of England: Volume 1, 10 Richard II MCCCLXXXVI to 11 Henry IV MCCCCX*, ed. N. H. Nicolas (London, 1834).
PROME	*The Parliament Rolls of Medieval England 1275–1504*, ed. C. Given-Wilson et al., CD-ROM (Leicester, 2005).
Select Cases	*Select Cases in the Court of King's Bench*, vol. 7, ed. G. O. Sayles, Selden Society 88 (London, 1971).
St Albans Chronicle I	*The St Albans Chronicle: The Chronica Maiora of Thomas Walsingham I. 1376–1394*, ed. and trans. John Taylor, Wendy R. Childs, and Leslie Watkiss (Oxford, 2003).
St Albans Chronicle II	*The St Albans Chronicle: The Chronica Maiora of Thomas Walsingham II. 1394–1422*, ed. and trans. John Taylor, Wendy R. Childs, and Leslie Watkiss (Oxford, 2011).
Statutes	*The Statutes of the Realm*, 9 vols. (London, 1810–25).
TNA	The National Archives, Kew
Westminster Chronicle	*The Westminster Chronicle, 1381–1394*, ed. and trans. L. C. Hector and Barbara F. Harvey (New York, 1982)

INTRODUCTION

The summer of 1415 found Henry V on England's south coast, readying ships and men for the French campaign that would culminate in his storied victory at Agincourt. In late July, he was shocked to discover that Henry Lescrope, Lord Masham, who was his trusted friend as well as a senior government official, was plotting to kill him and to destroy his great military enterprise. On 5 August, the nobleman was hauled up before a tribunal hastily assembled in Southampton, tried and convicted of treason. Royal justice proved swift and pitiless: Lescrope was beheaded that same afternoon.

Contemporary chroniclers depicted Lescrope in dramatic terms as a malicious double-dealing villain who had feigned love to Henry's face while conspiring behind his back to 'murder him with the sword because he had failed to do so with poison'.[1] Induced by 'the stench of French promises or bribes', he had sold out his king and countrymen for a handful of gold.[2] The official account of Lescrope's trial was less lurid than those found in the chronicles, but the execution process he was made to endure communicated in no uncertain terms his violation of manly loyalty to his king. He was first stripped of his elite status as a knight of the chivalric Order of the Garter in a ritual of public degradation that included tearing off his sword belt and striking off his spurs. He was then dragged through Southampton from its southern Watergate to the Northgate, where he was beheaded in the street.[3] Lescrope's severed head was sent north to York, where it was posted on the city wall at Micklegate Bar. As it decayed through the last days of a northern summer, it was a lingering reminder that any man who tried to strike the head from the body politic would find himself headless and his body divided.

When parliament met later the same year, the Southampton tribunal's judgment against Lescrope was re-enacted before the wider political community. The record preserved on the parliament roll condemned Lescrope as a man who had betrayed his king and by doing so, had destroyed his own manly honour and identity as a knight. It also included a more unusual determination: that Lescrope had betrayed 'the tongue in which he was born'.[4] This phrase incorporated into the judicial rhetoric a familiar trope

1 *St Albans Chronicle II*, p. 661. Lescrope's case is examined in Chapter Six.

2 *Gesta Henrici Quinti*, p. 19.

3 *PROME*, 'Henry V: November 1415', Item Six.

4 Ibid. The *PROME* editor has translated the Latin *lingua in qua natus est* as the 'nation in which he was born'.

of political discourse: when seeking parliament's support for war against France, English kings had sometimes claimed this was necessary because the French planned to invade England and to destroy the English language. In England's multilingual political culture, where French was used for much legal and administrative business including keeping the parliament roll itself, the linguistic politics of this claim were far from straightforward. Nevertheless, growing cultural associations between language, birth and national identity meant that speaking English was coming to be seen as a marker of *being* English.[5] The description of Lescrope as a traitor to his tongue was therefore intended to figure him as a traitor not only to his king but also to the English nation. Lescrope's fate had been sealed by a plea for mercy he wrote a few days prior to his death.[6] This letter, composed in first-person English and addressed directly to King Henry, presented a valiant if ultimately unsuccessful defence. Begging for his life, Lescrope swore he had only become involved in the plot in order to foil it from the inside. He supported this entreaty by recounting to Henry his many years of loyal knightly service both at home and abroad. Finally, he tried to convince the king that although he was guilty of stupidity, he had not been unfaithful; he remained the king's true man.

Lescrope's was just one of dozens of treason cases that tormented English political society in the later medieval period. The narratives it generated, from the chronicle portraits of Lescrope as the antithesis of chivalric manhood to the parliament roll's description of him as an enemy of the English nation, reflect the heinous but unfixed nature of this crime. John Bellamy's formative 1970 study *The Law of Treason in England in the Later Middle Ages* demonstrated that conflicts over the scope and meaning of treason played a critical role in negotiating the constitutional relationship between English kings, their subjects and the political abstraction of the crown.[7] Yet, despite renewed interest in constitutional history spearheaded by scholars of political culture such as Christine Carpenter and John Watts, there has been no extended examination of treason in late medieval England since Bellamy's account.[8]

5 W. M. Ormrod, 'The Use of English: Language, Law, and Political Culture in Fourteenth-Century England', *Speculum* 78 (2003), 750–87; Christopher Fletcher, 'Langue et nation en Angleterre à la fin du moyen âge', *Revue Francaise d'histoire des idées politiques* 2 (2012), 233–52; Andrea Ruddick, 'Ethnic Identity and Political Language in the King of England's Dominions: A Fourteenth-Century Perspective', *The Fifteenth Century VI. Identity and Insurgency in the Late Middle Ages*, ed. Linda Clark (Woodbridge, 2006), pp. 15–32; Ardis Butterfield, *The Familiar Enemy: Chaucer, Language, and Nation in the Hundred Years War* (Oxford, 2009). For the coalescence of national, legal and linguistic identity in a wider European context: John L. Watts, *The Making of Polities: Europe, 1300–1500* (Cambridge, 2009), pp. 141–3, 376–419.

6 TNA E 163/7/7 ms. 6 and 7.

7 J. G. Bellamy, *The Law of Treason in England in the Later Middle Ages* (Cambridge, 1970).

8 Christine Carpenter, *The Wars of the Roses: Politics and the Constitution in England,*

The 1352 statute was enacted in response to kings who used their prerogative powers to execute men without trial for an ever-widening array of offences that had not previously been considered treason according either to custom or to earlier common law precedents.[17] The political community therefore sought to clarify and limit the scope of treason and to ensure that in future, no subject would be convicted without a trial. But far from settling the definition of treason once and for all, the 1352 statute created more uncertainty because it became yet another touchstone, complicating but not displacing existing customary notions, common law precedents and the more expansive precepts found in Roman civil law.

Returning to Lescrope's case, we begin to get a better sense of how these different understandings of treason could apply in practice. The prosecution narrative portrayed Lescrope as a knight who had offended against manly honour by betraying his lord and he therefore merited the most shameful of deaths. This reflected perceptions of treason as an intimate crime focused upon the person of the king. At the same time, the judicial sentence reveals a more expansive construction of treason as an attack on the abstract political body of the state and a betrayal of the nation of England. Lescrope tried to counter the charges of treason through a performance of true manhood. He confessed that his plan to quash the plot himself had been unwise but insisted that despite this failure of wisdom, his bond of trust with the king (and implicitly, with the body politic of England) remained intact. In Lescrope's case the strategy failed, but in other cases accused men were able to evade conviction by threading the needle between customary, chivalric and more expansive state-oriented interpretations of treason. In the process, their defensive strategies invoked and helped to transform shared beliefs about the nature of true and false manhood.

Historians such as Maurice Keen, Alan Rogers and Theodore Plucknett have produced fine studies of treason law that remain essential reading, while literary scholars have addressed the ubiquity of treason as a theme in late medieval prose romances and poetry.[18] However, the central role of male bonding and of gendered notions of honour and betrayal in constructing legal and political responses to treason has been overlooked. Important new examinations of kingship demonstrate that until we account for the ways masculinity

17 Bellamy, *Law of Treason*, pp. 102–37; I. D. Thornley, 'The Act of Treasons, 1352', *History* 6 (1921), 106–8.

18 Keen, 'Treason Trials under the Law of Arms'; Alan Rogers, 'Parliamentary Appeals of Treason in the Reign of Richard II', *The American Journal of Legal History* 8 (1964), 95–124; T. F. T. Plucknett, 'Presidential Address: State Trials under Richard II', *Transactions of the Royal Historical Society* 2 (1952), 159–71; T. F. T. Plucknett, 'Presidential Address: Impeachment and Attainder', *Transactions of the Royal Historical Society* 3 (1953), 145–58; Michael Hanrahan, 'Seduction and Betrayal: Treason in the *Prologue* to the *Legend of Good Women*', *The Chaucer Review* 30 (1996), 229–40; Megan Leitch, *Romancing Treason: The Literature of the Wars of the Roses* (Oxford, 2015).

and manhood shaped assumptions about power and who should wield it, we will fail to fully grasp how medieval political culture functioned and why consensus so often broke down.[19] It has been over 30 years since Joan Scott's seminal call to consider gender as a category of analysis began to transform the field of political history.[20] Yet as Katherine Lewis recently pointed out, 'the potential for masculinity to illuminate medieval politics, and indeed for politics to illuminate medieval masculinity, is still left largely unrealized'.[21]

Why should we care about masculinities and manhood in a history of the medieval politics of treason? My goal here is to illuminate how gender mediated relationships between kings and their subjects when the accusations of treason flew in specific moments of crisis, but also to reveal the ways these conflicts over treason were integral to the gendering of the body politic and were implicated in the emergence of a nascent English nation-state. Recent scholarship recognises that critiques of manhood and masculinity must be incorporated into histories of nationhood and state building because gender is integral to determining how power is conceived of, legitimised and distributed.[22] Processes that characterise the emergence of nation-states, such as the development of a centralised judicial and administrative machinery, the creation of a professionalised military and the establishment of representative political institutions, bring with them deeper gender divisions between men and women; gender difference then works to naturalise other differences, including national difference.[23] These gendered processes not only produce political systems and institutions that accord to men roles, rights and privileges that are not accessible to women; they also underpin and reinforce hierarchies of power between men. In his influential writings on gender and nineteenth-century British imperialism, John Tosh argues that attention to

19 Christopher Fletcher, *Richard II: Manhood, Youth, and Politics, 1377–99* (Oxford, 2008); Katherine J. Lewis, *Kingship and Masculinity in Late Medieval England* (New York, 2013); Rachel Stone, *Morality and Masculinity in the Carolingian Empire* (Cambridge, 2012).

20 Joan W. Scott, 'Gender: A Useful Category of Historical Analysis', *The American Historical Review* 91 (1986), 1053–75.

21 Lewis, *Kingship and Masculinity*, p. 3.

22 A. Mark Liddle, 'State, Masculinities and Law: Some Comments on Gender and English State-Formation', *British Journal of Criminology* 36 (1996), 361–80; Susan Broomhall and Jacqueline Van Gent, eds, *Governing Masculinities in the Early Modern Period: Regulating Selves and Others* (Farnham, 2011); Christopher Fletcher, Sean Brady, Rachel E. Moss and Lucy Riall, eds, *The Palgrave Handbook of Masculinity and Political Culture in Europe* (London, 2018).

23 Anne McClintock, '"No Longer in a Future Heaven": Gender, Race and Nationalism', *Dangerous Liaisons: Gender, Nation, and Postcolonial Perspectives*, ed. McClintock, Aamir Mufti and Ella Shohat (Minneapolis, 1997), pp. 89–112; Joane Nagel, 'Masculinity and Nationalism – Gender and Sexuality in the Making of Nations', *Nations and Nationalism: A Reader*, ed. Philip Spencer and Howard Wollman (Edinburgh, 2005), pp. 110–30.

masculinity is essential for understanding state formation and political culture because in most societies, 'the political order can be seen as a reflection of the gender order in society as a whole, in which case the political virtues are best understood as the prescribed masculine virtues writ large'.[24]

Masculinity became an explicit focus for medieval historians in the 1990s, with early studies exploring how medieval masculinities were constructed against women and the feminine.[25] More recent scholarship has stressed the need to avoid reducing all gender difference to a masculine / feminine binary, recognising that masculinities are constructed not only against women and the feminine, but also in relation to other men.[26] This approach accepts that manhood was not something that men automatically had by virtue of their biology. Rather, masculine identity and social status had to be earned, performed and constantly defended and it depended on recognition and validation by other men. This gendered dynamic structured the overtly masculine polity of late medieval England, a time and place where most women were excluded from formal political participation.[27] In medieval political theory, the body politic was imagined by default to be a male body, with the king as its head and his greater and lesser male subjects as its working limbs. In practice, men monopolised the institutions and offices of government, and it was men who dominated channels of counsel and critique. In late medieval England, kings had little real coercive power so that royal government functioned largely through the voluntary cooperation of men of the middling and upper ranks of political society.[28] These were the men who

24 John Tosh, 'Hegemonic Masculinity and the History of Gender', *Masculinities in Politics and War: Gendering Modern History*, ed. Stefan Dudink, Karen Hagemann and John Tosh (Manchester, 2004), pp. 41–58 (p. 41). See also Michael Roper and John Tosh, eds, *Manful Assertions: Masculinities in Britain since 1800* (New York, 1991).

25 For example, Clare A. Lees, Thelma S. Fenster and Jo Ann McNamara, eds, *Medieval Masculinities: Regarding Men in the Middle Ages* (Minneapolis, 1994).

26 Jeffrey Jerome Cohen and Bonnie Wheeler, eds, *Becoming Male in the Middle Ages* (New York, 1997); D. M. Hadley, ed., *Masculinity in Medieval Europe* (London, 1999); Jacqueline Murray, ed., *Conflicted Identities and Multiple Masculinities: Men in the Medieval West* (New York, 1999); Ruth Mazo Karras, *From Boys to Men: Formations of Masculinity in Late Medieval Europe* (Philadelphia, 2003).

27 This is not to say women were unable or unwilling to engage in politics, but they did so by more indirect means: Mary Carpenter Erler and Maryanne Kowaleski, eds, *Gendering the Master Narrative: Women and Power in the Middle Ages* (Ithaca, 2003); Carolyn P. Collette, *Performing Polity: Women and Agency in the Anglo-French Tradition, 1385–1620* (Turnhout, 2006); Jacqueline Broad and Karen Green, *A History of Women's Political Thought in Europe: 1400–1700* (Cambridge, 2014). For an important critical assessment of the historiography of medieval political theory see Theresa Earenfight, 'Where Do We Go From Here? Some Thoughts on Power and Gender in the Middle Ages', *Medieval Feminist Forum: A Journal of Gender and Sexuality* 51 (2016), 116–31.

28 W. M. Ormrod, *Political Life in Medieval England, 1300–1450* (New York, 1995); G. L. Harriss, 'The Dimensions of Politics', *The McFarlane Legacy: Studies in Late Medieval Politics and Society*, ed. R. H. Britnell and A. J. Pollard (New York, 1995), pp. 1–20; G.

collected the taxes, staffed an increasingly sophisticated royal justice system and administrative bureaucracy, and provided soldiers for the king's wars. They inhabited a complex web of relationships that were at once personal and political. Women were integral to this web because they connected men to each other through marriage, kinship and the operations of patronage. However, the political system as a whole was ordered by masculine virtues of honour, loyalty, service, 'good lordship' and the notion of 'worship', which encompassed a man's individual honour and his reputation and standing among other men.[29]

In order to tease out the ways relationships between men were tested and transformed through conflicts over treason, I draw on the concept of homosociality. Homosociality allows historians to examine the ways masculinity interacted with other determinants of political subjecthood such as ethnicity, religious identity and social status to construct, reinforce or subvert relationships between men within social and political hierarchies.[30] Importantly, the concept of homosociality helps to bridge the gap between cultural history, which has tended to focus on symbolic and discursive representations of gender to the exclusion of men's lived experiences, and social history.[31] The framework of homosociality acknowledges that manhood and masculinities are not purely discursive abstractions but that manhood is grounded in and performed through sexed male bodies that exist in the

L. Harriss, *Shaping the Nation: England 1360–1461* (New York, 2005), Part I: Political Society.

29 Philippa Maddern, 'Honour among the Pastons: Gender and Integrity in Fifteenth-Century English Provincial Society', *Journal of Medieval History* 14 (1988), 357–71; Rosemary Horrox, 'Service', *Fifteenth-Century Attitudes: Perceptions of Society in Late Medieval England*, ed. Rosemary Horrox (Cambridge, 1994), pp. 61–78; Derek G. Neal, *The Masculine Self in Late Medieval England* (Chicago, 2008), pp. 16–25; Watts, *Henry VI*, pp. 86–90.

30 R. W. Connell, *Masculinities*, 2nd ed. (Berkeley, 2005), pp. 77–81, 109–12; Tosh, 'Hegemonic Masculinity'; R. W. Connell and James W. Messerschmidt, 'Hegemonic Masculinity Rethinking the Concept', *Gender & Society* 19 (2005), 829–59; Stefan Dudink, 'The Trouble with Men: Problems in the History of "Masculinity"', *European Journal of Cultural Studies* 1 (1998), 419–31. For examples of homosociality applied to medieval contexts: Karras, *Boys to Men*; Kim M. Phillips, 'Masculinities and the Medieval English Sumptuary Laws', *Gender & History* 19 (2007), 22–42; Rachel E. Moss, 'Ready to Disport with You: Homosocial Culture amongst the Wool Merchants of Fifteenth-Century Calais', *History Workshop Journal* 86 (2018), 1–21.

31 Karen Harvey and Alexandra Shepard, 'What Have Historians Done with Masculinity? Reflections on Five Centuries of British History, circa 1500–1950', *Journal of British Studies* 44 (2005), 274–80; Derek G. Neal, 'What Can Historians Do with Clerical Masculinity? Lessons from Medieval Europe', *Negotiating Clerical Identities: Priests, Monks and Masculinity in the Middle Ages*, ed. Jennifer D. Thibodeaux (New York, 2010), pp. 16–36; Christopher Fletcher, 'The Whig Interpretation of Masculinity? Honour and Sexuality in Late Medieval Manhood', *What Is Masculinity?*, ed. John H. Arnold and Sean Brady (Basingstoke, 2011), pp. 57–75.

material and social world. By analysing the performance of manhood and relationships between men along gradations of dominant ('hegemonic'), complicit and subordinate (or marginalised) masculinities, historians can foreground the role of gender in organising social and political hierarchies that implicitly or explicitly exclude or deprecate women and the feminine.

The narratives of treason prosecutions characterised traitors first and foremost as false men because they had defied or corrupted natural homosocial bonds. To understand the gendered implications of the legal rhetoric, we must first be cognisant of the broader context in which ideas about manhood were deployed and debated in late medieval England. Christopher Fletcher has convincingly argued that terms such as 'manly' and 'manliness' conveyed a dominant ideal of masculinity most strongly associated with qualities seen as knightly.[32] These qualities included personal honour, physical and moral strength, martial prowess, the upholding of justice and unswerving loyalty to one's lord.[33] While these qualities were expected of men of noble or knightly status, they were also relevant further down the social order. The men of England's rising merchant, artisan and professional classes adapted chivalric ideals to a model of civic manhood in which manly worship, loyalty, moral and physical self-governance, and service to the common good were central (even if that service was primarily financial or administrative rather than military).[34] This constellation of masculine virtues influenced the ways the crime of treason was constructed in the legal rhetoric of prosecution, and informed the strategies accused men used to defend themselves and to justify their political resistance.

When men asserted their own manliness or measured that of their fellow men, their judgments coalesced around the notion of 'trueness'. To be true in the sense of loyal, honest and keeping one's word was central to performing and defending masculine identity and honour regardless of a man's position in the social hierarchy, from noblemen and knights down to peasants and servants. Indeed, from his analysis of literary, didactic and legal sources, Derek Neal concludes that trueness 'may be one valence of masculinity not varying with social status'.[35] Trueness was connected to the ubiquitous cultural value attributed to a man's sworn word, with social, economic and

32 Fletcher, *Richard II*, pp. 25–51; Idem, 'Whig Interpretation of Masculinity?'.

33 Maurice Keen, *Chivalry* (New Haven, 1984), pp. 149–60, 224–37; Richard W. Kaeuper, *Chivalry and Violence in Medieval Europe* (Oxford, 1999); Karras, *Boys to Men*, pp. 20–66.

34 Shannon McSheffrey, 'Men and Masculinity in Late Medieval London Civic Culture: Governance, Patriarchy, and Reputation', *Conflicted Identities*, ed. Murray, pp. 243–78; P. J. P. Goldberg, 'Masters and Men in Later Medieval England', *Masculinity in Medieval Europe*, ed. Hadley, pp. 56–70; Isabel Davis, *Writing Masculinity in the Later Middle Ages* (Cambridge, 2010); Stephanie Tarbin, 'Civic Manliness in London, c. 1380–1550', *Governing Masculinities*, ed. Broomhall and Van Gent, pp. 23–46.

35 Neal, *Masculine Self*, p. 44.

political relationships between men being enacted and regulated through the public performance of vows and oaths.[36] In legal contexts, a man's oath made a contract and his sworn verbal testimony was a form of judicial proof, while his oral 'plaint' was an accepted way to initiate legal actions.[37] During the routine process of gaol delivery, an offender could be released or sent to trial based on the oaths of trustworthy men (*fidedignes*) as to his honour or lack of it; at trial, it was the jurors' sworn oaths that provided proof of the defendant's innocence or guilt and decided the judicial outcome.[38] The privileging of oral oaths and testimony derived from a customary concept of 'soothfastness', which expressed an ethical sense of truth that was grounded in a man's moral integrity and personal fidelity. In his influential study *A Crisis of Truth*, Richard Firth Green argued that in tandem with the expansion in written records over the course of the fourteenth century, the meaning of truth began to shift from this older customary association with 'sooth', meaning loyalty, honesty and fidelity especially as this was expressed in a man's word, to a narrower legalistic sense of truth as being in accordance with facts as these were represented by documentary evidence.[39] However, the two meanings were still intertwined so that in judicial contexts, men's words retained enormous value as both moral sooth and legal proof. More generally, too, while the growing use of written records meant that masculine bonds forged through verbal rituals were increasingly backed up by indentures and other documents, men's words remained integral to their social embodiment as true men. Recent studies of late medieval civic culture show that men's public speech – whether in positive forms such as oaths of citizenship and guild membership, or negative forms such as defamation and insults – was central to claiming and defending a place in homosocial political hierarchies.[40] If speech was integral to masculine

[36] Ibid., pp. 1–55; Steven Justice, *Writing and Rebellion: England in 1381* (Los Angeles, 1996), Chapter Four; Barbara A. Hanawalt, *Of Good and Ill Repute: Gender and Social Control in Medieval England* (New York, 1998), pp. 1–17; Ian Forrest, *Trustworthy Men: How Inequality and Faith Made the Medieval Church* (Princeton: Princeton University Press, 2018).

[37] Anthony Musson, *Medieval Law in Context: The Growth of Legal Consciousness from Magna Carta to the Peasants' Revolt* (Manchester, 2001), pp. 50–1, 221.

[38] Thomas Andrew Green, *Verdict According to Conscience: Perspectives on the English Criminal Trial Jury, 1200–1800* (Chicago, 1985), pp. 7–8, 20–7; J. B. Post, 'Jury Lists and Juries in the Late Fourteenth Century', *Twelve Good Men and True: The Criminal Trial Jury in England, 1200–1800*, ed. J. S. Cockburn and Thomas Andrew Green (Princeton, 1988), pp. 65–77.

[39] Richard Firth Green, *A Crisis of Truth: Literature and Law in Ricardian England* (Philadelphia, 1999), pp. 1–39. See also Michael T. Clanchy, *From Memory to Written Record: England 1066–1307* (London, 1979), pp. 1–57, 202–26.

[40] Jan Dumolyn and Jelle Haemers, '"A Bad Chicken Was Brooding": Subversive Speech in Late Medieval Flanders', *Past & Present* 214 (2012), 45–86; Jelle Haemers, 'Filthy and Indecent Words. Insults, Defamation, and Urban Politics in the Southern Low Countries, 1300–1550', *The Voices of the People in Late Medieval Europe. Communication*

embodiment as a true man, the corollary was that falseness, too, was gendered, so that liars, oath-breakers and others whose speech transgressed masculine norms and codes of honour were repudiated as false men.

The relationship between public speech, masculine embodiment and social identity as a true man took on a specific character in the context of treason. To foment armed rebellion, to put an iron spike in the king's bed or to have a necromancer's poisoned ointment applied to his saddle: these were all clearly acts of treason. But as shall be seen, treason could also encompass more amorphous transgressions of speech and thought, such as questioning the king's legitimacy, seeking to deprive him of his subjects' love or spreading false rumours with the intent of subverting the realm. But regardless of the particular form in which treason manifested, every instance was preceded by and predicated upon the breaking of bonds between men, whether the explicit bond of an oath or implicit bonds of affinity and allegiance. In a personal monarchy governed through a small, interconnected ruling elite, political and private loyalties were difficult to separate, so that a man who violated the king's trust was by definition a traitor. However, the knife cut both ways because the moral and ethical principle of trueness that was represented by keeping one's word applied as much to kings as it did to the men who served them. This became an important factor in treason trials when accused men justified their political resistance by claiming that it was the king who was the false man, because he had lied to, deceived or broken his sworn oath to his subjects.

The gendered terms in which accusations of treason were expressed and resisted, and the underlying cultural and constitutional conflicts that trial narratives illuminate, can only be grasped through detailed analysis of the sources for individual cases. By considering not only 'successful' cases (from the prosecution's point of view, those that resulted in a conviction) but also those that ended in acquittal or annulment, my analysis reveals that cultural understandings of true and false manhood guided people's expectations of how the law worked and delimited the legal interpretations they were prepared to accept or reject. I am interested in the ways kings and their officials constructed treason, but also in the terms in which accused men defended themselves and articulated their own identities as political subjects. However, there is no escaping the fact that in many cases, the only direct evidence we have for the latter was produced by the prosecuting authorities. This includes testimony about what the accused said and did, which was gathered either directly through the interrogation of suspects or from witnesses. This testimony was translated from verbal English into the written French of official

---

and Popular Politics, ed. Jan Dumolyn et al. (Turnhout, 2014), pp. 247–67; Christian D. Liddy, '"Sir Ye Be Not Kyng": Citizenship and Speech in Late Medieval and Early Modern England', *The Historical Journal* 60 (2017), 571–96; Bronach C. Kane, 'Defamation, Gender and Hierarchy in Late Medieval Yorkshire', *Social History* 43 (2018), 356–74.

legal record in third-person reported speech. In some instances, we also have the direct first-person evidence of alleged traitors themselves, which appears in two forms: statements of confession, which were composed in English and endorsed by the accused as 'written by my own hand'; and copies of handbills, public letters or petitions that men were circulating to justify their resistance to the king and his regime. Historians interested in heresy and in the workings of criminal justice have long pondered the practical and ethical difficulties of using the judicial products of interrogation or confessions to determine the legal facts in any particular case, let alone to understand the mentalities and inner beliefs of the people involved.[41] These difficulties are also intrinsic to the analysis of narratives produced by treason proceedings. Prior to the Tudor period, the English common law system did not use torture as a formal means of proof. However, there is little doubt that mental and physical coercion played a part in extracting testimony and confessions, which often bear traces of intense question-and-answer interrogation.[42] *Peine forte et dure*, which included being deprived of food and water as well as penalties such as being piled with heavy weights, could be used to force people to plead and be punished (if they pled guilty) or to go to trial.[43] The practice of approving, whereby convicted criminals could turn 'state's evidence' to mitigate their own punishment, created strong incentives for making false allegations.[44] A confession of guilt was also integral to the process of petitioning for pardon, so that a man who hoped to save his skin by an appeal to royal mercy had every reason to conform his supplications to the king's expectations.[45]

Bearing in mind these issues of coercion, mediation and translation, I approach the records of treason trials as 'cultural scripts' that were not created in a vacuum of judicial neutrality but were the discursive product of specific political and social circumstances.[46] These are not straightforward accounts of legal fact, but narratives that respond to and also influence wider cultural

41 Edward Muir and Guido Ruggiero, 'Introduction', *History from Crime*, ed. Edward Muir and Guido Ruggiero (Baltimore, 1994), pp. vii–xviii; John H. Arnold, 'The Historian as Inquisitor: The Ethics of Interrogating Subaltern Voices', *Rethinking History* 2 (1998), 379–86; Michael Goodich, 'Introduction', *Voices from the Bench: The Narratives of Lesser Folk in Medieval Trials*, ed. Michael Goodich (New York, 2006), pp. 1–13. The classic study of the problems raised by legal narratives remains Natalie Zemon Davis, *Fiction in the Archives: Pardon Tales and Their Tellers in Sixteenth-Century France* (Stanford, 1987).

42 John H. Langbein, *Torture and the Law of Proof: Europe and England in the Ancien Régime* (Chicago, 1977).

43 Langbein, *Torture and the Law of Proof*, pp. 74–6.

44 A. J. Musson, 'Turning King's Evidence: The Prosecution of Crime in Late Medieval England', *Oxford Journal of Legal Studies* 19 (1999), 467–79.

45 Helen Lacey, *The Royal Pardon: Access to Mercy in Fourteenth-Century England* (York, 2009), pp. 19–36.

46 Muir and Ruggiero, 'Introduction', p. xiv.

beliefs and values. This approach has proved fruitful for examining judicial narratives produced in other circumstances. For example, tropes of wrongful disinheritance, exile and heroic return that were familiar from chivalric literature informed the official rhetoric justifying Henry Bolingbroke's claim to the throne as Henry IV.[47] In a more prosaic context of lawsuits over rape, abduction and 'ravishment', in the indictments and other legal documents presented in court, 'the meanings of ravishment were not confined to the letter of the law; they also derived from cultural understandings of ravishment in the world of chivalry and romance'.[48] The records of treason trials were likewise shaped by legal and political interpretations but also by cultural themes of chivalric virtue and masculine trueness.

The recognition that judicial texts are cultural productions means that historians must consider not only what the records say or do not say, but also how they are constructed in discursive and linguistic terms. The primary sources used in this study feature a mixture of English, French and Latin. In some places, the language chosen reflects the technical vocabulary of the law and the requirement to include precise terminology in order to prosecute cases under particular statutes. Elsewhere, language choice was integral to the relationships of power constructed through judicial discourse, such as those between interrogator and interrogated or judge and jury. To date, historians who have examined medieval treason cases from a legal or political perspective have given little consideration to the possible purposes and meanings that lie behind the interplay of languages in trial narratives, focusing instead on the evidentiary facts and on the legal terminology in which indictments were phrased and convictions secured. However, literary scholars have demonstrated that there is much more to learn about how language itself – whether English, French or Latin – functioned in trial records both to authorise and to subvert prosecution narratives.[49]

The ambiguity of English treason law, as well as the potentially conflicting beliefs and values held by the king, by royal judicial officials and by juries and the wider political community, meant that treason was a discursive category rather than an objective crime. It did not fully manifest until it was named and

47 C. D. Fletcher, 'Narrative and Political Strategies at the Deposition of Richard II', *Journal of Medieval History* 30 (2004), 323–41.

48 Shannon McSheffrey and Julia Pope, 'Ravishment, Legal Narratives, and Chivalric Culture in Fifteenth-Century England', *Journal of British Studies* 48 (2009), 818–36 (p. 819).

49 Matthew Giancarlo, 'Murder, Lies, and Storytelling: The Manipulation of Justice(s) in the Parliaments of 1397 and 1399', *Speculum* 77 (2002), 76–112; E. Kay Harris, 'Censoring Disobedient Subjects: Narratives of Treason and Royal Authority in Fifteenth-Century England', *Reputation and Representation in Fifteenth-Century Europe*, ed. Douglas L. Biggs, Sharon D. Michalove and A. Compton Reeves (Leiden, 2004), pp. 211–33; Helen Wicker, 'The Politics of Vernacular Speech: Cases of Treasonable Language, c. 1440–1453', *Vernacularity in England and Wales, c.1300–1550*, ed. Elizabeth Salter and Helen Wicker (Turnhout, 2011), pp. 171–97.

defined through the processes of accusation, trial and conviction.[50] These processes fixed the crime into the official record through the Latin rhetoric of indictments and the third-person French of witness testimony, but also in the form of English-language letters, confessions and handbills. My methodology for interpreting these multilingual trial narratives is inspired by recent studies of the ecclesiastical prosecution of heresy. This work has moved beyond trying to determine what, if anything, inquisitorial records can tell us about people's objective religious beliefs to examining the relationships of power that were created through the legal discourses themselves.[51] The textual evidence generated by treason prosecutions bears similarities to that produced by ecclesiastical investigations into heresy. The discursive processes anchoring the investigation and prosecution of treason gained authority through the production of written records that claimed to capture legal truths, including those 'voluntarily' revealed in witness testimony and confessions. Using methods akin to those used in ecclesiastical investigations of heresy, the authorities prosecuting treason bolstered the truth-value of their legal narratives by embedding within them vernacular English texts in the words of those they accused. These texts were in their turn given the sheen of evidential veracity with endorsements that the accused had written them in their own hands.

However, the complex interrelationships between Latin, French and vernacular speech in judicial narratives of treason created the potential for accused men to contest and undermine the proof value of those same narratives. When royal judicial officials brought accused traitors into legal discourse by inviting or coercing them to explain their intentions and actions, and then authenticated their words as proof of treason through a first-person vernacular endorsement, the authorities compiling legal texts for their own purposes unwittingly conferred agency on the people they interrogated by giving them a voice in the first place.[52] This prompts us to recognise that while judicial narratives may privilege the voice of power, such narratives are

50 For a valuable extended study on this theme, see Karen Cunningham, *Imaginary Betrayals: Subjectivity and the Discourses of Treason in Early Modern England* (Philadelphia, 2002).

51 In particular, John Arnold, *Inquisition and Power: Catharism and the Confessing Subject in Medieval Languedoc* (Philadelphia, 2001); John H. Arnold, 'Lollard Trials and Inquisitorial Discourse', *Fourteenth Century England II*, ed. Chris Given-Wilson (Woodbridge, 2004), pp. 81–94; Steven Justice, 'Inquisition, Speech, and Writing: A Case from Late-Medieval Norwich', *Representations* 48 (1994), 1–29.

52 Recent research has stressed the amount of agency that witnesses and deponents could exercise, even within institutional constraints: Tom Johnson, 'The Preconstruction of Witness Testimony: Law and Social Discourse in England before the Reformation', *Law and History Review* 32 (2014), 127–47; Megan Cassidy-Welch, 'Testimonies from a Fourteenth-Century Prison: Rumour, Evidence and Truth in the Midi', *French History* 16 (2002), 3–27.

always multi-vocal. I therefore read trial records strategically to look for places where the interaction between languages and voices destabilised the prosecution's arguments, creating possibilities for accused men to evade or resist their accusers. In the context of treason, such possibilities were augmented by one important difference between ecclesiastical and royal justice. This was that treason proceedings usually took place in public, in the court of King's Bench or in parliament. In both venues, while the written records were primarily in French or Latin, English was the common language for oral proceedings by the later fourteenth century.[53] This generated distinctive tensions between aurality and textuality, and between Latin, French and vernacular modes of speech and writing.

Royal courts were public theatres in which sovereign authority was defined and exercised through the law. In the case of treason, this judicial theatre extended to public rituals of execution that were designed as spectacles of power to be witnessed by the entire political community.[54] Yet the investment made in ensuring royal justice was visible and accessible to all subjects meant that courts were not theatres in which the action and dialogue could be wholly controlled by the state. Despite the enactment of statutes that sought to define treason in more specific terms, by the later fourteenth century, trial records, chronicles and witness accounts reflected the reality that treason was a continuum of shades of grey, rather than a matter of black-and-white determination. Customary ideas, chivalric performance, common law precedent and the rhetoric of civil law were all deployed in flexible and sometimes conflicting ways to support but also to resist accusations of treason. Through narratives of trial and punishment, ideals of true manhood and loyal political

[53] Gwilym Dodd, 'Languages and Law in Late Medieval England: English, French and Latin', *The Cambridge Companion to Medieval Law and Literature*, ed. Candace Barrington and Sebastian Sobecki (Cambridge, 2019), pp. 17–29; J. H. Baker, 'The Three Languages of the Common Law' in *The Common Law Tradition: Lawyers, Books, and the Law* (London, 2000), pp. 225–46; Chris Given-Wilson, 'The Rolls of Parliament, 1399–1421', *Parliamentary History* 23 (2004), pp. 57–72 (pp. 66–70); Gwilym Dodd, 'Thomas Paunfield, the "Heye Court of Rightwisnesse" and the Language of Petitioning in the Fifteenth Century', *Medieval Petitions: Grace and Grievance*, ed. W. M Ormrod, Gwilym Dodd and Anthony Musson (Woodbridge, 2009), pp. 222–41.

[54] Esther Cohen, 'Symbols of Culpability and the Universal Language of Justice: The Ritual of Public Executions in Late Medieval Europe', *History of European Ideas* 11 (1989), 407–16; John Gillingham, 'Killing and Mutilating Political Enemies in the British Isles from the Late Twelfth to the Early Fourteenth Century: A Comparative Study', *Britain and Ireland, 900–1300: Insular Responses to Medieval European Change*, ed. Brendan Smith (Cambridge, 1999), pp. 114–34; Katherine Royer, 'The Body in Parts: Reading the Execution Ritual in Late Medieval England', *Historical Reflections / Réflexions Historiques* 29 (2003), 319–39; Klaus Van Eickels, 'Gendered Violence: Castration and Blinding as Punishment for Treason in Normandy and Anglo-Norman England', *Gender & History* 16 (2004), 588–602; Danielle Westerhof, 'Deconstructing Identities on the Scaffold: The Execution of Hugh Despenser the Younger, 1326', *Journal of Medieval History* 33 (2007), 87–106.

subjecthood were articulated and renegotiated, as were the limits and loci of sovereign authority, whether it was embodied in the king or in more abstract structures of power. Mutable understandings of treason also bore the imprint of wider trends in late medieval constitutional and political thought, in which sovereignty could be imagined residing in the *res publica*, the *popolo*, the 'communalty' or the nation.[55]

Tracing these shifts thematically but also chronologically, Chapter One begins at the court of Richard II in the mid-1380s. The king was governing through a coterie of favourites and had excluded his powerful noble relatives and other leading men of the realm from the inner circles of political power. They responded with accusations of treason aimed at removing Richard's 'wicked advisers', stoking a conflict that reached its bloody climax in the Merciless Parliament of 1388. Combatants on both sides drew on ideals of chivalric masculinity and on the performative model of knightly trial by combat to defend their own positions and attack their enemies. However, they also appealed to newer political values articulated in terms of manly loyalty to the commons and the public good. Chapter Two follows this conflict into the following decade, when the wounds of 1386–8 were re-opened in the Revenge Parliament of 1397. As Richard, his supporters and his enemies fought over who was the true man and who was the traitor, they re-imagined the meanings of treason to justify their own actions while condemning their opponents. Closing the loop on the trials of 1397, Chapter Three explores the ways Henry IV and his judicial officials used the laws of treason to bolster his claims to embody sovereign authority in the wake of Richard's deposition. As Richard's die-hard supporters were neutralised through legal proceedings in venues that included parliament and the Court of Chivalry, we find the king intervening at key moments to mould the definition of treason in ways that bound his usurping body more securely to the masculine body politic of the realm. In Chapter Four, treason cases heard in King's Bench between 1400 and 1405 illuminate the new regime's growing concern with public political speech that criticised Henry IV's rule or challenged the legitimacy of his kingship. Through these cases, important precedents were established for treating mere words as an act of treason punishable by death. Here, I present a new explanation for this crucial legal shift by showing that it was predicated upon a cultural conjunction between the gendering of particular speech acts and the perceived material effects of men's words. While this could justify punishing men's words as treasonous deeds, it also generated new means by which the accused could perform resistant identities as loyal subjects and true men. Chapter Five focuses on government campaigns and legislation that from 1406, identified lollard heretics and political dissenters as part of the same

55 Joseph Canning, *Ideas of Power in the Late Middle Ages, 1296–1417* (New York, 2011); Antony Black, *Political Thought in Europe, 1250–1450* (Cambridge, 1992); Watts, *Making of Polities*, pp. 109–16, 131–41, 381–93.

nest of traitors and false men. Men accused of treason defended themselves using strategies common to both religious and political dissenters, which were cross-fertilising through overlapping urban social networks of scribes, lawyers, artisans and tradesmen. Offenders drew on a shared discourse of civic manhood, twinned with adept manipulation of the language and forms of the common law, to voice and justify their political resistance. The final chapter returns to where the book began, with incidents of treason involving elite men, many of them close to the king. Comparing changes in the meaning and scope of treason across the first two decades of Lancastrian rule, this chapter shows that while the traditional perception of traitors as men who had betrayed personal homosocial bonds was still powerful, in the legal and political arena, customary understandings were beginning to give way to newer and more expansive definitions of treason as a crime against the nation, the *chose publique* or the people of England. Changes in treason law were thereby helping to effect a more general re-alignment of the constitutional relationship between the king and the masculine body politic, and transforming the way gendered political subjecthood as a true man was envisaged and performed.

In both medieval and modern polities, debates about treason are essentially conflicts about the nature and limits of legitimate political authority. As Alan Orr observes, 'whatever the precise nature of a regime – aristocratic, monarchic, or democratic – the claimants of sovereign power needed the law of treason in order to advance their claims to govern'.[56] As a corollary, the laws of treason are implicated in contested definitions of what makes a loyal political subject and thereby help to control access to the privileges of subjecthood. By integrating considerations of gender into a political and legal history of treason, this book illuminates the ways that cultural expectations and performances of manhood could both reinforce and subvert the government's responses to crises of legitimacy. At the same time, it explores the varied ways men positioned themselves and claimed agency in a masculine body politic by drawing on, and in the process helping to transform, shared convictions about what it meant to be a man in medieval England.

[56] Orr, *Treason and the State*, p. 56.

1

TRUE MEN AND TRAITORS AT THE COURT OF RICHARD II, 1386–8

In late November 1384, the politicians and public gathered at Westminster for a session of parliament were treated to a spectacle in the form of a trial by combat between the English esquire John Walsh and Martel de Villeneuve, an esquire from Navarre.[1] The combat took place under the judicial auspices of the Court of Chivalry, a court headed by the Constable and Marshal of England with authority devolving directly from the king. This court operated according to the law of arms, which used civil law procedures, and its remit included dealing with military disputes that originated outside the realm as well as knightly and noble conflicts over heraldic arms and other matters of honour.[2] It was one of the judicial venues that could be used to try treason and it was an accusation of treason that brought the two combatants into the lists at Westminster on that late November day. Martel had accused Walsh – the king's receiver at the English castle of Cherbourg – of planning to sell out the castle to the French.[3] The *St Albans Chronicle* added that Walsh had sexually assaulted Martel's wife, asserting that it was this insult that lay at the root of Martel's treason accusation.[4] Things did not end well for the accuser: Walsh emerged the victor so Martel was immediately stripped of his armour, drawn from Westminster Palace through the London streets and out to the public gallows at Tyburn, where he was hanged and beheaded.

Neither of the combatants play any further part in this narrative but the 1384 incident does bring to light several themes relevant to struggles over

1 Parliament assembled on 12 November and was dissolved on 14 December.

2 Anthony Musson and Nigel Ramsay, 'Introduction', *Courts of Chivalry and Admiralty in Late Medieval Europe*, ed. Anthony Musson and Nigel Ramsay (Woodbridge, 2018), pp. 1–13; M. J. Russell, 'Trial by Battle in the Court of Chivalry', *Journal of Legal History* 29 (2008), 335–57; G. D. Squibb, *The High Court of Chivalry: A Study of the Civil Law in England* (New York, 1959).

3 *A Chronicle of London*, p. 76. The event was also recorded in *Knighton's Chronicle*, pp. 334–5; *Westminster Chronicle*, pp. 105–7.

4 *St Albans Chronicle I*, pp. 732–3. The chronicler used the phrase 'oppresserat uxorem', which suggests a sexual assault or rape, although this Latin terminology was not usually used in lawsuits involving rape. For an analysis of common legal terminology: Dunn, 'The Language of Ravishment in Medieval England'.

treason that began in 1386 and culminated in the trials and executions of 1388's Merciless Parliament. The first was the fluid meaning of treason, with the chronicle accounts reflecting legal and military definitions of treason but also the cultural sense of treason as a betrayal of masculine bonds. Second was the question of how treason should be tried and by whom. This question had been left unanswered in the 1352 statute, which stated simply that uncertain cases should be brought before the king in parliament. In theory, the Court of Chivalry was limited to judging disputes arising outside the realm but in practice, its existence as a potential trial venue influenced strategy and tactics on both sides of the 1386–8 conflict. Finally, trial by combat was a judicial procedure that entailed textual, oral and embodied performances of true manhood, demonstrating the gendered underpinnings of legal struggles over treason.[5] The appellant was first required to present his accusations against the defendant in the form of a written appeal to which the defendant responded in kind. On the day set down for the trial the combatants came armed into the field and swore verbal oaths to the veracity 'of every worde and euery sillable of every worde substance and alle'.[6] The truth of their words was then tested upon their bodies so that trial by combat was, in a sense, men's words made flesh. In battle, the appellant's words were enacted and his status as true man or traitor was proved through his chivalric performance in a contest whose outcome ultimately rested upon divine judgment. Martel's loss having proved him a false man, he was deprived of both arms and honour and executed as a self-confessed traitor.

No record from the Court of Chivalry survives for the treason proceedings between Martel and Walsh, but there are at least five accounts in contemporary or near-contemporary chronicles.[7] Several of these chronicles are also important sources for the political crisis of 1386–8. They incorporated textual evidence including public letters that the parliament roll omitted, and augmented this with eyewitness testimony and insights into broader public perceptions of the political conflict. Like the other sources for these events – including the trial records themselves – the chronicles cannot simply be accepted as transparent accounts of fact. Their clerical authors shaped the narratives through familiar moralising tropes, and this moralising discourse also inflected the legal framework of accusation and trial, where it bolstered a political rhetoric of justice, counsel and good governance. Working at a

5 For procedure, see Squibb, *High Court of Chivalry*, pp. 191–224, esp. 219–20 for appeals of treason; Keen, 'Treason Trials'; Bellamy, *Law of Treason*, pp. 159, 180–3.

6 Bodleian Library, Ashmole 856, which is a seventeenth-century copy of a treatise dated to the reign of Henry V. Transcribed in Ralph Moffat, '"Armed and Redy to Come to the Felde": Arming for the Judicial Duel in Fifteenth-Century England', *Courts of Chivalry and Admiralty*, ed. Musson and Ramsay, pp. 121–33 (pp. 129–33, quote at p. 132).

7 Very few original records from the medieval court survive. On sources: Musson and Ramsay, 'Introduction', pp. 4–7.

deeper level, gender structured the ways the men of England's political elite responded to and negotiated a pivotal cultural and political moment. In both the chronicles and trial records, legal, political and moral discourses of treason rested upon and were integrated through cultural understandings of true and false manhood.

MANHOOD THWARTED

Richard II was nearly 20 years old by late 1386. At this age, he expected to be free to govern his realm with full personal authority as a man and king. Instead, during the parliament that met between 1 October and 28 November, he was thwarted on all sides. Richard's demand for taxes to campaign in France was refused and his chosen Chancellor Michael de la Pole, recently elevated to the earldom of Suffolk, was impeached and dismissed from office. Richard might even have been threatened with deposition, with unsettling allusions being made to the fate of his great-grandfather, Edward II.[8] Richard's humiliations were compounded when he was forced to accept the constraint of a Continual Council. This council or 'commission' included the king's uncles Thomas of Woodstock, duke of Gloucester and Edmund, duke of York and, as the new Chancellor, Thomas Arundel, bishop of Ely. The commission's remit was primarily financial and administrative: they were to rein in spending; claw back many of Richard's recent grants of land, titles and offices to royal favourites; and inquire into corruption in the royal justice system. The commission was also to exercise oversight of the royal household, in particular its expenses and the appointment of men around the king.

To Richard, these restraining actions were an attack on his masculine honour and an intolerable violation of his prerogative powers as a king.[9] He was not about to take the insult lying down. Gathering about him a group of allies and friends that included De la Pole, Robert de Vere, recently elevated to a new dukedom of Ireland, and Sir Simon Burley, vice-chamberlain of the royal household, Richard began devising ways to disband the Continual Council and punish those responsible for imposing it, and to establish full regnal authority in his own person. Within a few months, a deep rift had developed. On one side was a group of noblemen that became known as the Lords Appellant, which included Gloucester, Richard FitzAlan the earl of Arundel and Thomas Beauchamp, earl of Warwick. Ranged against them were Richard and his inner circle, which over 1387 expanded to include Sir Robert Tresilian, chief justice of King's Bench, Alexander Neville the archbishop of York, and Sir Nicholas Brembre, a wealthy merchant and mayor of London in

8 S. B. Chrimes, 'Richard II's Questions to the Judges, 1387', *Law Quarterly Review* 72 (1956), 365–90; the possibility of deposition is addressed at pp. 370, 381–2.

9 Fletcher (*Richard II*, pp. 143–58) demonstrates the connections between the king's policies in these years and his quest to assert his manhood and prove his knightly honour.

1377 and 1383–5. Enmity between the two groups led to armed conflict and ended in the treason trials of 1388.[10]

Multiple factors contributed to the breakdown of relations in 1386–8, including the crown's financial difficulties, differences over military policy, and anxieties about the growing political influence of De Vere, Burley and other men who surrounded Richard in the royal household. Underlying these immediate concerns were deeper constitutional questions of where power lay, who could wield it, and how and to what degree a 'misgoverned' king could be restrained. Once the accusation of treason emerged as a political weapon of choice for both sides, these abstract constitutional debates took on material form and were contested through and upon men's bodies. In the process, the figure of the traitor and the body politic against which they offended were given definitive masculine form through gendered legal discourses of true and false manhood.

Richard was first to raise the spectre of treason. In the months following the 1386 parliament, he avoided Westminster and evaded the Continual Council. Travelling through the Thames Valley and then further west to Chester, he worked to raise political and military support against the men he held responsible for illegitimately curbing his power.[11] On 21 August 1387, Richard called together the judges of King's Bench and Common Pleas at Shrewsbury and asked them a series of questions concerning the constitutional validity of the Continual Council.[12] The judges' response was unequivocal: those who had imposed the Council should be treated as traitors. As shall be seen, the judicial view was conditioned by the legal ambiguities surrounding treason, but it also reflected cultural understandings of treason as a violation of masculine bonds, and of the homosocial personal and political ties through which royal government functioned.

Robert Tresilian was among the judges and it was probably his idea for the king to secure a legal opinion at common law, validated by the seals of the judges of both superior courts.[13] This opinion took the form of ten questions and answers, along with three additional statements that the judges appear to have added unbidden to the document. The questions covered ground including whether the statute that imposed the Continual Council violated the king's prerogative and his regality; whether the king had the right to

10 For general accounts of the crisis of 1386–8: Fletcher, *Richard II*, pp. 151–75; Nigel Saul, *Richard II* (New Haven, 1997), pp. 148–96; Anthony Goodman, *The Loyal Conspiracy: The Lords Appellant under Richard II* (Coral Gables, 1971).

11 For Richard's itinerary: Anthony Tuck, *Richard II and the English Nobility* (London, 1973), pp. 227–8.

12 Chrimes, 'Questions to the Judges'; D. Clementi, 'Richard II's Ninth Question to the Judges', *The English Historical Review* 86 (1971), 96–113. The only senior judge not present was Justice Skipworth of Common Pleas, who was ill.

13 Chrimes, 'Questions to the Judges', pp. 372–3.

control proceedings in parliament, to direct its business and to dissolve it as he pleased; and whether parliament had the right to impeach and remove the king's officers against his will. The judges were also asked 'how those ought to be punished who incited the aforementioned king to consent to the making of that statute, ordinance and commission'; and 'what penalty they deserved who compelled or constrained the king to consent to the making of the … commission'.[14] The ninth question asked 'how he should be punished who suggested in parliament that the statute be invoked in which King Edward [II] … great-grandfather of the present king, was sometime adjudged in parliament'. This insinuated that Richard had been coerced into submitting to the Continual Council by the threat of deposition.[15] One clause stands out in the judges' responses: they declared that those responsible for the outcomes of the 1386 parliament 'deserve to be punished as traitors' but not that any particular offence *was* treason.[16] This wording allowed them to adhere technically to the clause in the 1352 statute, which stated that the determination of uncertain cases should be left to the king in parliament. More significantly, the phrasing took the legal abstraction of the crime of treason and transformed it into words and deeds located in the bodies of individual men. Beginning with inciting and inducing, Richard's opponents had moved on to compel, constrain and impede.

The references to compulsion and constraint, along with the judges' finding that the makers of the Continual Council had derogated from the king's prerogative, traded indirectly on the idea of accroaching. Accroaching was a vague but potent concept that described the usurpation and use of royal power by men other than the king. Although the questions to the judges did not include the term 'accroachment', the Lords Appellant soon seized upon it in their campaign against Richard's 'evil counsellors'. The charge of accroachment had been used to good effect in earlier treason proceedings at common law.[17] It also invoked civil law constructions of treason because it captured the idea of individuals usurping public power for private ends, a form of *lèse-majesté*.[18] When it was used against men who were, or were perceived to be, too close to the king, the legal rhetoric of accroachment tapped a deeper reserve of anxiety about the frangible nature of homosocial bonds.[19] Close physical and

14 *PROME*, 'Richard II: February 1388', Part Three. The questions to the judges formed part of the record for the trials in the Merciless Parliament, discussed below.

15 For detailed analysis, see Clementi, 'Richard II's Ninth Question'.

16 *PROME*, 'Richard II: February 1388', Part Two, Appeal.

17 Chrimes, 'Questions to the Judges', p. 383; Bellamy, *Law of Treason*, pp. 62–74.

18 Bellamy, *Law of Treason*, pp. 11–12; Keen, 'Treason Trials', p. 96.

19 For example, it was used against Edward II's favourite Piers de Gaveston, and against Richard II's chamberlain and close friend Robert de Vere in 1388. For discussion of this usage in relation to homosocial intimacy, see McVitty, 'False Knights and True Men', pp. 461, 464, 472.

emotional intimacy between the king and favoured men of his household and court was expected in a political system founded in personal rule. However, homosocial affinity could become a threat if the noblemen who considered themselves the king's 'natural counsellors' found themselves excluded from political influence and the rewards of royal service. The charge of accroaching proved a useful weapon in such circumstances for as Keen points out, it 'widened the scope of treason to the point where intimacy with the king might in itself be grounds for an accusation'.[20]

The testimony of the judges, validated by their seals and witnessed by men including Alexander Neville, Robert de Vere and Michael de la Pole, was confirmed at a royal council in Nottingham on 25 August. The lawyer John Blake was also listed as a witness. Having drafted the document later presented in parliament, he would pay with his life for his participation. The Lords Appellant were now on notice and, fearing that their enemies were engineering their executions, they made ready to defend themselves. Over the months leading up to Christmas, this defence took material and discursive forms. Gathering their retainers, Gloucester, Arundel and Warwick armed themselves for an anticipated physical attack and by mid-November, they were encamped just outside London. They also circulated public bills and oral proclamations explaining and justifying their position. This latter tactic attests to the fact that by the late 1300s, political conflict was not confined to parliament and the rarefied environment of royal and noble council chambers. Rather, this was a battle fought on a public stage, and verbal rumours, bill-casting, petitioning and pamphleteering all had their parts to play in the shifting fortunes of the opposing groups.[21]

While the Lords Appellant were converging on London with their armies, Richard and his supporters were at Westminster Palace, surrounded by soldiers mustered by the mayor of London and nobles who remained loyal to the king.[22] Richard then commanded the Appellants to present themselves before him, an order they initially defied for fear of an ambush. The tension is palpable in Henry Knighton's artful description of all London falling ominously silent with 'no boat or barge plying on the Thames all that day' as

20 Maurice Keen, *England in the Later Middle Ages: A Political History*, 2nd ed. (London, 2003), p. 72.

21 For general studies of petitioning and pamphleteering: Clementine Oliver, *Parliament and Political Pamphleteering in Fourteenth-Century England* (Woodbridge, 2010); Wendy Scase, '"Strange and Wonderful Bills": Bill-Casting and Political Discourse in Late Medieval England', *New Medieval Literatures* 2 (1998), 225–47; Elodie Lecuppre-Desjardin, 'Des portes qui parlent: Placards, feuilles volantes et communication politique dans les villes des Pays-Bas à la fin du moyen âge', *Bibliothèque de l'école des chartes* 168 (2010), 151–72; John L. Watts, 'The Pressure of the Public on Later Medieval Politics', *Fifteenth Century IV*, ed. Clark and Carpenter, pp. 159–80.

22 Sir Nicholas Exton was the mayor in 1387–8.

the populace waited to see how the standoff would play out.[23] His account also reflected the degree to which people interpreted politically motivated accusations of treason through the gendered discourse of honour and true manhood. For instance, when Richard asked Lord Basset to take up arms against the Appellants, Basset declared himself the king's true liegeman ready to put his body on the line for his lord. However, he added, 'I must tell you that if I have to go into battle, I wish unmistakably to be with the party that is true and seeks truth, and that I am not going to offer to have my head broken for the duke of Ireland'.[24] Basset's earthy tone indicates this was a story Knighton had been told by an eyewitness and the words show that for men directly involved in this conflict, matters of personal honour, true manhood and chivalric performance were as important as more abstract legal and constitutional concerns.[25]

Fearing that Richard was turning the populace against them, on 13 November the Lords Appellant sent an open letter to the mayor, aldermen, citizens and 'all the good commons of London'.[26] This laid out their position: they were seeking only to preserve the legal and constitutionally valid Continual Council, which had been ordained by the king himself in parliament, and it was the 'faithless and treacherous' men about Richard rather than themselves who were bringing ruin and dishonour upon the king and realm. The structure and rhetoric of this public letter foreshadowed the legal Appeal that would instigate the trials in the 1388 parliament. The prime targets were identified as Neville, De Vere, De la Pole, the 'false justice' Tresilian and Brembre, a 'false knight'. Standing against these five named traitors, Gloucester, Arundel and Warwick offered themselves as a single body ready to defend the honour of both king and kingdom. The letter encapsulated cultural and legal views that treason was located simultaneously in men's speech and their deeds. The accused men had sown dissension between the king and his nobles through their 'tendentious advice and contrivance', and they had induced Richard to violate his coronation oath. They had also bodily 'carried off the king' and 'led his honourable person into divers[e] parts remote from his council', to the shame and disparagement of the kingdom and the dismemberment of the crown. The connections the letter made between Richard's alienated body and the dismembered crown represented king and kingdom as single corporeal entity, implicitly masculinising the body politic against which traitors offended.

The Appellants intended the contents of this letter to be widely circulated because it closes by charging London officialdom 'to make full proclamation

23 *Knighton's Chronicle*, p. 403.

24 Ibid.

25 The chronicle's editor suggests Knighton had informants at the king's court and among the Appellants: *Knighton's Chronicle*, p. 406, n. 2.

26 *Knighton's Chronicle*, pp. 409–13. As far as is known, the copy Knighton preserved in his chronicle is the only one to survive: p. 409, n. 4.

throughout the city' of their words and to call on the populace to aid them in their cause. Following this effort to defuse any potential attack and after some bargaining with representatives sent by Richard, the Appellant lords agreed to present themselves before the king at Westminster Hall on 17 November. This meeting was staged as a public spectacle of royal authority and the Appellants took full advantage of the circumstances to perform before the watching crowds as his loyal subjects and honourable defenders. Richard was seated in splendour upon his throne and 'the whole place was filled with lords and commons'.[27] Gloucester, Arundel and Warwick arrived in full chivalric panoply, surrounded by 300 horsemen 'and with a great crowd of magnates and commons accompanying them'.[28] The three noblemen, acting as a single choreographed body, prostrated themselves three times on their way up the Hall to the king. They then presented their formal Appeal of treason against Richard's intimates, the same five men named in their letter to London. Backed into a corner, Richard agreed to call a parliament to resolve the conflict, perhaps believing that in this judicial venue he could maintain some control over the outcome. However, there were also hints in the chroniclers' descriptions of this meeting, corroborated by the internal evidence of the Appeal itself, that both sides viewed the accusations of treason as a matter of masculine honour that could be settled in the Court of Chivalry. The Appellants were 'assigned a day' to contest the accusations and the Appellants declared themselves ready to back their words with action.[29] Thomas Walsingham added that having delivered their Appeal, the Appellants threw down their gauntlets in pledge that their words were true and took an oath that they would prove this through a trial by combat.[30] Knighton's account was similar, with the Appellants pledging 'not to shrink from putting their bodies to the danger of death' in pursuit of their cause.[31]

In the wake of the Westminster meeting, the fragile detente between the king and the Appellants soon disintegrated and Richard sent letters and writs under the privy seal to Robert de Vere in Chester, authorising him to raise troops and bring them to London. Matters came to a head on 20 December at Radcot Bridge. Gloucester, Arundel and Warwick had now been joined in their cause by Thomas Mowbray, earl of Nottingham and Marshal of England, and by Richard's cousin Henry Bolingbroke, then the earl of Derby. At Radcot Bridge, De Vere's forces met those of Derby and Gloucester in the field. The Appellants were the victors, routing their opponents and sending De Vere fleeing into a continental exile from which he would never return.[32] However,

27 Ibid., p. 413.

28 Ibid., p. 415. Cf. *Westminster Chronicle*, p. 213.

29 *PROME*, 'Richard II: February 1388', Part Two, Appeal.

30 *St Albans Chronicle I*, p. 835.

31 *Knighton's Chronicle*, p. 413.

32 Robert de Vere died in Flanders in 1392. For accounts of the battle: *Westminster*

the battle raised thorny questions about who, exactly, was the traitor and who was the true man. De Vere took the field with the king's banner raised, signifying his claimed position as a loyal knight defending his lord. According to the *Westminster Chronicle*, De Vere was also displaying the banner of St George, the standard of the chivalric Order of the Garter and, by the 1380s, a potent symbol of English national identity.[33] Prior to and after the enactment of the 1352 statute, riding armed with one's banner raised against the king was interpreted as an act of treason, perhaps one so obvious it did not need to be stated explicitly in the statute.[34] But what of riding against a man who was himself carrying the royal standard and who also carried letters from the king authorising his activities? Surely this, too, was treason? At Radcot Bridge, it was De Vere rather than the Appellants who appeared to have the better claim to embody true manhood by fulfilling his chivalric duty to defend his lord with his body and his life.[35] This was a problem that took some tricky manoeuvring once De Vere was put on trial (*in absentia*) for treason, with the Appellants having to deploy against him the slippery charge of accroaching royal power.

THE APPEAL OF TREASON

With De Vere defeated and on the run, Richard's hopes of an outright victory were gone. The balance of power shifted decidedly in the Appellants' favour as they congregated with their forces at the Tower, where Richard had now retreated for refuge. The Appellants briefly canvassed the possibility of deposing Richard, who was now fully under their control, but instead they induced the king to call a parliament for early the following year.[36] In the meantime, on 30 December they presented their Appeal for a third time, establishing the legal groundwork for the treason trials to follow in the Merciless Parliament. It is unclear whose idea it was to import the appeal, a civil law procedure used in the Court of Chivalry, into parliament; however, the 1352 statute's imprecision as to procedures and venues, along with its open-ended clause about bringing uncertain cases to be decided by the king in parliament, meant that although an appeal in parliament was innovative it was not strictly extra-legal.[37] Moreover, Thomas Mowbray having joined the Appellant cause, the Appeal could be framed as an action lawfully instigated by the Constable

Chronicle, pp. 221–5; *Knighton's Chronicle*, pp. 418–23.

33 *Westminster Chronicle*, p. 223. On St George as a national symbol: Jonathan Bengtson, 'Saint George and the Formation of English Nationalism', *Journal of Medieval & Early Modern Studies* 27 (1997), 317–40.

34 Bellamy, *Law of Treason*, pp. 47–9, 75 n. 2, 95.

35 For an analysis of this dilemma, see McVitty, 'False Knights and True Men', pp. 472–3.

36 Fletcher, *Richard II*, p. 172; Goodman, *Loyal Conspiracy*, p. 31.

37 Rogers, 'Parliamentary Appeals of Treason', pp. 95–102.

and Marshal of England, the Court of Chivalry's two principal officers. The Appeal text itself and the manner in which it was presented suggest that the Appellants anticipated deploying the law of arms and its underlying codes of chivalric honour and nobility. This would enable them to control the trial process while representing themselves to the political community as loyal liegemen defending the king's honour and the integrity of his kingdom from the predation of false and duplicitous men. Following the presentation of the Appeal, the Commons initiated a second legal process. In a set of sixteen articles that closely mirrored the language of the Appeal, Sir Simon Burley and three of Richard's chamber knights (intimate companions of his household) were impeached on charges of treason for aiding and abetting the five prime offenders.[38]

Broadly matching the textual and aural processes of the Court of Chivalry, the Appeal was delivered in the form of a written petition that was read out in the public venue of parliament. The preamble re-enacted the three earlier occasions on which the Appellants' had appealed Neville, De Vere, De la Pole, Tresilian and Brembre of treason before the king. Using language redolent of contests of chivalric honour, the text recounted that the king 'assigned [the Appellants] a day ... to pursue and declare their said appeal', while Gloucester and his allies offered their own persons to prove the truth of their words.[39] The *Westminster Chronicle* reveals this challenge was corporeal as well as discursive, with the Appellants stating they were 'willing to prove this by their own right hand to any that would gainsay it, and on this issue to defend themselves against any adversary with a head on his shoulders'.[40] The Appeal having originated in the Appellants' performances of chivalric loyalty and noble honour, it therefore became a written embodiment of their claims to true manhood. It comprised thirty-nine articles in all, but it was framed and its reception was conditioned by the first four articles. These constructed treason primarily in terms of the destruction of positive masculine bonds and the forging, through false and devious means, of destructive ones. These homosocial bonds were envisaged as conceptual and emotional, but equally as material and embodied. Their corrosive nature dishonoured Richard, his loyal nobles and his kingdom; imperilled the integrity of the body politic; and threatened the common profit of the realm.

The Appeal located the origins of this political rupture in false speech, as the accused men 'caused' Richard to 'believe many falsities devised and plotted by them against loyalty and good faith, that they caused him to devote his affection, firm faith, and credence entirely to them, and to hate his loyal

38 The chamber knights were Sir John Beauchamp, Sir James Berners and Sir John Salisbury. For the articles of impeachment: *PROME*, 'Richard II: February 1388', Part Three.

39 *PROME*, 'Richard II: February 1388', Part Two, Appeal.

40 *Westminster Chronicle*, p. 235.

lords and lieges, by whom he ought rather to have been governed'.[41] They also induced Richard to swear to be 'governed, counselled, and led by them', and to 'swear and assure them that he would maintain and sustain them to live and die with them'.[42] These oaths dishonoured the king by causing him to betray the superior oath made at his coronation. In Article Three, the false speech of the accused led directly to false deeds when, after forcing Richard to swear his loyalty exclusively to them, they 'did not allow the great men of the realm, nor the good counsellors of the king, to speak with nor approach the king, properly to counsel him, nor the king to speak with them'.[43] In Article Four, the bodily estrangement and physical separation between the king and the nobles who considered themselves his rightful and natural counsellors was compounded by emotional alienation between the king and his subjects, 'so that his presence, which he should by duty show to the great lords and to his liege people … was granted only at the will and bidding' of the five accused men, 'alienating the hearts of the great lords and people from their liege lord, seeking to distance our lord the king's heart from the peers of the land'.[44]

In these first four articles, treason was constructed through a complex coalescence of statutory, civil law and common law ideas but most prominent – and therefore presumably most compelling to parliament and the political community – was the chivalric perception of the traitor as the inversion of the true man. This was emphasised by the Appeal's repeated categorisation of the accused men as false traitor, false knight and false justice (of Tresilian), whose devious and destructive ends were achieved by means of their false covine. False covine was a legal expression that appeared in common law indictments against criminal gangs.[45] It carried substantial cultural weight because it engaged viscerally with fears of corrupted masculine intimacy. By implication, the Appellants strategically placed themselves in the role of true men, loyally defending the king's honour, estate and regality as well as the integrity and common profit of the realm.

Articles Nineteen through Twenty-one returned to this theme of treason as the fruit of false bonds between men. They described the king's masculine body becoming estranged from the body politic as the accused, 'caused the king to accompany some of them through the greater part of his kingdom' and 'to absent himself [*soi esloigner*] in the most distant parts of the realm'.[46] This rupture meant that the members of the Continual Council and his noble advisers could not communicate with Richard, 'to the great injury of the king

41 Article One.

42 Articles One and Two.

43 Article Three.

44 Article Four.

45 Jonathan Rose, *Maintenance in Medieval England* (Cambridge, 2017), pp. 125–7.

46 Article Nineteen.

and kingdom'.[47] According to the Appeal, the accused men then forced lords, knights 'and other good people' they met on their travels to swear false oaths to them, so that 'by force of such bonds and oaths the entire realm was stirred into great trouble and unrest'.[48] In Article Twenty-four, the false bonds forged through corrupt oaths took material form in the potent sign of the livery badge, as the five accused 'caused the king newly to create a large retinue of divers men, and give them divers badges such as were not customarily used in ancient times by any of the kings his predecessors, to the end of giving them power to perform their false treason aforesaid'.[49] By all these means, 'the aforesaid traitors were assured that they had drawn away the heart and goodwill of the king' from the Appellant lords and others responsible for establishing the Continual Council.[50]

Augmenting charges that the traitors had caused physical and emotional estrangement between the king and his subjects, several articles drew on the familiar medieval heuristic that read political entities as corporeal male bodies in order to portray the accused men as an existential threat to the integrity of realm. According to Article One, their 'false thoughts and imaginations' had caused unrest and destruction but also 'disease', while elsewhere treason was figured as the literal dismemberment of the body politic. Article Eleven, for example, accused Neville, De la Pole and De Vere of inciting Richard to make De Vere the king of Ireland, 'to the severance of the allegiance of the king [Richard] from the said kingdom of England and the said land of Ireland'. The lordship, land and people of Ireland having been part of the English crown and loyal to English kings 'from time immemorial', this was a wound that would tear apart the imagined political unity inherited by Richard through 'his royal progenitors the kings of England'. Elsewhere, Richard's gifts of lands, lordships, titles and revenues to the accused were condemned in material terms as injuries to the kingdom, as well as acts that dishonoured the king.[51] This discourse of bodily division was echoed in the political community's petitions to parliament; one such petition asked for the restoration of local rights granted away by the king, in a move that had 'dismembered the bodies of many counties'.[52]

Several articles charged the accused men with treason for involving the king in judicial corruption that included maintenance and pursuing false quarrels; taking bribes; violating Magna Carta by delaying or denying justice; and procuring false indictments.[53] The skulduggery represented by

47 Article Twenty-one.
48 Articles Nineteen and Twenty.
49 Article Twenty-four.
50 Article Twenty-six.
51 For example, Articles Five, Seven and Eight.
52 *PROME*, 'Richard II: February 1388', Part One, Roll, Item Thirty-two.
53 Articles Six, Nine, Ten, Thirteen, Twenty-six; quote from Article Ten.

maintenance, bribery and other forms judicial corruption did not remotely fall within either statutory or customary rubrics of treason but it had for decades provided plentiful fodder for petitions to parliament.[54] It also fuelled widespread popular complaint, which took the form of public pamphlets, libels and satirical poetry and manifested in a more visceral form when lawyers were targeted for violent retribution during the Great Revolt of 1381. Incorporated into the Appeal, this virulent anti-lawyer cultural discourse amplified the legal discourse, creating conditions in which parliament and the public could accept the definition of treason being stretched to include routine corruption and manipulation of the legal system. This proved an effective strategy when it came time to try the lawyer John Blake as well as Thomas Usk, a minor judicial official. It was also used against Nicholas Brembre, who was charged with violating the 'Great Charter and other good laws and usages of the kingdom' for having taken 'certain persons from the prison of Newgate by night … and led them out of London to Kent, to a place called the Foul Oak, and there, accroaching to himself royal power as a traitor to the king, without warrant and process of law he caused them all to be beheaded'.[55]

If the articles concerning judicial corruption stretched the definition of treason in one direction, Articles Twenty-two, Thirty-seven, Thirty-eight and Thirty-nine stretched it in another. These articles dealt with the confrontation at Radcot Bridge and the events leading up to it, and they reveal the extent to which the Appellants had to manipulate received chivalric and legal understandings of treason to paint Robert de Vere as a traitor. Article Twenty-two charged De Vere with accroaching royal power by making himself justice of Chester and then causing 'divers original and judicial writs to be made and sealed with the king's great seal', which he used to raise forces against the Appellants.[56] But in the following articles, agency for these actions became dangerously detached from De Vere so that it was unclear whether it was he or Richard himself acting as the instigator. In Article Thirty-seven, the Appellants admitted that the king had ordered 'various knights, squires, his sheriffs and other ministers, by his letters, to raise and assemble all the power they could'; while Article Thirty-eight affirmed that Richard had indeed written to De Vere, 'instructing him to take to the field with as strong a force as he could assemble, and that the king would meet him with all his force, and that the king would there venture his royal person; and that the king himself and all

[54] Jonathan Rose, 'Medieval Attitudes towards the Legal Profession: The Past as Prologue', *Stetson Law Review* 27 (1998), 345–69; Harriss, *Shaping the Nation*, pp. 6–31; Anthony Musson and W. M Ormrod, *The Evolution of English Justice: Law, Politics, and Society in the Fourteenth Century* (New York, 1999), pp. 78–111; Richard W. Kaeuper, *War, Justice, and Public Order: England and France in the Later Middle Ages* (Oxford, 1988), pp. 269–315.

[55] Article Twelve.

[56] Article Twenty-two.

his kingdom were in great danger unless they were aided and succoured by the said duke of Ireland'. The king, it was said, had also undertaken to pay De Vere's wages and costs and those of the soldiers he retained.

According to the Appeal, De Vere and his fellows had forced Richard to write the letters and writs that initiated military action, but this image of a weak and passive king dominated by other men sat uneasily alongside the description of Richard as a bold and active warrior who was ready to face his opponents in the field. Moreover, De Vere came perilously close to emerging as a model of chivalry and true manhood by loyally carrying out his king's commands and standing ready to defend him with his body and his life. The Appellants therefore had some work to do to transform De Vere from honourable knight into 'false traitor'. Article Thirty-nine did not deny that at Radcot Bridge, it was the Appellants who rode in arms against the king's banner – an overt act of treason according to both the 1352 statute and cultural perceptions of chivalric honour. However, in the Appeal the royal standard became the material proof of De Vere's accroachment and treason, because he 'caused the king's banner to be displayed in his company, contrary to the estate of the king and his crown'. De Vere's identity as a traitor rather than a true man was cemented by Article Thirty-nine, which depicted his defeat at Radcot Bridge as the outcome of a chivalric trial by combat, in which 'the said duke of Ireland and his company, by the grace of God, were hindered in their evil purpose'.

The Appeal did not make as much of the discourse of national betrayal as post-Ricardian treason prosecutions would. However, Article Fifteen did state that the 'evil counsel' and 'wicked dispositions' of the traitors had made the realm vulnerable to the French king, who was 'about to arrive in England to destroy the entire realm and tongue of England'.[57] Other articles added that Richard had been treacherously induced to make a truce with the French king, handing over English fortresses in France in return for military support against the Appellants.[58] Understandably though, given the acute domestic conflict in which the Appellants were embroiled, their Appeal focused primarily on arguing for the insidious effects on Richard of men who were far too close for comfort rather than on enemies from outside the realm.

Many of the Appeal articles concluded by stating that the men named as traitors had acted 'to the destruction of the king and his kingdom' or 'to the great injury of the king and kingdom'. This rhetoric, repeated over and over again, implicitly masculinised the body politic by connecting it directly to the gendered body of the king. In one way, the Appeal undermined Richard's manhood by placing him in a passive position, portraying him as an innocent 'of tender age' who was vulnerable to being dominated,

57 Article Fifteen.

58 Articles Fifteen (quote), Twenty-nine, Thirty and Thirty-one.

manipulated and 'enslaved' by the five accused men.[59] At the same time, though, it stressed that once these predators were removed, Richard would fully embody the masculine virtues integral to good kingship, including honouring his coronation oath and keeping his word, taking wise counsel from the noblemen who saw themselves as the king's natural advisers, delivering justice and ruling for the common profit of the realm.

Few of the offences listed as treason in the Appeal or in the articles of impeachment against Burley and his fellow knights conformed explicitly to the legal definitions of treason in the 1352 statute or to existing common law precedents. For those that did, such as riding with banners raised against the king, the evidence had to be manipulated to make the charge stick. Other articles relied on the loose terminology of accroachment and on related allegations of broken oaths, false bonds, and emotional and bodily estrangement. The legal patterning of accusation and evidence was therefore more closely aligned with customary notions of treason as a betrayal of masculine truth and chivalric honour than with narrower legal definitions in either common or civil law, and it was on questions of knightly honour and true manhood that the resulting trials turned. A closer look at these trials reveals the degree to which the 'traitor' was a contested category. It was imagined through a binary of true and false manhood, but the events of 1388 demonstrate that perceptions differed as to what this meant in reality. Discourses and performances of true and false manhood could therefore be used to construct, but also to resist, charges of treason.

Before turning to the trials, it will be valuable to briefly consider how the authors of the main chronicle accounts interpreted the events that led up to the Merciless Parliament. While these clerical authors shaped and embellished their narratives to fit their moralistic worldview, they do give a sense of the nature and limits of interpretive possibility when it came to explaining the disease of treason in the body politic. By preserving public letters, petitions and reports of rumour and talk, chronicles also to a degree captured the currents of wider popular opinion. The accounts of Henry Knighton and the anonymous monk of the *Westminster Chronicle* were extensive and well informed by contacts within the royal and Appellant factions and in the city of London, parliament and Chancery. These are complemented by the short *History* of the London clerk Thomas Favent and by Thomas Walsingham's *St Albans Chronicle*.

Treason in these texts was shaped by an underlying cultural and moral binary of natural/unnatural. The Appellants were represented (as they positioned themselves) in the role of the king's natural counsellors and true lieges. They had been displaced physically and emotionally by Richard's evil counsellors

[59] On the discourse of youthful changeability in the Appeal and its connection to Richard's manhood: Fletcher, *Richard II*, pp. 172–3.

and wicked advisers, who by a process of inversion were constructed as both false and unnatural. The Appeal deployed the discursive register of falseness, deception and manipulation to define treason as a crime rooted in the false words, deeds and affections of the group of men surrounding the king. In the chronicles, these toxic political relationships tilted towards more perverse models of homosociality and masculine intimacy that ranged from unreasoning and excessive love to 'seduction' and hints of sodomy.

The chroniclers used expressions including *fautores* and *auriculares* to describe De la Pole, De Vere and the other accused traitors, phrases that are usually translated by modern editors as 'favourites'.[60] 'Favourite' has its own negative political connotations but it does not fully capture the disturbing and unnatural excesses of emotional entanglement and physical intimacy of the Latin originals.[61] *Fautore*, for example, appeared widely in records of ecclesiastical inquisition to describe heretics and it therefore called up the idea of iniquitous rebellion against God himself.[62] This was the ultimate act 'against nature' from which all other sinful and unnatural acts including sodomy, blasphemy and treason stemmed.[63] *Auriculares* created a viscerally embodied image of men who were so close to the king they were literally 'in his ear', manipulating his thoughts and affections and turning him against his 'true nobles'. Favent's chronicle gives a sense of how this form of political and personal homosociality could be interpreted by contemporary observers with his allegation that the traitors had 'blinded the guileless king by the conversations from their serpents' mouths, with ambitions, adulations, lascivious words and praises', so that the helpless Richard was 'ensnared by all their poisonous conspiracies and desires'.[64] At the heart of Favent's account was a potent image of treason originating in a debased parody of idealised chivalric loyalty between a king and his knights and nobles. Starting with false words and progressing inevitably to treasonous violence, the favourites 'swore by the

60 *Knighton's Chronicle*, pp. 402, 404, 418.

61 On the idea of the favourite: Henric Bagerius and Christine Ekholst, 'Kings and Favourites: Politics and Sexuality in Late Medieval Europe', *Journal of Medieval History* 43 (2017), 298–319; Klaus Oschema, 'The Cruel End of the Favourite. Clandestine Death and Public Retaliation at Late Medieval Courts in England and France', *Death at Court*, ed. Karl-Heinz Spiess and Immo Warntjes (Wiesbaden, 2012), pp. 171–95; Joel T. Rosenthal, 'The King's "Wicked Advisers" and Medieval Baronial Rebellions', *Political Science Quarterly* 82 (1967), 595–618.

62 Arnold, 'Lollard Trials and Inquisitorial Discourse'.

63 Jeffrey Richards, *Sex, Dissidence, and Damnation: Minority Groups in the Middle Ages* (London, 1991), pp. 132–48; Mark D. Jordan, *The Invention of Sodomy in Christian Theology* (Chicago, 1998); Ruth Mazo Karras, *Sexuality in Medieval Europe: Doing Unto Others* (New York, 2005), pp. 132–5; Steven F. Kruger, 'Conversion and Medieval Sexual, Religious, and Racial Categories', *Constructing Medieval Sexuality*, ed. Karma Lochrie, Peggy McCraken and James A Schultz (Minneapolis, 1998), pp. 158–79.

64 Favent, *History*, p. 233.

power of a certain oath and made the king submit himself as oath-swearer that, by the strength of his body and of royal power … he would sustain and defend them against all who opposed or resisted them'.[65]

Knighton fixed upon the cultural dread of sodomy with his characterisation of the accused men as 'nephandi seductores regis' who had peddled 'nephandum consilium' and 'seduced the king [*seduxerant regem*] and were … sowing discord and rancour between the king and his lords'.[66] He first used the phrase *nephandi seductores regis* (translated simply as 'seducers' on this occasion although elsewhere as 'seducers of the king') in his account of the September 1387 council at Nottingham, where the judges' opinion on the Continual Council of 1386 was confirmed.[67] Knighton claimed De la Pole and his fellows had forced the judges to declare the Continual Council constitutionally illegitimate and to condemn Gloucester and the other commissioners as deserving punishment as traitors. Stating that it was not Richard but his five 'seducers' who had devised and asked the questions, he went on to assert (without warrant) that the judges had merely affixed their seals to a pre-prepared document. Moreover, he added that at least one man – Sir Robert Bealknap, chief justice of Common Pleas – had only complied because De Vere and De La Pole had threatened to kill him.[68]

Knighton's version of events featured coercion and strong-arming aplenty, but the expression *nephandi seductores regis* invoked darker forms of manipulation and domination because it made a rhetorical link between Richard's court and the most commonly used Latin term for sodomy in late fourteenth-century England, *nephandum vitium*, meaning 'unspeakable sin'.[69] In this cultural and religious context, sodomy was not primarily about specific sexual acts but about the inversion of a divinely ordained and therefore natural

65 Ibid.

66 *Knighton's Chronicle*, pp. 392, 404–5. For valuable analysis of discourses of sexual disorder in literary and chronicle accounts of this period, see W. M. Ormrod, 'Knights of Venus', *Medium Aevum* 73 (2004), 290–305; Michael Hanrahan, 'Speaking of Sodomy: Gower's Advice to Princes in the *Confessio Amantis*', *Exemplaria* 14 (2002), 423–46; Hanrahan, 'Seduction and Betrayal'; P. Strohm, 'Treason in the Household', *Hochon's Arrow: The Social Imagination of Fourteenth-Century Texts* (Princeton, 1992), pp. 121–44.

67 *Knighton's Chronicle*, pp. 392–3.

68 Ibid., p. 395.

69 Ruth Mazo Karras, 'The Lechery That Dare Not Speak Its Name: Sodomy and the Vices in Medieval England', *In the Garden of Evil: The Vices and Culture in the Middle Ages*, ed. Richard Newhauser (Toronto, 2005), pp. 193–205; William E. Burgwinkle, *Sodomy, Masculinity, and Law in Medieval Literature: France and England, 1050–1230* (Cambridge, 2004), pp. 48–68; Joan Cadden, *Meanings of Sex Difference in the Middle Ages: Medicine, Science, and Culture* (Cambridge, 1993), pp. 218–25; Mathew Kuefler, 'Male Friendship and the Suspicion of Sodomy in Twelfth-Century France', *Gender and Difference in the Middle Ages*, ed. Sharon A. Farmer and Carol Braun Pasternack (Minneapolis, 2003), pp. 145–81.

hierarchical gender order and it was used to describe a wide range of sinful acts in which men were perceived to adopt the passive, feminine role. This bodily 'perversion' was deemed to stem from wilful rebellion against God, so that sodomy signalled the destruction of all other social and political order. Sodomy acquired its potency through its dangerous unspeakability. As the sin against nature that was so polluting it could not be named, it loomed as a formless yet ever-present threat that could signify any number of both sexual and non-sexual sins. Late medieval political thought harboured conceptual dependencies between the cultural category *nephandum* and the crime of *lèse-majesté*, which was analogous to the charges of accroaching royal power found in the Appeal.[70] The idea of *nephandum* was also wielded more generally to encapsulate the perverse nature of the relationship between Richard and his male intimates, and to represent as sinful corruption the accused traitors' disruption of natural homosocial bonds between the king and his nobles.

Knighton was not the only chronicler to make the connection between treason and sodomy, attesting to the relevance and political potency of this discourse. In the *Westminster Chronicle*'s account of Alexander Neville's trial in the Merciless Parliament, the disgraced archbishop was called 'nephando episcopo'.[71] Elsewhere, Robert de Vere emerged as the man directly responsible for exciting dangerous affections in the king that led to political breakdown. For Knighton, De Vere was Richard's 'amicum specialissimum' whose absence Richard was 'unable to bear', figuring their relationship as one of excessive and exclusionary love that defied masculine reason.[72] To the chronicler, this corrupted form of male bonding lay at the root of wrongs such as that described in Article Eleven of the Appeal, in which De Vere was accused of exploiting his hold over Richard for personal gain by inducing Richard to make him king of Ireland. Finally, in the *St Albans Chronicle* the relationship between the two men was marked with an unequivocally sodomitic character: 'The king was very devoted to [De Vere], and greatly respected and loved him, but not without ignominy, it is said, of an obscene intimacy [*familiaritatis obscene*]'.[73] Walsingham added the reference to obscene intimacy to a later redaction of his chronicle that he produced shortly after Richard's deposition and death, but its presence in that context shows how sexual deviance could

70 Jacques Chiffoleau, 'Dire l'indicible. Remarques sur la catégorie du nefandum du XIIe au XVe siècle', *Annales. Economies, Sociétés, Civilisations* 45 (1990), 289–324.

71 *Westminster Chronicle*, p. 316.

72 *Knighton's Chronicle*, pp. 418–19. For the nuanced fourteenth-century meanings of terms such as *amicum specialissimum* and *singularis familiarus*: Jochen Burgtorf, '"With My Life, His Joyes Began and Ended": Piers Gaveston and King Edward II of England Revisited', *Fourteenth Century England V*, ed. Nigel Saul (Woodbridge, 2008), pp. 31–51 (pp. 37–40).

73 *St Albans Chronicle I*, p. 799.

figure political disintegration.[74] Elsewhere, Walsingham reiterated the natural/unnatural binary, describing the accused traitors doing 'All they could, day and night, to influence the king … So the king's hatred grew greater day by day against the true [*naturales*] and loyal nobles'.[75]

The rhetorical power of sodomy to signal the gendered inversion of natural personal and political bonds between men shadowed the Appeal, with its account of the 'enslaved' Richard being physically controlled, dominated and emotionally manipulated by the men around him. It lurked more overtly in the ninth question to the judges, posed by Richard in September 1397 and revisited in the Appeal and during the Merciless Parliament. This concerned the fate of Richard's deposed great-grandfather Edward II. The reasons for political breakdown, civil war and finally, deposition in 1327 are too complex to address here. However, what is significant is that by Richard's reign, chronicle accounts and popular rumour attributed much of the blame to Edward's excessive and unnatural intimacy with his male favourites, Piers de Gaveston and Hugh Despenser the Younger. When Despenser was executed for treason in 1326, the legal judgment ordered that after he was drawn and hanged:

> [B]ecause you have been at all times disloyal and incited discord between our lord the king and our most noble lady the queen, and between [the king] and the other men of the realm, you will be disembowelled and your bowels will be burnt.[76]

After Edward's death, chroniclers expanded this legal construction of treason as the material and affective division of the body politic with direct accusations of sodomy that became embedded in the collective political memory (and became part of Edward II's enduring reputation).[77] Typical of the cultural intersection of sodomy and treason was Jehan le Bel's mid-fourteenth-century account of Despenser's execution, which added castration to the catalogue of punishments inflicted:

[74] For analysis of Walsingham's changing views of Richard and of the manuscript redactions, see Ormrod, 'Knights of Venus'; James G. Clark, 'Thomas Walsingham Reconsidered: Books and Learning at Late-Medieval St. Albans', *Speculum* 77 (2002), 832–60; George B. Stow, 'Richard II in Thomas Walsingham's Chronicles', *Speculum* 59 (1984), 68–102; V. H. Galbraith, 'Thomas Walsingham and the Saint Albans Chronicle, 1272–1422', *The English Historical Review* 47 (1932), 12–30.

[75] *St Albans Chronicle I*, p. 807.

[76] G. A. Holmes, 'Judgement on the Younger Despenser, 1326', *The English Historical Review* 70 (1955), 261–7 (pp. 266–7, my translation).

[77] Burgtorf, '"With My Life, His Joyes Began and Ended"'; W. M. Ormrod, 'The Sexualities of Edward II', *The Reign of Edward II: New Perspectives*, ed. Gwilym Dodd and Anthony Musson (York, 2006), pp. 22–47; Ian Mortimer, 'Sermons of Sodomy: A Reconsideration of Edward II's Sodomitical Reputation', *The Reign of Edward II*, ed. Dodd and Musson, pp. 48–60.

> First his penis and testicles were cut off because he was a heretic and sodomite, even as it is said with the king himself, and the king has driven away the queen because of his exhortations.[78]

In 1388, pointed references to Edward II's deposition had legal and constitutional relevance. The fate of Richard's great-grandfather had been obliquely raised in the 1386 parliament and in late December 1387, the Appellants had discussed the possibility of deposing Richard if they could not curb him by other means. However, in the midst of another political crisis that was framed in terms of natural and unnatural masculine bonds, Edward's fate also carried deeper cultural import because of the way the relationship between that king, his nobility and his male favourites had come to be reimagined by the 1380s.

TRIAL AND PUNISHMENT IN THE MERCILESS PARLIAMENT

The aptly named Merciless Parliament sat between February and June 1388. In all, it saw eight men publicly executed as traitors, including Brembre, Burley, Tresilian, the lawyer John Blake and several of Richard's household knights. De Vere and De la Pole, convicted *in absentia*, were condemned to drawing and hanging as traitors and the death sentences prevented any future return to England. The judges other than Tresilian were stripped of office and exiled for life, while dozens of members of Richard's household were deprived of their positions and banished from the royal court. Legal and political historians have long debated the legality and constitutional validity of the trials held in this parliament in light of the technical limits of the 1352 statute, questioning in particular the resort to novel procedures of parliamentary appeal and impeachment.[79] Coming at these issues from a different perspective, my analysis of the trials that culminated in execution reveals that shared cultural beliefs about honourable and debased masculinity were integral to the legal process itself, thus gendering the constitutional constructions that became embedded in treason law. More immediately, the model of the traitor as the opposite of the true man informed the Appellants' prosecutorial strategies as well as the defences mounted by the men they accused.

At the opening of parliament on 3 February, the spiritual and temporal lords were quick to assert the customary right of nobles to be tried by their peers 'and not by civil law, nor by the common law of the land, practised in other lower courts'.[80] An expert group comprising both common lawyers and

78 Jehan le Bel, *Chronique de Jean le Bel*, ed. Jules Marie Édouard Viard and Eugène Déprez (Paris, 1977), p. 28. Le Bel's version was repeated virtually word-for-word in the 1390s redaction of Jean Froissart's *Chroniques*: McVitty, 'False Knights', pp. 467–8.

79 For example, Bellamy, *Law of Treason*, pp. 112–13, 168–9; Rogers, 'Parliamentary Appeals of Treason'; Clarke, 'Forfeitures and Treason in 1388'; Plucknett, 'State Trials under Richard II'; Plucknett, 'Impeachment and Attainder'.

80 *PROME*, 'Richard II: February 1388', Part Three, Roll, Item Seven.

civil lawyers had already been consulted on the correct way to proceed, and had found that the Appeal 'had not been made or affirmed in accordance with the procedure required by either law', leaving the cases to be decided 'by the law and usage of parliament'.[81] In practice, this turned out to be a flexible blend of 'ancient custom', common law and the law of arms applied in the Court of Chivalry. Uncertainty about how the truth of accusations should be tested, compounded by the polyvalent nature of treason as a legal and cultural category, left conceptual and procedural gaps that the Appellants exploited to secure convictions. However, those spaces were also colonised by the accused, who drew on legal but also customary and chivalric definitions of treason to defend themselves. The particular blend of defensive strategies that emerged in each case shows that the universalising ideal of true manhood provided a shared discursive and performative register that men tapped into in different ways, depending on their social status and professional identity.

Sir Nicholas Brembre was the first of the accused to appear in person, and he immediately asked for legal counsel and for a written copy of the charges against him. These were the requests of a man who was well-versed in the workings of the common law, and they were unsurprising in someone with Brembre's experience in London civic administration and politics. Specifically, Brembre was likely aware of the original parliamentary reasoning for the 1352 statute, which was enacted in part to ensure that no subject would in future be condemned without a trial. However, when parliament refused his requests, Brembre shifted ground to a legal strategy that invoked contests of honour in the Court of Chivalry, stating 'that he was not guilty of [the charges] in any respect, and that he was ready to prove that by his body as a knight ought to do'.[82]

The appeal articles had repeatedly identified Brembre as 'false knight of London', a naming practice that implicitly invoked the masculine ideal of the true knight, and Brembre's opponents were initially willing to engage him in a legal battle fought on these grounds of knightly honour. Brembre having made his challenge, the Lords Appellant, the other peers, and numerous knights and esquires of the Commons, 'flinging down their gauntlets before the king to the number of 305 and refusing to take them back, wagered battle that the said Nicholas is a false traitor to the king and to his realm'.[83] Following this dramatic display of gauntlet-throwing, the Appellants had second thoughts. Probably, they recognised that trial by combat was a test of masculine truth they could not fully control, and one which could well see Brembre vindicate himself. Backtracking to state that 'battle was not appropriate' in Brembre's case, they declared instead that they would prove their Appeal by

81 Ibid., Part Three.

82 Ibid.

83 *Westminster Chronicle*, p. 283.

other means.[84] This contention over the right to combat as a legal procedure highlights the powerful influence chivalric ideals had on the way treason was being treated in law, but simultaneously stressed that masculine identity was inherently unstable. A man's claim to be a knight had to be continuously performed and defended, and it rested upon the recognition of other men.

In the end, it was not doubts about Brembre's knightly status that sank his defence, but his tarnished reputation as a citizen of the urban polity of London. The London guilds had previously complained that when Brembre was mayor, he and his supporters had used violence and intimidation to retain control of the city.[85] In 1386, the Mercers Company even delivered a petition into parliament alleging that Brembre had:

> Made dyuerse enarmynges bi day & eke bi nyght & destruyd the kynges trewe lyges, som with open slaughtre, some bi false emprisonements ... the next yere after, the same Nichol ... did crye openlich that no man sholde come to chese [the] Mair but such as were sompned [invited] ... [and] he did carye grete quantitee of Armure to the Guyldehalle ... And thus yet hiderward [up until now] hath the Mairaltee ben holden as it were of conquest or maistrye.[86]

That the petition was produced in English rather than French supports Oliver's theory that it was nailed up at the Guildhall and other prominent public sites around London. From there, its contents could be expected to spread swiftly by word of mouth through the streets, marketplaces and alehouses. The petition's accusations were mirrored in the Appellants' charges and references to the civil law concept of 'notoriety' brought Brembre's masculine honour and reputation, or *fama*, into the frame as a mode of proof.[87] This was then put to the test when the Appellants called representatives of the London guilds, as well as the current mayor, several aldermen and the city recorder, before parliament. They were 'to depose to their personal belief' whether Brembre knew about and was therefore guilty of the treasonous plotting catalogued in the Appeal.[88] Brembre's personal iniquities, including the devious business of conducting extrajudicial executions at Foul Oak under cover of darkness, had been central to the charges against him and were proof of his essential nature as a false man and a traitor. On the basis of the Londoners' witness testimony, Brembre was convicted and condemned to death by drawing and hanging at Tyburn on the same day.

Execution rituals sometimes enabled men whose knightly identity was

84 *PROME*, 'Richard II: February 1388', Part Three.

85 Protests are on record from guilds including the Saddlers, Cordwainers, Spurriers and Bladesmiths: Oliver, *Parliament and Political Pamphleteering*, pp. 126–67.

86 'A Petition of the Folk of Mercerye', *A Book of London English 1384–1425*, ed. R. W. Chambers and Marjorie Daunt (Oxford, 1931), p. 34.

87 On notoriety: Rogers, 'Parliamentary Appeals of Treason', pp. 95–102.

88 *Westminster Chronicle*, p. 315

recognised by their fellow elite men to preserve some honour by sparing them the humiliation of public drawing and hanging, allowing instead a swift beheading. Brembre being denied this small mercy, the spectacle of his suffering and abject body shamefully exposed on the gallows at Tyburn – the place where common thieves and murderers went to die – reinforced his identity as a false knight. Moreover, through spatial and symbolic inversion, the execution ritual invoked ideals of civic manhood in order to complete his disgrace and undo his identity as a citizen of London. He was first taken to the Tower, which bordered the city's eastern wall. From there, his executioner was 'to drag him through the city of London as far as the said gallows, and there to hang him by the neck'.[89] The sentence was carried out by Mowbray, the Marshal of England, 'calling upon the aid and authority of the mayor, sheriffs, and aldermen of London'.[90] The London chronicler Thomas Favent added the detail that Brembre was dragged to Tyburn lying upon a hurdle.[91] This would have forced him down into the muck of the London streets, leaving him vulnerable to kicks and blows from the crowds along the way.

The routes used in execution proceedings were often inversions of routes used for royal entries, 'thus spatially tying together two manifestations of authority and power'.[92] A pageant staged for Richard II's entry into London in 1392 followed a route from Bridgegate along Fish Street to Cornhill, along Cheapside to St Paul's, and out to Westminster via Temple Bar in the west.[93] Brembre's route from the Tower to Tyburn would have taken him out of the city via Newgate, but otherwise compassed many of the same sites of civic identity. He was most likely dragged along the route laid out in a city edict of 1382 for the punishment of deviants including adulterers, lecherous priests, procuresses and bawds. This specified for example that recidivist prostitutes should be banished from the city forever after traversing a walk of shame from Aldgate (by the Tower) through the central market of Cornhill, along Cheapside past the Guildhall and St Paul's, and finally out of the city through Newgate.[94] To an audience familiar with witnessing this process applied to London's most despised inhabitants, the dragging marked Brembre as a man utterly rejected by the urban body politic. By rendering him publicly abject and powerless at sites including the Guildhall, where he had formerly wielded authority and performed civic manhood as a citizen and mayor, it also forced him to participate in the destruction of his own masculine identity. As a final insult, Brembre's trip to the gallows took him through the neighbourhoods

89 *PROME*, 'Richard II: February 1388', Part Three.

90 Ibid.

91 Favent, *History*, p. 247.

92 Cohen, 'Symbols of Culpability', p. 410.

93 *Westminster Chronicle*, pp. 502–7.

94 Frank Rexroth, *Deviance and Power in Late Medieval London* (Cambridge, 2007), pp. 147–87. The route is described in a 1382 statute, included as an Appendix at pp. 347–9.

associated with the Mercers, Cordwainers and other London guilds. It had been their testimony that had helped to convict him as a traitor, and it was their London he was dragged through on the way to his death.

Brembre had first appeared in parliament on 17 February and he was executed on 20 February. In between, proceedings were interrupted by the news that Robert Tresilian had been discovered hiding right next door in the sanctuary of Westminster Abbey. Favent made a great meal of this, describing Tresilian disguised in a tunic 'made of old russet, extending down to mid-shin, as if he were an old man', with a rough beard and 'looking more like a pilgrim or beggar than a king's justice'.[95] For the political community, though, the issue was not Tresilian's concealment but whether it was legal for him to be forced out of sanctuary to stand trial. The parliament roll avoided the question altogether, saying simply that he was 'taken and led before the same parliament'.[96] The author of the *Westminster Chronicle*, while no fan of Tresilian's, was more disturbed by the violation of his Abbey's sacred privilege.[97] He was well placed to observe events and described the duke of Gloucester bodily dragging Tresilian out of hiding but then having to shield him from crowds that were 'making savage efforts to set upon him'.[98]

Interestingly, as debate ensued about the legality of Gloucester's actions, it was Tresilian to whom the Lords temporal turned for answers, asking him 'whether the sanctuary ... gave immunity to a traitor against the king and the realm'.[99] Alluding to the Abbey's royal charters, Tresilian replied that it did and he went on to defend himself by pointing to the Appellants' other technical violations of the law. Told that he had been condemned by parliament in his absence, he answered that those proceedings had been 'founded in error and had no force and should accordingly be quashed'.[100] He then demanded the right to prove this 'in accordance with his rights', no doubt a reference to due process as it was followed in King's Bench, the court over which he had presided as chief justice. He was then asked whether he had anything new to say in response to the charges, 'but he had nothing to say or claim to prevent the said execution'.[101] Favent described Tresilian standing 'stock-still and mute' and interpreted this as an outward symptom of his hardened and unrepentant heart.[102] However, this strategy more likely reflected the judge's familiarity

95 Favent, *History*, p. 246.

96 *PROME*, 'Richard II: February 1388', Part Three.

97 *Westminster Chronicle*, pp. 325–7. On Westminster Abbey as a sanctuary: Shannon McSheffrey, *Seeking Sanctuary: Crime, Mercy, and Politics in English Courts, 1400–1550* (Oxford, 2017), pp. 27–35.

98 *Westminster Chronicle*, p. 311.

99 Ibid., p. 313.

100 Ibid.

101 *PROME*, 'Richard II: February 1388', Part Three.

102 Favent, *History*, p. 246.

with silence as the defendant's last redoubt, with the common law acknowledging that those charged with crimes could delay sentencing indefinitely by refusing to plead either 'guilty' or 'not guilty'. Tresilian was immediately taken from parliament and subjected to the same humiliating execution ritual that would be used for Brembre the following day. In the eyes of at least some observers though, his silence enabled him to retain a shred of dignity as 'no fear or shame or dread of death altered his refusal to admit that he had ever been a traitor'.[103] Tresilian's refusal to speak, even when a confession might have saved him from a degrading and painful death, alerts us to the nature of silence not as mere absence or vacancy, but as the active obverse of speech. Standing resolutely mute, first before his accusers in parliament and then his executioner, Tresilian's performative silence was as important to his defence of manly honour as were the chivalric challenges of other men that were orally delivered and bodily tested.

Tresilian's legal associate John Blake also tried to defend himself through silence rather than speech, a strategy that drew on his knowledge of the common law and on a model of civic manhood that privileged intellectual rather than physical prowess. Walsingham identified Blake as an apprentice-at-law, a counterintuitive term which in fact meant he was an experienced senior practitioner of the common law, not a junior or trainee.[104] This status is confirmed by his trusted position as amanuensis to Tresilian and the other judges in 1387 and he likely contributed his own legal expertise in the process of crafting their written opinion in response to Richard's questions about treason. As a senior lawyer with personal connections to men in the top ranks of bench and bar, Blake was the embodiment of learned, literate civic manhood. Like other men of his social class and professional cadre, his masculine identity was performed through service to the king and common good not on the military battlefield, but in the arena of the courtroom. Blake's next step up the career ladder would have been to the illustrious rank of serjeant-at-law, the only men granted audience to plea on behalf of clients in the Court of Common Pleas.[105] His legal training and personal connections suggest this could have been a realistic ambition had he not become embroiled in the political traumas of 1386–8.

Blake was accused of knowing about the treasonous plotting of the king's favourites and of concealing it, and of actively abetting it by having 'made

103 *Westminster Chronicle*, p. 313.

104 *St Albans Chronicle I*, p. 851. Chrimes ('Questions to the Judges', p. 374) thought Blake likely to have been an official of King's Bench; if so, he probably had a personal connection to Tresilian. On terminology: J. H. Baker, 'Audience in the Courts', *Common Law Tradition*, pp. 75–88.

105 Serjeants were the elite of the early legal profession. They had a monopoly on presenting and defending clients' pleas and actions in the court of Common Pleas and it was from their ranks that judges were selected: Baker, 'Audience in the Courts'.

and compiled' the questions asked of the judges in 1387 'so that the questions might be answered in the way in which they were subsequently answered' – a charge that assigned a good deal of agency to Blake in crafting the legal opinion.[106] The charges also indicate that Blake was to be the man tasked with drawing up indictments against the Lords Appellant as part of the plotters' scheme to have Richard execute them as traitors. When the Commons put these charges to Blake, he 'remained for a long time mute and, in order to save the inheritance of his heir, would not speak'.[107] Warned that his silence would not prevent the forfeiture of his lands and goods, and that it was seen as proof of his collusion, Blake found his voice, stating 'that he was retained counsel' of the king 'and sworn loyally to conceal and guard his counsel; and whatever he did, he did at the command of his said liege lord, whom it was proper for him to obey'.[108] Blake's defence deployed dual understandings of manly honour: at one level he invoked a professional ethic of trust between lawyer and client; at a more profound level, in the face of threats of violence and death he was staying true to his oath of obedience to his lord.

Blake was tried alongside Thomas Usk, another member of London's literate, legally learned professional classes. Usk had gained legal experience in his capacity as a city office-holder, as was demonstrated in a 1384 Appeal of treason he lodged against then-mayor John Northampton.[109] Usk's knowledge of the law had also shaped his *Testament of Love*, a long poem in the Boethian tradition that he wrote in response to a spell in prison in 1385. Usk defended himself in a like manner to Blake, claiming he had been acting as a true man and obedient servant to his king. In the end, the pressure on both men became too great. They had first appeared before parliament on 3 March but steadfastly refused to speak. On 4 March, the record reports that they had confessed to all the charges and admitted their guilt; one can only imagine what had been done in the intervening twenty-four hours to extract their confessions. As convicted traitors, both men were condemned to be immediately drawn from the Tower through the city to the gallows at Tyburn and hanged. Usk suffered an additional penalty that reflected his entanglements in civic politics: after hanging, he was to be beheaded 'and his head fixed to the gate of Newgate in London'.[110] According to the *Westminster Chronicle*, Usk's execution was horrifically botched and he was only beheaded 'after about thirty strokes of the axe'; yet 'to the very end he refused to admit having

106 *PROME*, 'Richard II: February 1388', Part Three.

107 *Westminster Chronicle*, p. 285.

108 *PROME*, 'Richard II: February 1388', Part Three.

109 Usk began his career as a legal clerk in the city administration and ended as under-sheriff of Middlesex. Ronald Waldron, 'Usk, Thomas (c.1354–1388)', *Oxford Dictionary of National Biography* (Oxford, 2008).

110 *PROME*, 'Richard II: February 1388', Part Three.

wronged John Northampton, of whom he maintained that every word was true that he had spoken'.[111]

Sir Simon Burley was the next man whose neck was to feel the bite of the executioner's blade. His trial heralded a pivot back from performances of civic manhood to chivalric manhood, with trial by combat again becoming the desired mode of proof. Burley was a man of relatively humble birth who had been tutor to the young Richard II while the king's father, Edward the Black Prince, had still been alive. Following Richard's accession, Burley had risen rapidly in royal service, being welcomed into the Order of the Garter in 1381 and elevated to the earldom of Huntingdon in 1385 – a title the Appellants refused to use.[112] At the time of his trial, Burley also held the office of vice-chamberlain, a powerful position at the centre of the royal household that entailed his own close daily contact with Richard while enabling him to control other men's access to the king.[113] The articles of impeachment focused on Burley's emotional and physical intimacy with the royal person, and his consequent violations of normative homosocial bonds, to construct him as a traitor. The charges against him included that after the 1386 parliament, Burley had 'by his cunning and manipulation' arranged for the disgraced Michael de la Pole to be put under his own guard at Windsor, 'because the king was often resident there', thereby effectively reincorporating De la Pole into Richard's household. It was also alleged that when the Appellants asked Burley to persuade Richard to order Robert de Vere 'not to procure nor cause to be made a levy of armed men and archers', Burley 'haughtily' refused them; and that Burley had brought about 'dispute and troublesome severance' between Richard and his subjects by 'maintaining bad governance about the person of our lord the king, and withdrawing the true and royal heart of the king from the lords and peers of the kingdom and the commons'.[114] According to Article Twelve, this 'bad governance' included bringing Robert de Vere into Richard's household, thus facilitating a toxic relationship between the two young men that led to corruption, dishonour, treason and, if the Appellants did not prevent it, complete destruction of the king and realm.

When these charges were read out in parliament, Burley denied every one of them, 'declaring with spirit that he was ready to prove in personal combat that the accusations made against him were not true'.[115] A rift then developed between the Lords Appellant and the rest of the Lords temporal, with many of

111 *Westminster Chronicle*, pp. 317–19.

112 On Burley's career: Fletcher, *Richard II*, pp. 38–40, 97, 116–17.

113 Chris Given-Wilson, *The Royal Household and the King's Affinity: Service, Politics, and Finance in England, 1360–1413* (New Haven, 1986), pp. 2–6, 72–4; Ormrod, *Political Life in Medieval England*, pp. 19–21.

114 *PROME*, 'Richard II: February 1388', Part Three, Articles of Impeachment, Items Five, Six and Thirteen.

115 *Westminster Chronicle*, p. 319.

the noblemen present being impressed by Burley's performance and inclined to believe he was speaking the truth. The parliament roll gives only a glimpse into the ensuing debate, saying that between 13 April and 5 May 'the [L]ords temporal deliberated with great diligence' over the charges and the circumstances in which they arose.[116] The *Westminster Chronicle* described a much more impassioned conflict of true manhood, which reached its climax with the duke of York offering to wage battle against his own brother Gloucester in defence of Burley's honour. According to York, 'Sir Simon Burley … had been in all his dealings loyal to the king and the realm; and to anybody who wished to deny or gainsay this, he would himself give the lie and prove his point in personal combat'.[117] In reply, Gloucester declared Burley false and 'this he offered to prove … with his own sword-arm', at which York 'turned white with anger and told his brother to his face that he was a liar, only to receive a prompt retort in kind' from Gloucester; 'they would have hurled themselves upon each other' were it not for the intervention of the king.[118]

Sixteen articles of treason were lodged against Burley but in the end, he was found guilty only of Article Eight. This did not mention any deeds against the king himself but instead concerned the supposed plot to have the makers of the 1386 commission indicted and executed as traitors. This was a stretch of the 1352 statute by anyone's measure. More significantly, it transformed Burley's trial into a personal contest of honour between himself and the Appellants, so that the confrontation between York and Gloucester became a proxy for Burley's own demand to prove his trueness through a chivalric trial by combat. Despite York's bold intervention and 'the entreaties and arguments of the king and queen and other exalted persons', on 5 May Burley was sentenced to be drawn from the Tower to Tyburn, hanged and beheaded.[119] Yet in the end, parliament still recognised his years of loyal service and his status as a member of the Order of the Garter. This recognition of his chivalric identity by other men enabled Burley to retain a semblance of knightly manhood in death, as 'for the reason that the said Simon served the king in the time of his youth and also served … the king's father … and likewise because he was a knight of the Garter', the punishments of drawing and hanging were remitted and he was awarded a more dignified beheading 'near the Tower of London'.[120] This concession spared Burley the final degrading trip through the city streets and the torments of hanging. The site of execution at Tower Hill also meant that he remained physically and symbolically within the body politic as it was represented by the royal fortress and the city walls, rather than being wholly ejected from it as Brembre, Tresilian, Blake and Usk had been.

116 *PROME*, 'Richard II: February 1388', Part Three, Articles of Impeachment.

117 *Westminster Chronicle*, p. 329.

118 Ibid.

119 Ibid., p. 331.

120 *PROME*, 'Richard II: February 1388', Part Three, Articles of Impeachment (judgment).

On 12 May, the bloodletting finally came to an end with the executions of Richard's household knights Sir John Beauchamp, Sir James Berners and Sir John Salisbury. All three were sentenced to hanging, drawing and beheading at Tyburn. Beauchamp and Berners were remitted the drawing and hanging and awarded execution by the Tower in recognition of their knightly status, 'gentle blood' and their years of loyal service.[121] However, Salisbury had been found guilty of going in person to the king of France to hand over Calais and other English fortresses in return for French aid against the Appellants. This represented treason against the nation as well as the king and it earned Salisbury the most unforgiving penalty: Mowbray was to take him to the Tower and 'from there drag him through the city of London as far as the gallows at Tyburn, and there hang him by the neck'.[122]

The political traumas of 1386 to 1388 saw the definition and scope of treason contested through men's physical bodies as well as through intertwined legal, political and cultural discourses of true and false manhood. Chivalric, civil law and common law definitions and procedures were all deployed to advance and contest charges of treason, but the legal wrangling was structured and underpinned by gendered understandings of normative political relationships. Richard's emotional alienation and material separation from the men who saw themselves as the king's natural counsellors awakened anxieties that homosocial bonds of loyalty and service which allowed England's political system to function were innately vulnerable to corruption and destruction. According to the Appellants, the king's natural counsellors and true lieges had been displaced by toxic favourites and corrupt counsellors; by processes of inversion, the men they accused of treason emerged as both false and unnatural. In response, men charged with treason sought to prove their true manhood, either by demanding the chivalric right to trial by battle, or by resort to intellectual defences grounded in ideals of service and obedience that shaped civic manhood for men of the legally learned professional classes.

In the trials of the Merciless Parliament, the male body, performing and performed upon, was central to legal, political and constitutional constructions of the traitor but also of the entities against which he offended. When the actions of traitors were figured as the literal dismemberment of the body politic, this discourse gendered the body politic through its implicit reliance on the medieval heuristic that envisioned political bodies as male by default. When convicted traitors were subjected to execution rituals that ended with the public display of their torn and dismembered corpses, it was through the division and destruction of their individual bodies that the masculine body politic of the realm was once again made whole.

121 Ibid.

122 Ibid.

2

TYRANNY, REVENGE AND MANLY HONOUR, 1397–8

The line between principled but forceful political resistance and criminal disorder is ever a fine one. Regardless of legal definitions, in practice the distinctions are often blurred and perceptions of events and personalities can be tilted in either direction by political propaganda and public opinion. These factors were at work in England in the closing days of the Merciless Parliament when the Lords Appellant took steps to legitimise their actions, which in effect had included armed rebellion and usurping royal authority to judge and execute the king's subjects. On 2 June 1388, King Richard heard and granted a series of Commons petitions. These requested general pardons for the citizens of London and anyone else caught on the wrong side between 1386 and 1388; and a more specific undertaking that the Lords Appellant and those who had given them armed support would never in future be 'accused, molested, or harmed for anything aforesaid, either at the suit of the king or that of any party'.[1]

By including references to 'assembly, expedition, combat, raising of pennants or banners' and 'coming and remaining with force and arms, or armed in the presence of the king', as well as imprisonment and homicide, this last petition acknowledged that the Appellants had engaged in violent armed resistance that could in other circumstances be interpreted as treasonous rebellion.[2] However, it carefully justified these actions by implicit reference to *diffidatio*. *Diffidatio* was the formal renunciation of liege homage, which meant breaking the oath of reciprocal trust and fidelity between a man and his lord. According to custom, in dire circumstances knights and noblemen had the right – even the duty – to renounce their fealty to a king who was ruling unjustly and providing bad lordship, and this right extended to defending the common good through armed resistance if necessary.[3] When the 1388 petition framed the Appellants as having acted 'to the honour of God, the salvation of the king … the maintenance of his crown and the salvation of all his kingdom', it was

1 *PROME*, 'Richard II: February 1388', Part One, Roll, Items Thirty-five, Thirty-seven (London), Thirty-eight and Thirty-nine. Quote from Item Thirty-eight.

2 Ibid., Item Thirty-eight.

3 Claire Valente, *The Theory and Practice of Revolt in Medieval England* (Burlington, 2003), pp. 21–5; Bellamy, *Law of Treason*, p. 10.

expansive civil law terms, this shift was less about political ideology and more about expiating the king's hatred against the Appellants and satisfying his need to avenge his honour. Nevertheless, the precedents set had longer-term consequences for the way the relationship between the king and the political abstraction of the state was defined, and for how men imagined and embodied loyal political subjecthood.

The sources for the 1397 trials include the parliament roll and a number of contemporary chronicle accounts. The most detailed of these, *The Chronicle of Adam Usk* and the *Historia Vitae et Regni Ricardi Secundi* by an anonymous monk of Evesham, were based on an account of the parliament compiled by a royal Chancery clerk, which appears to have been widely circulated. Other commentaries can be found in the *St Albans Chronicle* and in the *Continuatio Eulogii* (the 'Continuation' to the *Eulogium Historiarum*).[16] The chronicles help to clarify the chronology of events but their greater value lies in the insights they provide into contemporary perceptions of treason as a legal and cultural phenomenon. Together with the official account, they show that chivalric and civil law perceptions of treason were equally meaningful to the political community, and were used both to construct and to refute the allegations. The rhetoric they deployed and the ways Latin, French and English interacted to authorise the judicial narratives further reveals that men's words were central to the way treason was constructed and contested by all parties to the conflict. A novel statutory interpretation of political speech against the king as an act of *lèse-majesté* was used to help justify the convictions. At the same time, the performance of knightly manhood emerged as a key theme for both prosecution and defence, especially as this was publicly validated by speaking true and keeping one's oaths.

To understand the strategic use of concepts of treason in 1397, the trials must be viewed in light of Richard II's performance of kingship. By the mid-1390s, he had built a formidable power base by creating a royal affinity, extending the reach of his royal household into the provinces and surrounding himself with a large personal bodyguard.[17] According to contemporary chroniclers and to many modern historians, the king used these administrative and military resources to exercise an increasingly autocratic form of rule, one that by 1397 was crossing the line into tyranny.[18] This development has been seen

16 On these and other sources for the parliament see C. Given-Wilson, 'Adam Usk, the Monk of Evesham and the Parliament of 1397–8', *Historical Research* 66 (1993), 329–35; *Chronicles of the Revolution*, pp. 1–53; G. B. Stow, 'The Continuation of the *Eulogium Historiarum*: Some Revisionist Perspectives', *The English Historical Review* 119 (2004), 667–81.

17 Given-Wilson, *The Royal Household and the King's Affinity*, pp. 211–26, 245–51; C. M. Barron, 'The Tyranny of Richard II', *Bulletin of the Institute for Historical Research* 41 (1968), 1–18; Nigel Saul, 'The Kingship of Richard II', *Richard II: The Art of Kingship*, ed. Anthony Goodman and James L. Gillespie (Oxford, 1999), pp. 37–57 (pp. 50–6).

18 For general accounts of the crisis of 1397, see May McKisack, *The Fourteenth Century:*

as the result of Richard's exposure to continental political theories affirming that kings were wholly sovereign in their person and that, as the source of law, they could not be made subject to it.[19] Saul asserted that the extravagant and 'obsequious' manner in which Richard's subjects were expected to address him provides evidence for his exalted view of kingship, although changes to the address style of petitions could also be explained by changing scribal conventions.[20] Nevertheless, there are other indications that Richard was using his royal prerogative in arbitrary ways while dismissing any balancing obligations to rule according to the law and with the benefit of noble counsel. In his chronicle entry for 1397, Thomas Walsingham asserted that 'from that time the king began to tyrannise the people', while the *Continuatio Eulogii* gave us the familiar image of Richard as an imperious and aloof monarch who sat on his throne 'from dinner till vespers, talking to no one but watching everyone, and when his eye fell on anyone, regardless of rank, that person had to bend the knee'.[21] In the articles of Richard's deposition, he was portrayed as a tyrant for abusing the royal judicial prerogative, having said that 'his laws were in his mouth, or sometimes in his breast: and that he alone could alter and create the laws of his realm'.[22] These criticisms were shaped by Lancastrian political rhetoric justifying the deposition and usurpation, and Richard's actions in 1397 were more likely to have been the result of political expedience than the considered application of political theory. Regardless of immediate motivations, the manipulation of treason in the 1397 parliament paved the way for more enduring changes in the constitutional relationship between the king, the state and political subjects. The events of 1386–8 had shown that nobles could use the law to constrain the king and potentially even to separate an intransigent ruler from his crown. In 1397, Richard used his judicial prerogative to assert the indivisibility of king and crown in his own person. This was achieved by portraying insults to his manhood represented in the form of

1307–1399 (Oxford, 1959), pp. 462–98; Michael J. Bennett, *Richard II and the Revolution of 1399* (Stroud, 1999), pp. 90–123; Saul, *Richard II*, pp. 366–404. On the chroniclers' views of Richard: John Taylor, 'Richard II in the Chronicles', *Richard II: The Art of Kingship*, ed. Goodman and Gillespie, pp. 15–35.

19 This interpretation of Richard's kingship was most extensively developed by Richard H. Jones, *The Royal Policy of Richard II: Absolutism in the Later Middle Ages* (Oxford, 1968); Saul, *Richard II*, pp. 459–64; Nigel Saul, 'Richard II and the Vocabulary of Kingship', *The English Historical Review* 110 (1995), 854–77. For alternative interpretations: Caroline Barron, 'The Deposition of Richard II', *Politics and Crisis in Fourteenth-Century England*, ed. John Taylor and Wendy R. Childs (Gloucester, 1990), pp. 132–49; Fletcher, *Richard II*, pp. 7–13, 262–7.

20 Saul, 'Richard II and the Vocabulary of Kingship'. For a counter-argument, see Gwilym Dodd, 'Kingship, Parliament and the Court: The Emergence of "High Style" in Petitions to the English Crown, c.1350–1405', *The English Historical Review* 129 (2014), 515–48.

21 *St Albans Chronicle II*, p. 61; *Continuatio Eulogii*, p. 378.

22 *PROME*, 'Henry IV: October 1399', Part One, Roll, Article Thirty-three.

restraints on his personal power as treasonous attacks on the public authority of the state.

In the parliament of January 1397, there were already signs of how Richard II was coming to view his position when the Chancellor described the king as 'complete emperor in his realm of England' and therefore as acting in the 'plenitude of his royal power'.[23] A second parliament was called for September and the events leading up to it show that it was intended primarily to serve as a legal theatre in which Richard could wreak his personal vengeance on the Lords Appellant while at the same time reversing the dangerous constitutional precedents they had set. In July, Richard had Gloucester and Arundel arrested and on 5 August, eight of the king's closest supporters presented an Appeal of treason against the two noblemen. These 'Counter-Appellants' included John and Thomas Holand, the king's half-brother and his nephew who were the earls of Huntingdon and Kent (the former elevated to this title after the execution of its previous incumbent, Simon Burley); Thomas Mowbray, who had by now abandoned his former allies; Richard's cousins Edward, earl of Rutland and John Beaufort, earl of Somerset; and John Montague, earl of Salisbury.[24] In a move stage-managed by Richard, they asked that their Appeal be heard in the September parliament.

The Lords and Commons assembled on 17 September and on the opening day, the king extended a general pardon to all his subjects for past offences, including those relating to the crisis of 1386–8.[25] This was not the generous act of royal grace that it may initially appear, for the pardon excluded certain unspecified offences as well as fifty individuals the king refused to name. The people on this secret blacklist would only be identified when they were brought before parliament to answer for their crimes.[26] Then on 18 September, parliament revoked the 1388 pardons that Richard had granted to Gloucester, Arundel and Warwick.[27] In Arundel's case, the second personal pardon granted in April 1394 at the king's palace of Windsor was also revoked.[28] The nature of royal pardons and whether or not they could honourably be revoked became a central theme in the trials that followed.

23 *PROME*, 'Richard II: January 1397', Item Twenty-eight: 'nostre seignour le roy, come entier emperour de son roialme d'Engleterre, pur honour de son sank, voet, et ad de sa plenir roial poiar hablie' (my translation).

24 During this parliament the Counter-Appellants were rewarded with elevations to dukedoms or marquisates. Rutland, Kent, Huntingdon and Nottingham were awarded the dukedoms of Aumale, Surrey, Exeter and Norfolk; Somerset was made marquis of Dorset: *PROME*, 'Richard II: September 1397', Part One, Roll, Item Thirty-five.

25 *PROME*, 'Richard II: September 1397', Part One, Roll, Item Three. The pardon required payment and was to be sued out of chancery: Lacey, *Royal Pardon*, pp. 169–75.

26 Lacey, *Royal Pardon*, pp. 169–75; Barron, 'Tyranny of Richard II', pp. 7–9.

27 *PROME*, 'Richard II: September 1397', Part One, Roll, Item Twelve.

28 Ibid., Item Thirteen.

Another critical step was the enactment of a new statute of treasons.[29] This extended the provisions of the 1352 statute, for alongside the act of 'compassing or imagining' the king's death, the new statute identified as a traitor anyone who plotted or planned ('compasse et purpose') to depose the king or to renounce their liege homage.[30] As will be seen, the nobles' activities on this score had never advanced beyond verbal discussion, but by framing such thoughts and words as material acts of treason, the statute drew on the notion of *lèse-majesté*, wherein insulting or denigrating the king's person was interpreted as treason against the public authority he embodied. The new provision also explicitly categorised knightly *diffidatio* as treason, shutting the door on the kinds of forceful remedial action used in 1386–8 to restore good governance. These extensions were not intended to address treason at a broad jurisprudential level but were specifically designed to give judicial legitimacy to the killing of Arundel and Gloucester. The trials were motivated by Richard's desire to avenge the death of his favourites at the hands of the Lords Appellant in 1388 and to pre-empt a new plot he feared was being hatched against him.[31] However, in light of Richard's ideas about kingship and majesty, it is likely the expanded definition of treason would have remained in force had it not been for his deposition.

From its opening clauses, the 1397 Appeal of treason made use of the civil law idea of *lèse-majesté* but it was also shaped by customary masculine values of honour and loyalty. The Counter-Appellants described themselves as Richard's 'humble foster-children and lieges' ('voz humblez nurriz et lieges'), a self-representation that alluded to literal kinship connections between the king and several of the Counter-Appellants, as well as to a figurative knightly brotherhood with others such as Salisbury and Mowbray, who were members of the Order of the Garter headed by the king.[32] The allegations against Arundel and Gloucester modelled the language of the 1352 statute by accusing them of having 'assembled … with a great number of men armed and arrayed, forcibly to wage war'.[33] However, specific charges that they had 'usurped, perpetrated, imagined, and done things against and upon your high and royal majesty, crown, and estate, as traitors to you and your kingdom' and that they were 'intending to accroach and take to themselves the governance

29 *Statutes*, II, pp. 98–9; *PROME*, 'Richard II: September 1397', Part One, Roll, Item Eighteen. Item Thirty-two added that all ordinances, declarations and decrees of the September 1397 parliament were to be held as statutes.

30 Bellamy, *Law of Treason*, p. 114.

31 Saul, *Richard II*, pp. 366–8; Bennett, *Richard II*, pp. 92–102; Fletcher, *Richard II*, pp. 250–4. Fletcher argues that vengeance for the dishonour of 1386–8, rather than fears of a new plot, was Richard's primary motivation.

32 *PROME*, 'Richard II: September 1397', Part Two, Pleas, Item Two. For this meaning of *nurriz*: *AND*.

33 Ibid., Item Five.

of your royal person, your realm, your laws and liberties, and all your dignity' pushed the interpretation further.[34] The references to Richard's majesty, crown and estate drew on civil law concepts and this is redolent in the charge that the accused had usurped the king's role as the source of law by accroaching Richard's 'laws and liberties'. The argument that Richard indivisibly united the king's private and public powers in his person was given rhetorical weight by having the charges lodged by subjects who described themselves as acting simultaneously in a personal capacity, as the king's 'foster-children', and in a public capacity as his 'humble lieges'. Richard's embodiment of sovereign majesty was emphasised in the description of the Counter-Appellants delivering their Appeal to 'your royal person ... you, most redoubtable lord, being seated in your royal state, the crown upon your head'.[35]

The charges drew power from the interpretation of treason as *lèse-majesté* but they simultaneously portrayed the accused as violators of chivalric honour and the values of true manhood. Richard's need to revenge himself for the old wounds of 1386–8 can be seen especially in Items Five and Six of the Appeal. Item Five described the Appellants forcing Richard to swear an oath of surety to allow them to come and go from his presence safely. Notwithstanding this oath, the Appeal alleged, the noblemen then entered 'your royal palace at Westminster with a great force of armed men and forced you and treacherously caused you to take them into your safe protection, against your will'.[36] Entering the king's presence in arms and with such a threatening attitude fell within the 1352 ambit of riding in arms against the king and it also echoed standard common law rhetoric of acting 'by force and arms'. However, the greater harm lay in coercing Richard to swear an oath of surety for fear of 'their force and wickedness' but then in refusing to accept that this oath offered any real protection. These actions implicitly insulted Richard's manly honour, as he was first made to swear a false oath and was then faced with the refusal to accept that his word, as a man and as king, was his bond. Item Six concerned the 1388 execution of Richard's dear friend Sir Simon Burley. The Appeal charged that Arundel, Gloucester and Warwick had hauled Burley up before parliament to accuse him of 'various acts of crime and *lèse-majesté*'.[37] When Richard refused to endorse these charges publicly, the Appellants resorted to more devious measures by inducing the king:

> To come to a secret place at Westminster, [where] they expounded to you the points of the aforesaid crime: to which you answered then that the said Simon was guilty on none of the said points. And there they took it upon themselves

34 Ibid., Items Two and Three.
35 Ibid., Item Two.
36 Ibid., Item Five.
37 Ibid., Item Six.

> treacherously to constrain you to give your assent to the judgment which they had planned.[38]

This charge, together with Item Five, portrayed the Appellant lords as purveyors of false speech, who exploited their personal access to the king in order to draw him into a 'secret place' where they verbally coerced him into endorsing their allegations against Burley. False speech was also the fundamental issue raised in Item Seven, which charged the nobles with planning to withdraw their liege homage and then depose Richard. 'By common agreement amongst them', they had searched the records for precedents and 'said falsely and treacherously that they had adequate reason to depose you'.[39]

When legal and constitutional historians discuss the events of 1388 and their subsequent punishment in 1397, they tend to measure the Appellants' actions in terms of the technical limits of the 1352 statute. From this perspective, debate has centred on whether or not the noblemen's most obvious physical actions of gathering troops and riding to London amounted to the treasonous act of riding in arms with banners raised against the king. However, issues of false speech and of oaths and their breaking were equally important to the treason cases established against Arundel, Gloucester and Warwick. Repeated references to speech acts that violated the norms of manly trueness show that the chivalric understanding of treason as a personal betrayal of knighthood was as important as the statutory definitions of either 1352 or 1397. In their explanations of their own actions, Arundel and Gloucester drew on discourses of knightly honour and true manhood to represent themselves as loyal political subjects. In turn, it was Richard's deceptive and dishonourable behaviour and his failure to keep his oaths that attracted the strongest criticism from contemporaries.

THE TRIAL OF THE EARL OF ARUNDEL

Arundel was the first to face his accusers. The official record of his trial preserved in the parliament roll was heavily edited and it eschewed the richer details preserved in the *Historia Vitae et Regni Ricardi Secundi* and in *The Chronicle of Adam Usk*. The chroniclers provided a largely accurate chronology of events that corroborated the official record but they framed their interpretations through the lens of chivalric culture and expectations of masculine honour, presenting Arundel's defence as a dramatic performance of knighthood that called upon the king to honour his oaths as a true man. Reading across the official and unofficial accounts, we soon see the strategies the king and his supporters used to cloak their actions in legality but can also discern how the wider political community perceived the king's actions: as

38 Ibid.

39 Ibid., Item Seven.

unjust in a legal sense, but also as dishonourable and unmanly. The parliament roll contained a seemingly neutral account of the trial that was carefully structured to suggest that proceedings were conducted strictly within legal limits. The king's uncle John of Gaunt, the duke of Lancaster, conducted the prosecution in his capacity as Steward of England. Gaunt's role in the trial reflected contemporary informal understanding that the Steward exercised delegated powers in parliament as the king's highest judge; as Walsingham explained, he was 'acting in accordance with the responsibility of his office'.[40] By appointing Gaunt as judge in Arundel's case, Richard was also able to exploit long-standing personal enmities between the two men to ensure the scales of justice were weighted against Arundel from the outset.[41]

The record opened with Arundel being brought into parliament at the request of the Counter-Appellants, where their Appeal was read out to him and he was told to answer the charges. Arundel's first defensive move was to claim the protection of the pardons issued to him in 1388 and 1394, only to be told that those pardons had just been revoked on the king's order. This had been justified on the grounds that the pardons had been extracted 'to the deceit of the king' and had been cancelled 'by the assent of the king and of all the estates of parliament'.[42] This extraordinary act of undoing the king's grace was given the stamp of judicial validity through reference to the statute in which it was formalised. An attempt was then made to use the threat of a traitor's death to coerce a confession as 'the king ordered Sir Walter Clopton, his chief justice, to say and declare to the said earl of Arundel the law, and the penalty he would suffer, if he did not say anything else'.[43] Seeing the forces ranged against him, at this point Arundel was likely well aware his life was forfeit; the only power he retained was the power of silence. Saying nothing, he refused to compromise his own masculine honour with a false confession and deprived Richard of the satisfaction of a verbal admission of guilt. The trial record elided the personal confrontation between Richard and Arundel over the latter's defiant silence in a curt statement that the earl, 'notwithstanding the repeal of the aforesaid pardon and charter, did not speak, nor did he wish to say anything else, unless it was to ask for allowance of the aforesaid charter and pardon'.[44] The record went on to describe the Counter-Appellants entreating Richard to give immediate judgment against Arundel 'as convicted

40 *St Albans Chronicle II*, p. 87; on the nature and extent of the Steward's authority: Bellamy, *Law of Treason*, p. 169.

41 James Sherborne, 'Perjury and the Lancastrian Revolution of 1399', *Welsh History Review* 14 (1988), 217–41 (pp. 222, 233).

42 *PROME*, 'Concerning Richard earl of Arundel' in 'Richard II: September 1397', Part Two, Pleas.

43 Ibid.

44 Ibid.

of all of the points'.[45] The king assented to this and the earl was sentenced to be drawn, hanged, beheaded and quartered, with all his lands, titles and other property subject to perpetual forfeiture. The king remitted the drawing, hanging and quartering because Arundel was of noble blood, but the earl was taken straight to the Tower and beheaded there the same day.[46]

The chronicle accounts of Arundel's trial give a rather different impression of how the wider political community interpreted these events. The monk of Evesham used dialogue and reported speech to create a sense of veracity, an approach that made this account read like an eyewitness statement and so heightened its purported truth value.[47] The chronicler drew on the language of chivalric manhood to contrast the knightly Arundel with the dishonourable king and the sycophantic officials who did his dirty work. However, the narrative also tapped into the language of popular complaint by introducing (in Arundel's mouth) the idea of the 'true commons' as a wider representative political community that was deliberately excluded from the parliament but that acted as an external witness to its illegitimate actions. In place of this true commons and colluding in Arundel's wrongful conviction was a pliant and submissive parliamentary Commons, egged on by the royal favourite Sir John Bussy as Speaker. The *Vita Ricardi Secundi* opened with the dramatic image of Arundel standing before parliament clad in the scarlet robe and hood that visually marked his elite social and political status as an earl. Gaunt immediately ordered that he be stripped of his hood and sword belt, a ritual of inversion that was intended to mark publicly and with maximum humiliation Arundel's fall from an identity as nobleman and knight to an identity as traitor.[48] Gaunt read out the Appeal, in response to which Arundel 'vehemently denied that he was a traitor' and claimed the benefit of his 1388 pardon.[49] An intense argument then ensued, first between Arundel and Gaunt but soon with the addition of other voices including that of the king himself, whose voice had been occluded in the parliament roll because Justice Clopton had served as his mouthpiece. At the heart of this verbal combat was

45 Ibid.

46 Ibid.

47 *HVRS*, pp. 142–4. See also *Chronicles of the Revolution*, pp. 58–60. The account in the *St Albans Chronicle* has many similarities, including the use of dialogue and reported speech: *St Albans Chronicle II*, pp. 86–95. On the use of these rhetorical techniques to craft persuasive legal narratives: McSheffrey and Pope, 'Ravishment, Legal Narratives, and Chivalric Culture in Fifteenth-Century England', pp. 820–1; Wicker, 'The Politics of Vernacular Speech', pp. 159–85.

48 *HVRS*, p. 142. On such rituals of inversion, see Westerhof, 'Deconstructing Identities on the Scaffold', pp. 91–2; Royer, 'The Body in Parts', pp. 330–1; Fionn Pilbrow, 'The Knights of the Bath: Dubbing to Knighthood in Lancastrian and Yorkist England', *Heraldry, Pageantry and Social Display in Medieval England*, ed. Peter R. Coss and Maurice Keen (Woodbridge, 2002), pp. 195–218 (pp. 195–6).

49 *HVRS*, p. 142.

the issue of true and false speech, and therefore of the performance of true manhood. When Gaunt told Arundel his pardon had been revoked, Arundel hotly replied that Gaunt was a liar and that he had never been a traitor. Gaunt argued that Arundel must have been guilty of treason to request a pardon in the first place, but Arundel countered that he had only sought the pardon 'to silence the tongues of my enemies, of whom you are one'.[50] Arundel then claimed that when it came to treason, Gaunt's slanders and lies had left him in bigger need of a pardon than he was, phrasing that confirms the earl's conception of treason was shaped primarily by chivalric values rather than by more prescriptive statutory definitions.

At this point, the king intervened directly to demand that Arundel answer the Appeal. In the *Vita Ricardi Secundi*, Justice Clopton was nowhere to be seen so the veneer of judicial neutrality his voice had added to the measured account of the parliament roll is missing. Arundel, speaking directly to Richard, asserted he could still claim a second pardon, 'which you, within the last six years when you were of full age and free to act as you wished, granted to me of your own will'.[51] This referred to the 1394 pardon, granted in the years after Richard declared his majority in May 1389. To this, Richard replied that he had only granted the pardon 'provided that it were not to my prejudice', thus implying that it was extracted dishonestly and under duress.[52] Gaunt said this made the pardon worthless but Arundel denied having anything to do with extracting it and said he had known nothing of it until it had already been 'willingly granted' by the king.[53] Underlying this debate about the pardon was a dense network of assumptions about the king's manhood and his ability to fully embody the sovereign powers of justice and mercy. By 1394, Richard had freed himself of commissions of government. He had declared his majority and asserted that he was now acting in the fullness of his masculine authority as a mature king, exemplified in his unique power to pardon through the sacral act of royal grace. Gaunt's suggestion that Arundel had manipulated or coerced Richard into granting a pardon had dangerous implications, for it suggested that Richard was not fully embodying royal power or, as Arundel put it, 'of full age and free to act as you wished'.[54] By questioning the king's ability to confer grace of his own royal will, this line of dispute between Gaunt and Arundel threatened to undermine Richard's masculine performance of kingship and his claim to be fully sovereign in his person. The *St Albans Chronicle* pursued this theme in greater depth. Walsingham seems to have been informed by an eyewitness for he described the king, 'by his head-shaking and bodily gestures ... show[ing] that he had

50 Ibid.
51 Ibid.
52 Ibid.
53 Ibid., pp. 142–3.
54 Ibid., p. 142.

little regard' for Arundel's argument.[55] Adding that it was contrary to God and unlawful for Richard to revoke the pardons, Walsingham maintained that these actions 'had very great repercussions against the person of the king, since showing mercy confirms the authority to the royal throne and he who removes from the king the opportunity for showing mercy removes the foundation for royal authority'.[56]

This perception that revoking the pardons weakened royal authority had the potential to jeopardise the careful work Richard had done after the crisis of 1386–8 to assert his identity as a mature adult sovereign, rather than a boy incapable of independent rule. Gaunt's line of attack therefore risked voicing in parliament awkward questions about Richard's manhood and his kingship. The Evesham chronicler implied that Richard was aware of this risk and this helps to explain an abrupt change of tack as another voice entered the debate, that of Sir John Bussy. Bussy added the weight of parliamentary legitimacy to the cancelling of the 1394 pardon, saying that it had been revoked 'by the king, the lords, and us, the true commons'.[57] However, the concept of the true commons also provided Arundel with an interpretive tool to criticise the king's actions, one that drew on the language of popular political complaint as well as on the evidentiary weight of true manhood in the legal arena. Arundel and the other Appellants had already shown they knew the strategic value of appealing to the commons with their open letter to the populace of London in 1387. More specifically, it was juries of 'true men' who were called upon in the public arena of royal courtrooms to determine the guilt or innocence of those indicted. Faced with a rigged trial in parliament, Arundel protested the absence of a similar community of true men, who had been excluded in order to ensure his unjust conviction based on the testimony of false men and liars. We can assume that proceedings in parliament were being conducted in English. The account of the verbal duel between Arundel and Bussy therefore imbued Arundel's words with the authenticating power of first-person vernacular speech as he challenged:

> 'Where are those true commons? I know all about you and those about you, and how you have come to be gathered here – not to act honestly, but to shed my blood. The true commons of the realm are not here; if they were, it may be that they would take my side in this struggle, to stop me from falling into your hands. They, I know, are grieving greatly for me; while I know well that you have always been false.' Then this Bussy and his supporters shouted, 'Look,

55 *St Albans Chronicle II*, p. 83. Walsingham's detailed account of the 1399 parliament was based in part on information from the bishop of Carlisle, who stayed at St Albans before and after the session (*Chronicles of the Revolution*, p. 200). Given St Albans' prominent role providing hospitality to people travelling to and from the royal court, Walsingham could well have had a similar episcopal informer in 1397.

56 *St Albans Chronicle II*, p. 83.

57 *HVRS*, p. 143.

> lord king, at how this traitor is trying to stir up distrust between us and the commons who have stayed at home.' To which the earl replied, 'You are all liars. I am no traitor.'[58]

With these words, Arundel carved a chasm between the 'true commons of the realm' who were absent and the corrupt and false Commons doing the king's bidding by having Arundel wrongfully condemned as a traitor. Whereas the legalistic account in the parliament roll sought to constrain the trial within the framework of parliamentary judicial process and the new statute of treason, the *Vita Ricardi Secundi* represented it as a battle over personal honour and the trueness of individual men. By speaking falsely, Bussy and his backers – who included the noble Counter-Appellants as well as the Commons – colluded with Richard in perpetrating an unjust and therefore dishonourable and unmanly act of violence against Arundel.

When Bussy called Richard into the conversation, it was a reminder that the king's desire for vengeance lay behind Arundel's trial. Judicial execution embodied the monarch's right and duty to 'do justice', and this right worked in harmony with chivalric values that endorsed the rational exercise of just violence for legitimate ends. The idea that a good lord would take violent, even vengeful, action when necessary was integral to cultural expectations about manhood generally and about kingship specifically.[59] By contrast, the chronicler interpreted Richard's actions as being motivated not by his duty as a king or his honour as a knight, but by personal hatred and wilful desire that had led to his unnatural corruption of royal justice.[60] This was made apparent in the next passage, where the king directly challenged Arundel about the 1388 execution of Simon Burley. Richard accused Arundel of telling him 'in the bathhouse behind the white hall [of Westminster Palace], that Simon Burley was for various reasons worthy of death', and that this sentence was carried out despite the king's protestations.[61] By first asserting that Arundel and his fellow Lords Appellant had 'traitorously put [Burley] to death' and then immediately demanding that sentence be passed on Arundel, the account made clear that as far as Richard was concerned, this was the main offence for which Arundel

58 *HVRS*, p. 143. While *fideles* can be translated as 'faithful', 'fidelis' and analogues like *fidedignes* were generally rendered in English as 'true' or 'trustworthy' in other legal contexts involving proof; for example, the 'true men' that made up juries were routinely described as *fidedignes* in Latin records.

59 Fletcher, *Richard II*, pp. 25–44.

60 It was this interpretation of Richard's motivations that later appeared in the articles of deposition: *PROME*, Henry IV: October 1399', Part One, Roll, Article Twenty-one.

61 *HVRS*, p. 143: 'Tui, in balneo retro albam aulam, quod Symon de Burlei reus erat mortis propter plures causas … Pro quo etiam ego et uxor mea regina obnixe rogauimus, et tamen tu et socii tui, spretis precibus nostris'. This mirrors the charge in Item Six of the Appeal, although with the additional lurid detail that the 'secret place' to which Richard was lured was a Westminster bathhouse.

was being punished.[62] This implied the king's own speech was false and his word could not be trusted, as he went back on his performative acts of royal grace in granting the pardons of 1388 and 1394.

The reasons for Arundel's conviction given in the official sentence were:

> Because the said treasons were so high; and they would have surrendered their liege homage and deposed the king from his crown, regality, estate, and dignity, and because the act of war was so notorious.[63]

Of these offences, two – planning to withdraw liege homage or to depose the king – had only just been defined in law as acts of treason. The decision made by the monk of Evesham to centre his account of the trial on the personal enmity between Richard and Arundel rather than on technical arguments conditioned by the new statute suggests that Richard may have been widely perceived even at that time as using legal fictions to cloak a wilful act of injustice. Certainly, by the time Richard was deposed two years later, the devious methods he employed to secure Arundel's death were held up as clear examples of the king's tyranny and falseness, as he was accused of 'showing a cheerful and kindly face' to Arundel while 'nourish[ing] hatred in his heart', and of 'damnably' causing Arundel's wrongful execution against justice and the laws of the realm.[64]

Walsingham's account reinforces the extent to which contemporary responses to the 1397 treason trials were conditioned by ideas about true and false manhood, with the conflict between Arundel and the king framed through the oppositional relationship between treason and knighthood in chivalric culture rather than legalistic interpretations. Walsingham described the Counter-Appellants throwing down their gloves and offering to fight a duel to prove their charges.[65] This ritualised gesture placed their Appeal firmly within the context of trial by battle as a judicial ordeal designed to test the truth of a man's speech upon his body. For Walsingham the Counter-Appellants' claims to knightly manhood rang utterly false and he depicted their performance as mere outward acting when, 'with their bodily gestures and ignominious leaping about they made themselves look more like theatrical executioners than knights'.[66] By contrast, Arundel's true knighthood was validated by his refusal to speak falsely even when facing death. Urged to confess and beg another pardon, 'he openly refused to do this and said: "I never was a traitor to the king, either in word or deed"'.[67] In the end, it was

62 Ibid.

63 *PROME*, 'Concerning Richard earl of Arundel' in 'Richard II: September 1397', Part Two, Pleas.

64 *PROME*, 'Henry IV: October 1399', Part One, Roll, Article Twenty-one.

65 *St Albans Chronicle II*, p. 89.

66 Ibid.

67 Ibid., p. 93.

Arundel's innate inability to be false – his embodiment of true manhood – that proved his undoing as he asserted, 'this alone I confess, that by reason of my artlessness I did not know how, or was unable, to please the king as he desired'.[68] Arundel's artlessness drew a stark contrast to the falseness of a king who would unjustly and dishonourably revoke his promises of grace, and to the dishonest words of his royal favourites, which Walsingham characterised as at best obsequious flattery (*verbis adulacionis*) and at worst as malicious lies.[69]

THE CONFESSION AND CONVICTION OF THE DUKE OF GLOUCESTER

On 21 September, the same day that Arundel was beheaded at the Tower, Richard engineered the post-mortem conviction of the duke of Gloucester. The duke's absence made this a document-centred performance in which the outcome was achieved through the manipulation of writs, of Gloucester's letter of confession, and of the parliament roll itself, which was edited to create the narrative the king desired.[70] These evidentiary texts use a mixture of Latin, French and English and they provide a detailed insight into how language choice itself could work to authenticate, but also to subvert, legal narratives of treason.

Proceedings began with the production of a writ that ordered Thomas Mowbray, Marshal of England and captain of Calais, to bring Gloucester into parliament to answer the Appeal of treason against him. By this time, Richard must have known that Gloucester was already dead.[71] Nevertheless, the writ made full use of the linguistic and judicial authority of Latin to construct the image of a just king giving an accused subject his rights under the law to hear and answer the charges against him. The writ said that the case was 'to be prosecuted according to the law and custom practised in our kingdom of England', and Gloucester was to be brought 'safely and securely before us and our council in our aforesaid parliament … to answer the aforesaid appellants'.[72] Three days later Mowbray returned the writ, which publicly confirmed Gloucester's death. The Counter-Appellants requested that Gloucester be

68 Ibid.

69 Ibid., pp. 82–3, 89.

70 Giancarlo lays out the manipulations of the parliament roll and other documents in detail: 'Murder, Lies, and Storytelling', pp. 79–92. Richard's deliberate falsification of the record of this parliament was one of the charges brought against him at his deposition.

71 Tait, 'Did Richard II Murder the Duke of Gloucester?'; Stamp, 'Richard II and the Death of the Duke of Gloucester'; Wright, 'Richard II and the Death of Gloucester'; Giancarlo, 'Murder, Lies, and Storytelling', pp. 85–6.

72 *PROME*, 'Concerning Thomas duke of Gloucester' in 'Richard II: September 1397', Part Two, Pleas.

declared a traitor forthwith and subjected to the penalty of total forfeiture. At this point, the Counter-Appellants took up the role of active speakers and the language of the roll changes to French, mirroring the practice for transforming verbal pleading and testimony into written record in common law courts. They accused Gloucester and his men of having assembled 'armed and arrayed to wage war against the king' and of having appeared before Richard in force, asserting that this amounted to levying war against the king.[73] They then alluded to the notoriety of Gloucester's treason, for 'all the lords temporal of the said parliament … said that the said crime and treason were well known to them, and to all the realm'.[74] There are several interesting features in these charges. Firstly, they all related to the events of 1387–8, for which Gloucester had already been pardoned more than once. This had included the pardons granted at the close of the 1388 parliament but also Richard's second pardon granted in the royal chapel at Langley, which reconciled the two men before God as king and subject and as nephew and uncle. Secondly, as shall be seen, Gloucester positioned his own actions in 1387–8 as an act of knightly *diffidatio* that was intended to rid Richard of 'wicked advisers' and to restore just rule for the common good. In the Appeal, his actions were re-framed as levying war against the king by using terminology that reflected the 1352 statute. Thirdly, the allegation of notoriety was deployed to justify Gloucester's summary conviction. Notoriety drew on the deep cultural well of ideas relating to a man's *fama*, and to what was said about him by true men of good repute. It therefore acted as a communal form of witness testimony. According to the influential legal treatise *The Mirror of Justices*, if a man's treason was notoriously known, there was no need for a trial and the king could move straight to conviction and execution.[75]

The sentence of perpetual forfeiture for Gloucester and his heirs followed. The duke's kinship to the king was recalled by including a provision that not only should his heirs lose their noble titles and lands but they should never 'bear the royal arms of England whole or with difference … nor should they inherit the crown'.[76] Then with no break in the record, we are alerted to the next act in the drama when we are told that on 25 September, the Counter-Appellants asked Richard 'that if anything was on record, be it by confession of any of the persons thus accused, or of any other person' regarding their Appeal, that it should be declared.[77] This cued the disclosure of Gloucester's confession, written in the first-person vernacular and witnessed at Calais

73 Ibid.

74 Ibid.

75 Bellamy, *Law of Treason*, pp. 19–20, 29, 31. On the resort to notoriety to convict Gloucester *in absentia*: Rogers, 'Parliamentary Appeals of Treason', pp. 120–1.

76 *PROME*, 'Concerning Thomas duke of Gloucester' in 'Richard II: September 1397', Part Two, Pleas.

77 Ibid.

by Sir William Rickhill, chief justice of the court of Common Pleas and the realm's most senior common law official. The confession represents one of the rare examples of English in the parliament roll prior to the mid-fifteenth century, and it is not simply due to convenience that it was preserved in its original vernacular form. The duke's voice was heard from beyond the grave as it was read out by Rickhill, with the intent clearly being that through this verbal performance Gloucester would be condemned by his own sworn words. Richard used Rickhill's unblemished judicial reputation to give the confession its legal veracity, although the judge was himself a victim of trickery and documentary falsifications in the process of its production.[78] The version of the confession recorded in the parliament roll was edited to exclude several mitigating factors raised by Gloucester in his own defence, but Rickhill kept a second, complete copy that he produced after Richard's deposition.[79]

The growing status of English as a language of record meant that in legal contexts, it fixed in textual form the proof of a man's sworn word, thus allowing documents to represent men's verbal testimony under oath in a court of law.[80] When the vernacular was used to embed Gloucester's edited confession within the parliament roll, the intent was to imbue the record with this same judicial truth-value and this became a doubled process of authentication when Justice Rickhill spoke with Gloucester's voice. Giancarlo notes that in the legal arena 'a written instrument or record implied a certain legitimacy and authenticity, but its oral recitation (unavoidably recorded in the written record) was necessary for its felicitous performance'.[81] There is no doubt this performance was stage-managed by Richard to give legal legitimacy to Gloucester's conviction, for it presented the duke to the political community as a self-confessed traitor. However, by allowing Gloucester's own voice into parliament, the prosecution proceedings inadvertently created space for an alternative narrative to be preserved. This was one in which Gloucester defended himself through the vocabulary of knighthood, honour

78 Giancarlo, 'Murder, Lies, and Storytelling', pp. 84–92: Rickhill was provided with writs that were deliberately left un-dated or were post-dated to fit the king's falsified timeline, and he was initially not told why he was being sent to Calais.

79 *PROME*, 'Concerning Thomas duke of Gloucester' in 'Richard II: September 1397', Part Two, Pleas, for the version of the confession read to parliament. There are at least two other official versions of the document. Wright ('Richard II and the Death of Gloucester') notes that a full copy of the confession is attached as a separate document to the parliament roll for 1397, but he argues this was done after 1399 when Richard's tampering with the roll had been revealed. It is generally agreed that the edited version from the 1397 parliament was the version publicly circulated to justify Gloucester's conviction. See Giancarlo, 'Murder, Lies, and Storytelling', p. 82 n. 15.

80 For an expanded analysis of this development see E. Amanda McVitty, '"My Name of a Trewe Man"': Gender, Vernacularity, and Treasonous Speech in Late Medieval England', *Parergon* 33 (2016), 91–111; Wicker, 'The Politics of Vernacular Speech'.

81 Giancarlo, 'Murder, Lies, and Storytelling', pp. 91–2.

and noble duty, and in which he represented himself as a true man and loyal subject. While some of his most compelling mitigations were edited out of the confession read before parliament, even those elements that formed part of the official record brought into sharp relief the troubling cultural and legal implications of conflicts over the meaning of treason.

The confession in the parliament roll was undated and it excluded three major clauses and one significant phrase that appeared in the other copies of the text.[82] These more complete copies were dated 8 September, one day prior to the day on which Gloucester was murdered. By erasing the date, Richard deliberately created uncertainty about the circumstances of the duke's death and cloaked his own role in it. In the form it was read out to parliament, the confession opened with the endorsement that everything to follow was 'iknowe [acknowledged] and confessid be ... the forssaide Duk be his owne honde, fully and pleynly iwrite'.[83] Gloucester then admitted a string of offences relating to the events of 1386–8, although he never explicitly named any of these actions as treason. The first was:

> The makyng of a Commission; In the which ... I amonges other restreyned my Lord of his fredom, and toke upon me amonge other Power Reall, trewly nagth knowyng ne wygtyng [realising] that tyme that I dede ageyns his Estate ne his Realte [regality], as I dede after, and do now.[84]

This was as good as an admission of accroaching and it echoed the civil law model of treason as the usurpation of public power for private benefit. However, Gloucester did not refer to this as treason or *lèse-majesté*. He also immediately referenced the 1388 pardon, saying that as soon as he saw the wrongness of his actions, he had submitted himself to Richard's mercy.

Gloucester admitted coming armed into the king's presence but presented a knightly defence of *diffidatio* when he said that 'I dede it for drede of my lyfe'.[85] In a subsequent clause, he expanded on the claim that he was being threatened by the king when he admitted that he had consulted with other men, including legal experts, 'whethir we miyght gyve up our homage for drede of our lyves or non'.[86] This clause marked the first significant omission from the parliament roll version, with an excised phrase in which Gloucester claimed that the talk about renouncing homage to Richard had been forced on him by exigency as 'for feer of my lyf to yyve up myn hommage to my Lord, I knowlech wel, that for certain that I among other communed'.[87] The implication was that

[82] I use Giancarlo's transcription of the full confession, in which he has numbered the clauses for ease of reference: 'Murder, Lies, and Storytelling', pp. 81–2.

[83] Giancarlo, 'Murder, Lies, and Storytelling', p. 81, clause one.

[84] Ibid., clause two.

[85] Ibid., clause three.

[86] Ibid., clause six.

[87] Ibid., clause six.

Richard's bad lordship had driven the duke to contemplate extreme measures in self-defence. Gloucester then made the damning admission that he had 'communed and spoken in manere of deposal of my liege Loord' and that he and his allies had been agreed on this course 'for two dayes or three'.[88] Yet before taking any action, they had reconsidered and had 'done our homage and our oothes, and putt [Richard] as heyly in hys estate as ever he was'.[89]

While Gloucester confessed to having considered renouncing his homage and even deposing Richard, his own words verified that this was never more than talk. His detailed description of this conversation drew on the power of first-person English to validate his testimony as truth, as he admitted dangerous speech but denied this ever led to action. Technically, such speech would not have amounted to treason at the time Gloucester confessed because it was not until the new statute of treasons was enacted on 18 September that merely verbalising the possibility of renouncing homage or deposing the king was defined as treason. Damaging speech was also a factor in Gloucester's admission that he had 'sclaundred my Loord' to his face and in front of other people.[90] Gloucester confessed this was something he had done 'unkunnyngelych' (unwisely) but he did not name it as treason.[91] The 1352 statute did not define slandering the king as treason, although under civil law it could be interpreted as insulting public authority and therefore as *lèse-majesté*. However, Gloucester did not defend himself in legalistic terms. Instead, he represented his verbal wrongdoing as an injury to Richard's manhood. It was an assault on the king's masculine honour that could conceivably be punished as defamation or even avenged through combat in the Court of Chivalry, but in Gloucester's worldview it was not treason. Elsewhere, too, he eschewed any attempt to excuse his actions by referencing statutory definitions of treason but framed his confession through the language of true manhood and homosocial bonds of knighthood.

The stakes become clear in the last three clauses of the confession, which amount to one-third of the original text. These sections were omitted from the version read out in parliament, an act of silencing that in itself signals how potent the rhetoric of true manhood was for the political community, especially when the truth-value of a man's speech was authenticated by his sworn testimony in English. In the confession presented to parliament, Gloucester had described himself as having done 'untrewly and unkyndely as to hym that is my lyege Loord'. The terms 'untruly' and 'unkindly' positioned the duke's offences as violations of trueness and masculine fidelity, with the term 'unkinde' being understood in Middle English to mean behaviour

88 Ibid., clause seven.

89 Ibid.

90 Ibid., clause five: 'I spake it unto hym in sclaunderouse wyse in audience of other folk'.

91 Ibid.

against filial affection or natural loyalties.[92] In the omitted sections, the duke expanded on this theme to mitigate his actions and to confer a reciprocal knightly obligation upon Richard, as his king and nephew, to honour his pardon and oath of forgiveness as well as to entertain a renewed plea for mercy.

Richard had justified Gloucester's precipitous arrest and removal to Calais by claiming that his uncle was hatching a new plot against him. In the first omitted clause of his confession, Gloucester vigorously denied being involved in any such plot, swearing that he had been loyal 'syth that day that I swore unto hym at Langeley on Goddys body trewly. And be that oothe that I ther made, I never knew of gaderyng ageyns hym'.[93] This was dangerous for Richard, for it challenged his own integrity as a king and a man. By revoking the duke's pardon, Richard had violated his sacred oath and the duke implied the king had also lied about a new plot. It is unsurprising that this clause was suppressed, for it called attention to the false words, deceit and violations of royal grace that lay behind Richard's actions. As first-person testimony in English, recorded in perilous circumstances in which Gloucester must have known his life was on the line, the duke's words carried the evidentiary weight to contest the version of events Richard presented in parliament to secure his conviction as a traitor.

Gloucester went on to defend his activities in 1386–8 by balancing his admission of acting 'unkyndely and untrewly' with an assertion that his *intentions* had been true. Although he had offended the king, Gloucester claimed that:

> Trewly, and as I wyll answere befor Godd, it was my menyng and my wenyng [intention] for to have do the best for his persone and for his estate. Nevertheles I wote [understand] wel, and know wel nowe, that my dedes and my werchynges were ayeyns myn entente. Bot, be the way that my sowle schall to, of this pyntes, and of all othir the which that I have done of neclygence and of unkunnyng, It was never myn entent, ne my wyll, ne my thoght, fo to do thynge that schuld have bene distresse or harmyng ayeyns the salvation of my lyege Loordys persone.[94]

By fixing on the disjuncture between intentions and material outcomes, Gloucester alluded to the statutory definition of treason as 'compassing or imagining' the king's death but he exploited the space between thought and deed to resist being named as a traitor. The precise meaning of the vague phrase 'compassing or imagining' in the 1352 statute has been a topic of debate for medieval lawyers and modern legal historians alike, with opinions varying as to whether treason required a physical action or whether

92 *MED*.

93 Giancarlo, 'Murder, Lies, and Storytelling', p. 82, clause eight.

94 Ibid., clause nine.

thinking treasonous thoughts was enough.[95] Regardless of the legal position, Gloucester's confession reflected cultural acceptance of the view that if a man's intentions and his thoughts were true, this inner trueness carried greater weight than any outer, tangible results. This was evinced, for example, in jury verdicts on unlawful killings, with acquittals being the norm unless a pre-meditated intent to murder could be proved.[96] Gloucester argued that he had done everything in the sincere belief that it was best for the king's person and for the realm. His 'deeds and workings' contradicted this true intention, but this was evidence of negligence and lack of wisdom, not treason. In essence, Gloucester remained a loyal subject because his purpose had not been to harm the king or his royal estate, but to urge him to rule for the common good of the realm.

Gloucester concluded with a plea for mercy that enacted his abject submission while also deploying rhetorical flourishes to appeal to Richard's prickly sense of honour and majesty. Addressing the king as 'my lyege and souverayn Loord' and as 'his heygh Lordeschipp', he asked that Richard 'of his heygh grace and benyngnytee accept me to his mercy and grace'.[97] This invoked the king's unique power to pardon, derived from his sovereign embodiment of justice and mercy. The emotive content of this plea – and the attraction it was no doubt intended to hold for Richard – was heightened when Gloucester drew an analogy between the suffering of Christ on the cross and the compassion and pity of the Virgin Mary and Mary Magdalene, and Richard's own 'compassion and pytee'.[98] By aligning himself with the two Marys, Gloucester may deliberately have been trying to feminise himself and thereby stress his own abjection and his submission to Richard's superior authority as man and king. However, the image of the crucifixion also invoked Christ as redeemer and saviour; by creating this image as an analogue for his relationship with Richard, Gloucester appealed to Richard's exalted views of kingship. At the same time, Gloucester recalled reciprocal chivalric obligations between the king and his noble subjects by swearing to put his life, body and goods at his lord's will and then begging for Richard's pardon 'as he that hathe ever bene ful of mercy and of grace to all his lyeges, and to all other that have naght bene so neygh unto hym as I have bene, thogh I be unworthy'.[99] By mentioning his familial relationship to the king, Gloucester sought to strengthen his plea through reference to bonds of blood but in the context of the masculine performance of lordship and oaths, this phrasing appealed

95 Bellamy, *Law of Treason*, pp. 102–3, 121–3; *Tudor Law of Treason*, pp. 10–11; Rezneck, 'Constructive Treason by Words'.

96 Thomas A. Green, 'Societal Concepts of Criminal Liability for Homicide in Mediaeval England', *Speculum* 47 (1972), 669–94.

97 Giancarlo, 'Murder, Lies, and Storytelling', p. 82, clause ten.

98 Ibid.

99 Ibid.

equally to the knightly values that shaped relations between kings and their greater subjects.

It is telling that Gloucester did not structure his confession through the discourse of treason law. His leading role in the trials of 1388 must have given him detailed knowledge about how treason could legally be defined and prosecuted, but he did not explicitly use the language of the 1352 statute or exploit loopholes left by its ambiguities to resist the Appeal against him. Instead, he voiced his defence through the language of chivalry and true manhood shared by his peers, so this rhetorical strategy must have been convincing for an audience he most likely envisaged as the king and Lords in parliament. Gloucester's admission that he had contemplated withdrawing homage implied the knight's right to *diffidatio* when faced with bad lordship. This served as a reminder to his audience that the reciprocal relationship between the king and the men who helped him govern required loyalty and service from the political classes, but it also entailed honourable, prudent and just kingship. While Gloucester admitted offending the king, he described himself as acting 'untruly' and 'unkindly', terms that conjured up personal, homosocial bonds of knighthood and kinship rather than a more abstract constitutional relationship between state and subject. In his final supplication and plea for mercy, Gloucester argued that his intentions remained true, and this inner trueness made him a loyal man, not a traitor. In the end, these arguments were in vain for by the time Gloucester's confession was presented in parliament the duke was already dead. One final nail was hammered into Gloucester's coffin: after Rickhill had read out the doctored confession, the trial record stated that Gloucester had 'forgotten' to include one point but he wished Rickhill to convey it verbally to the king and parliament. This was purportedly an admission that in 1388, Gloucester had told Richard that if he wanted to be king, 'he should not seek to save the said Simon Burley from death'.[100] Thus, the official record staged the duke's death as the lawful result of Richard's just and manly vengeance. Yet the fact that Gloucester's most compelling words in his own defence had been silenced makes a powerful statement about the capacity of the vernacular to work across legal and ethical dimensions to authenticate masculine speech as the words of a 'true man'.

What of Richard's other enemies from 1388, the earl of Warwick, Henry Bolingbroke (now the duke of Hereford) and Thomas Mowbray (now the duke of Norfolk)? After Gloucester's trial, Warwick was led into parliament to take his turn before the king and Counter-Appellants. Warwick was a generation older than his fellow Appellants and by 1397 he was suffering serious illness, no doubt compounded by being held in prison for the preceding two months.[101] Faced with the charges in the Appeal he did not even attempt to

100 *PROME*, 'Concerning Thomas duke of Gloucester' in 'Richard II: September 1397', Part Two, Pleas.

101 *St Albans Chronicle II*, p. 65. Warwick was arrested in early July.

defend or justify himself but instead immediately confessed his guilt and threw himself upon Richard's mercy. He was sentenced to drawing, hanging, beheading and quartering but 'the king, moved to pity … and at the prayer of the said [counter-]appellants, and of all the other lords' remitted the death sentence, instead condemning Warwick to perpetual exile and forfeiture.[102] Behind the brief account of this royal pardon in the parliament roll was a dramatic performance of abjection and humiliation. Walsingham described Warwick disavowing his bonds with Arundel and Gloucester – '"would that I had never seen sight of them!"' – and begging the lords 'with tears and pitiful groans' to intercede with the king on his behalf.[103] His supplications apparently elicited such pity that all those present, even Warwick's accusers, were moved to tears. Usk corroborates this account: Warwick was stripped of his earl's hood and the appeal was read to him, 'whereupon, like a wretched old woman, he began to weep and sob and wail', throwing himself on the king's mercy and 'bewailing the fact that he had ever become involved with the aforesaid appellees'.[104] The monk of Evesham was even harsher, describing Warwick 'foolishly, wretchedly, and cravenly' confessing to everything, and 'sobbing and whining and begging the king's mercy'.[105] These accounts alluded to cultural understandings of gender that structured Warwick's performance. Warwick's weakness, cowardice and abjection marked his loss of masculine identity while allowing Richard to expiate his hatred and restore his own manly honour by publicly humiliating the earl before the entire parliament. This unsettling image was complicated further by the chroniclers' reports that almost everyone else present was eventually reduced to weeping and pleading for Warwick's life. It seems the Lords and Commons were deeply uncomfortable with the spectacle Richard made of the earl's fall, as the king 'in the plenitude of his power' reduced a once proud old nobleman to ignominious grovelling. Perhaps they recognised only too well the potential for themselves to suffer the same fate if they crossed Richard.

As for Henry of Bolingbroke and Thomas Mowbray, both men had been restored to the king's grace by 1389 and as we have seen, Mowbray was among the Counter-Appellants in 1397. Mowbray did not appear at the September parliament, perhaps remaining at Calais where he had been sent to fetch Gloucester, but in late January both men were in Shrewsbury for the second session of parliament, which had reconvened after the Christmas break. On 30 January, Bolingbroke came before the king to lodge a sensational accusation of treason against Mowbray, saying that he had 'spoken many dishonest and slanderous words' about the king. The conflict turned on men's words – first

102 *PROME*, 'Concerning Thomas earl of Warwick' in 'Richard II: September 1397', Part Two, Pleas.

103 *St Albans Chronicle II*, p. 97.

104 *Adam Usk*, p. 35.

105 *HVRS*, p. 151.

Mowbray's 'slander' against the king and then Bolingbroke's witness testimony to that speech in his own oral and textual accusations. Because this was a matter of true and false speech and underlying questions of manly honour, proceedings were conducted according to the 'law of chivalry' although the entire affair – including the trial by combat in which it was to culminate – was adjudicated by the king in parliament.[106] After making his verbal allegations to the king, Bolingbroke produced his schedule of charges, written in French. He recounted that in late December, while he was riding on the road between Brentford and London, Mowbray had 'suddenly come upon him, and spoke with him on various matters, amongst which he said "We are about to be undone"'.[107] Mowbray went on to warn Bolingbroke that despite all the pardons and reconciliations, Richard was about to pounce on them and '"do with us what he has already done with the others, because he wants to wipe that slate clean"'. Mowbray clearly feared that he and Bolingbroke were about to follow Arundel and Gloucester to the scaffold. In his schedule of charges, Bolingbroke claimed to have defended Richard, arguing that the king would never renege on his acts of royal grace and the words of forgiveness he had spoken publicly before the people. To this Mowbray replied that even though Richard had sworn his oaths to them 'on many occasions on the body of God', he could not be trusted to keep his word and that they could never again rest easy in their beds. Mowbray recognised Richard as a man for whom revenge was a dish just as good served cold; if the noblemen who had done the king's dirty work in the September parliament did not kill them now, '"they would be ready to kill us in our houses ten years hence"'.[108] Mowbray met Bolingbroke's charges by firmly denying he had committed any treasons. This was a case of 'he said, he said' and the merits on both sides were discussed in the January parliament and then over the following months by a group of commissioners appointed by that parliament. This group was unlikely to give Mowbray much sense of security, for it included John of Gaunt and the Counter-Appellants of 1397 along with John Bussy and several other knights. Since no other evidence surfaced to support either Bolingbroke's allegations or Mowbray's denials of any treason, the two men were assigned a day for a trial by combat that would prove the truth of their words upon their bodies.

The battle was set for 16 September 1398 at Coventry and was staged with all the panoply and display of a chivalric tournament. According to Adam Usk, 'both men came, splendidly arrayed … the duke of Hereford was the more gloriously arrayed … arriving with seven horses decked out in a variety

[106] The case was therefore documented in the parliament roll: *PROME*, 'Richard II: September 1397', Part Two, Pleas, Item Eleven. The record uses the titles the men had acquired by late 1397, duke of Hereford (Bolingbroke) and duke of Norfolk (Mowbray).

[107] Ibid.

[108] Ibid.

of remarkable trappings'.[109] However, after the two men had been fighting for some time, Richard stopped the battle. According to Usk, this was because it looked like Bolingbroke was going to win, although the official account claimed it was because the king did not want to see either man dishonoured by defeat and death. More likely, Richard saw an opportunity to rid himself of both men in one fell swoop while burnishing his own masculine honour as the arbiter of a chivalric contest between two of England's foremost noblemen. And so, 'grieving in his heart, as a good and gracious lord, more over those than over any other, even when they deserved the opposite' he 'took the battle into his own hand' and, 'with the full advice, authority, and assent of parliament' condemned both men to exile, on pain of suffering the full penalty for treason should they return to the realm.[110] Mowbray's exile was for life and he died a broken man in Venice in 1399. As for Bolingbroke, Richard initially sentenced him to ten years in exile but after the death of Bolingbroke's father the duke of Lancaster, Richard changed his sentence to one of perpetual exile and seized his inheritance. It was this final insult that would drive Henry to return to England in 1399 with an army, initially so he said to reclaim his rightful inheritance but eventually to depose his cousin and claim the throne for himself as Henry IV.

Henry IV's justifications for his actions in 1399 traded heavily on shared cultural narratives of chivalric honour and manful righting of insufferable wrongs, by force if necessary.[111] These same themes of manhood, trueness and honour had conditioned the ways treason was legally constructed and prosecuted in 1397–8. By 1399, it was Richard's own questionable honour rather than that of the men he had hounded into exile or death that had become the crucial issue. The new statute enacted in the 1397 parliament created a definition of treason that was closer to the civil law concept of *lèse-majesté* than to the customary and chivalric notions embedded in the 1352 statute and it reinforced Richard's other attempts to recast English kingship along increasingly imperial and authoritarian lines. By inextricably identifying the public authority of the state with Richard's manly sovereign person, the legal precedents created in the 1397 statute and subsequent treason trials implicitly produced the body politic as a wholly masculine political and ideological construct. Nevertheless, as the trials of Arundel and Gloucester showed, chivalric and customary ideas could be deployed in opposition to this constitutional shift. These ideas included the knightly right of *diffidatio* and the belief that it was the duty of true noblemen to resist, reform or even remove a bad king for the common good of the realm. In this constitutional model, sovereignty did not reside inalienably in an individual king's person

109 *Adam Usk*, p. 51.

110 *PROME*, 'Richard II: September 1397', Part Two, Pleas, Item Eleven.

111 Fletcher, 'Narrative and Political Strategies at the Deposition of Richard II'.

as Richard had claimed, but in the office of kingship; the two entities could in extreme circumstances legitimately be separated. It was this argument that Henry would use in 1399 to justify Richard's deposition, and he would go on to exploit ambiguities in the laws of treason to join his own manly body natural to the masculine body politic of the crown.

3

THE LANCASTRIAN SUCCESSION AND THE MASCULINE BODY POLITIC

By September 1399, when Henry returned from exile with an army to claim his Lancastrian inheritance – and ultimately the English throne – Richard had alienated himself from most of the people who had any stake in England's political fortunes.[1] In the face of Richard's worsening reputation, Henry could credibly explain his actions as those of a wronged man defending his noble honour and birthright against an untrustworthy lord. By October, public sentiment and the political winds had shifted to the point where Henry and his supporters could argue that Richard's removal was a noble act in defence of the honour and common profit of the realm. Henry's chivalric reputation and his status as 'a man, not a boy' became a key theme in the discourses justifying Richard's deposition; compared to Richard, Henry emerged as an ideal king who embodied masculine virtues of prudence, honour, courage and moral self-governance.[2] Gendered norms of true and false manhood conditioned political perceptions, as was made abundantly clear in the canon lawyer Adam Usk's eyewitness account of events. Usk was on the committee of experts assembled to debate 'the question of deposing King Richard [II] and replacing him as king with Henry duke of Lancaster, and of how and for what reasons this might lawfully be done'.[3] Amongst the reasons seized upon were Richard's 'sodomitical acts'; this was not intended to describe the

1 For a summary of events surrounding the deposition: *Chronicles of the Revolution*, pp. 1–52. Cf. M. J. Bennett, 'Henry of Bolingbroke and the Revolution of 1399', *Henry IV: The Establishment of the Regime, 1399–1406*, ed. Gwilym Dodd and Douglas Biggs (York, 2003), pp. 9–33; Bennett, *Richard II and the Revolution of 1399*; B. Wilkinson, 'The Deposition of Richard II and the Accession of Henry IV', *The English Historical Review* 54 (1939), 215–39.

2 The quote is from the Archbishop of Canterbury's sermon in Henry's first parliament, immediately after Richard's deposition. This discourse is discussed in Fletcher, *Richard II*, pp. 262–74; Christopher Fletcher, 'Manhood and Politics in the Reign of Richard II,' *Past & Present* 189 (2005), 3–39; Anthony Tuck, 'Henry IV and Chivalry', *Henry IV: The Establishment of the Regime*, ed. Dodd and Biggs, pp. 55–72; Lewis, *Kingship and Masculinity*, pp. 67–73.

3 *Adam Usk*, p. 63.

king's personal sexual behaviour but was instead shorthand for his unnatural inversion of the political and social order.

The Record and Process that set out the official terms of Richard's removal painted a vivid picture in negative of what the English political community expected of their kings.[4] Deposition articles excoriated Richard as a devious and wilful ruler who had corrupted justice and flagrantly defied expectations of manly honour in order to enrich himself and his friends and destroy his enemies. Richard's intemperance featured prominently in charges that he had fraudulently manipulated treason law in order to wreak his vengeance on Gloucester, Arundel and Warwick in the 1397 parliament, while other articles accused him of more general violations of the laws and customs of England. Richard also faced multiple counts of breaking his coronation oath and of deceit, falsity and malice. Finally, he had oppressed his subjects with heavy taxes and forced loans and instead of using this money for the good of the realm, he had spent it on a lavish court heaving with grasping royal favourites.

These were justifications for deposition that would return to haunt Henry but in 1399, he made full use of them to position himself as a man who would rule according to law and with the benefit of wise counsel, for the common good of the realm. Speaking to parliament at the moment he 'challenged' for the throne, Henry declared he had had been sent by God to rescue the realm of England, 'the whiche rewme was in point to be undone, for defaut of Governance and undoing of the gode Lawes'.[5] The new king then promised that none of his subjects should in future be deprived of their inheritance, franchise, or other rights held by law or custom, 'except thos persons that has ben agan the gude purpose and the commune profit of the Rewme'.[6] Henry's proclamations marked one of the rare occasions when the vernacular was used in the parliament roll before the 1450s and it was no mere act of linguistic pragmatism. When Henry's direct first-person oral statement in English was preserved in writing in the parliament roll and in other legitimising texts that the Lancastrian regime immediately put into public circulation, this authenticated his speech as the words of a true man – and a true king.[7] Moreover, potent cultural and political associations between language, law and national identity meant that Henry's use of the vernacular implicitly identified him as the man who would be saviour of the English nation.

4 *PROME*, 'Henry IV: October 1399', Part One, Roll, Articles Eighteen–Fifty. For a discussion of the deposition articles as political theory: John M. Theilmann, 'Caught Between Political Theory and Political Practice: "The Record and Process of the Deposition of Richard II"', *History of Political Thought* 25 (2004), 599–619.

5 Ibid. Item Fifty-three.

6 Ibid., Item Fifty-six.

7 For these public accounts: *Chronicles of the Revolution*, pp. 5–11, 168–9; G. O. Sayles, 'The Deposition of Richard II: Three Lancastrian Narratives', *Historical Research* 54 (1981), 257–70; Chris Given-Wilson, *Henry IV* (New Haven, 2016), pp. 138–45.

Official accounts portrayed the events of 1399 as a smooth and universally welcomed transfer of power from a misgoverned tyrant who had 'voluntarily' resigned his throne to a just king. Yet as a king without a direct dynastic blood-right, Henry's claim to embody sovereign authority still faced constitutional hurdles, not least because there was another heir with a closer blood title in Edmund Mortimer, the young earl of March.[8] Richard's bill of abdication (to which he was likely coerced to put his name) had carefully separated him as an individual man from 'his royal status and majesty, and … the crown' as well as from his 'name, honour, regalia, and royal supremacy'.[9] This statement elided the legal and theological conundrum posed by dividing an anointed king from his crown and then conferring regality upon a man not born to it. Contemporary commentators recognised the difficulties and a number of chroniclers reported Richard saying that even had he wanted to, he could not renounce or resign the sacral nature of his kingship.[10] Even the *Manner of King Richard's Renunciation*, a text that has been characterised as Lancastrian propaganda, included a passage in which Richard initially refused to sign the bill of abdication 'and declared that he would like to have it explained to him how it was that he could resign the crown'.[11]

Gendered narratives that contrasted Richard's intemperate youth with Henry's chivalric manhood could only go so far in overcoming the constitutional dilemmas. More useful in the first years of Lancastrian rule were a series of treason trials that had their roots in Richard's reign. These trials allowed Henry to embody and enact sovereignty by exercising justice and mercy over his most powerful subjects. At the same time, legal judgments articulated new definitions of treason that joined Henry's body natural and that of his Lancastrian bloodline more securely to the political body of the crown. Because of the extraordinary political situation and because the main offenders were all of noble status, proceedings took place in the king's council, in parliament and in the Court of Chivalry rather than in the common law court of King's Bench. It was not a jury who determined guilt or innocence

8 Both Henry IV and Edmund Mortimer could claim descent from Edward III but Mortimer had the superior link: Peter McNiven, 'Legitimacy and Consent: Henry IV and the Lancastrian Title, 1399–1406', *Mediaeval Studies* 44 (1982), pp. 470–88 (pp. 476–9); Michael Bennett, 'Edward III's Entail and the Succession to the Crown, 1376–1471', *The English Historical Review* 113 (1998), 580–609.

9 *PROME*, 'Henry IV: October 1399', Part One, Roll, Item Thirteen, presented in parliament on 30 September.

10 *St Albans Chronicle II*, p. 217 and n. 297. The *Dieulacres Chronicle* and a number of French chronicles included similar versions of the story.

11 *Chronicles of the Revolution*, pp. 162–7 (p. 163). The document is printed from Corpus Christi College, Cambridge, MS.59, fols. 230v–231 in Sayles, 'The Deposition of Richard II', pp. 266–70. Sayles characterised this as Lancastrian propaganda, but Given-Wilson has questioned this: C. Given-Wilson, 'The Manner of King Richard's Renunciation: A "Lancastrian Narrative"?', *The English Historical Review* 108 (1993), 365–70.

in these venues. Instead, the king and his senior officials directly influenced judicial procedures, charges and verdicts, in the process generating novel legal constructions that represented treason as attacks on abstract public entities including the *chose publique* and the nation of England. These emerging conceptions of treason as a crime against the state were not so much the result of considered jurisprudence as a tactical response to Henry's immediate need to bolster his royal authority by defining attacks on himself as attacks on the crown. Alongside these constructions, customary perceptions of treason as a personal betrayal of homosocial bonds remained relevant to the wider political community, so that cultural values of chivalry, honour and true manhood were also central to the ways charges of treason were deployed and resisted.

The fall-out from 1397's Revenge Parliament began within days of Richard's deposition when in Henry IV's first parliament, the Counter-Appellants who had voiced the charges of treason against Gloucester, Arundel and Warwick were in their turn accused of treason and murder.[12] Savage recriminations in parliament were symptomatic of deeper wounds in the body politic, which Henry needed to heal quickly if he was to restore stability to the realm and consolidate his hold on power. As the first step, he made a number of strategic interventions in the laws of treason that allowed him to represent himself as a just king who ruled by law and good counsel, not by arbitrary will as Richard had done. Yet the new treason legislation was carefully structured to protect the king's prerogative powers and his right to resort to venues such as the Court of Chivalry, where convictions for treason could be secured without a public jury trial and for a range of offences not explicitly covered in statute law.

The Record and Process of Richard's deposition had condemned the erstwhile king for a number of offences related to the conviction of Gloucester, Arundel and Warwick as traitors, including his corrupt extensions to treason law in the new statute of 1397. Article Forty-four then castigated Richard in more general terms for using the Court of Chivalry to target a much larger group of his subjects for nebulous misdeeds that amounted to no more than speaking ill of the king. The Article first alluded to the 1352 statute by asserting that no man should be charged or condemned except 'by the law of the land'.[13] It went on to say that nevertheless, Richard had unlawfully resorted to the Court of Chivalry to maliciously condemn 'a great number of his lieges ... on the grounds of having been supposed to have said something publicly or secretly which could lead to the disparagement, scandal or disgrace of the person of the said king'.[14] Those charged were forbidden from speaking in

12 *PROME*, 'Henry IV: October 1399', Part Two, Pleas, Items One–Sixteen.

13 *PROME*, 'Henry IV: October 1399', Part One, Roll, Article Forty-four.

14 Ibid.

their own defence but could only state their innocence; they then had to prove the truth of their verbal plea upon their bodies through a trial by combat. Richard was accused of fixing these combats in the most dishonourable way by forcing old, feeble and maimed men to fight for their lives against strong and healthy young knights. The image conjured up was of Richard as a Nero or Caligula, stretching the concept of *lèse-majesté* to its limits in order to dispatch his critics in grotesque public spectacles of unbridled power.

Once Richard's deposition had been secured and Henry had been crowned, the political community set to work to restore their customary protections against such malicious uses of treason law. At the start of the session, the Commons petitioned the king to reconfirm the acts of the 1388 parliament, reverse the convictions of Gloucester, Arundel and Warwick, and restore the nobles' heirs.[15] The king agreed to these requests and he also agreed to revoke the 1397 treason statute:

> The king, rehearsing of his own will how in the said [1397] parliament ... several penalties of treason had been ordained by statute, with the result that there was no man there who knew how he ought to act, speak, or talk, for fear of such penalties, said that he wished to act in a quite different manner, and that at no time in the future would any treason be adjudged otherwise than had been ordained by statute in the time of his noble grandfather King Edward the third.[16]

It is evident from this wording, as well as the terms of Article Forty-four of the Record and Process, that the political community's criticism of Richard centred on his suppression of men's ability to exercise full political subjecthood by speaking openly and honestly about the governance of the realm. More specifically, the implication was that Richard had acted outside the law when he punished the verbal discussion of renouncing homage or deposing the king as material acts of treason. The *St Albans Chronicle* reported that the king 'said that it was entirely unreasonable for those men who spoke against the evil governance of the king or his irregular actions to be called or adjudged traitors'.[17] This placed Henry's undertaking regarding the 1397 treason statute into a broader constitutional framework in which the men of England's political elite saw it as their duty to counsel the king to rule justly, and also that in dire circumstances where the common good of the realm was in jeopardy, they could exercise this obligation by applying the pressure of *diffidatio*.

According to Walsingham, Henry pledged that in future, men would not be called traitors unless they had 'been previously adjudged so by the ancient law of their virtuous ancestors'.[18] The slight difference in emphasis between the official account, which specifies that the 1352 statute of Edward III was

15 Ibid., Items Sixty-six–Sixty-eight.

16 Ibid., Item Seventy; *Statutes*, II, p. 114, c. x.

17 *St Albans Chronicle II*, p. 247.

18 Ibid.

the authoritative source of treason law, and the more generalised authority of the 'ancient law of virtuous ancestors' referred to by the chronicler is telling. Historians have tended to locate Henry's cancellation of the 1397 legislation within the history of statute law, debating its role in establishing a common law doctrine of treason by words.[19] However, Walsingham's account indicates that for the political community of 1399, customary perceptions of treason were equally meaningful. Changes in the way treason was defined and punished were to be measured not only against the narrow technical limits of statute law but in relation to cultural understandings of masculine identity and the self-fashioning of England's greater political subjects as inheritors of the knightly virtues of elite manhood. The chronicler's reference to the 'ancient law' as being that of 'ancestors' more generally, rather than just of Edward III, reflected normative expectations that reciprocal homosocial bonds should govern relations between the king and his nobles in their capacity as his natural counsellors. It is a reminder that the 1352 statute had itself been the result of a compromise forced on Edward by his subjects, who were reacting against his increasingly arbitrary findings of treason. Having witnessed Richard behaving in the same arbitrary way in 1397, the men present in Henry IV's first parliament would doubtless have recognised the appeal to custom as a powerful tool for negotiating their relationship with their new king. However, the implicit tension between the 'statute' of the official record and the 'ancient law' of noble progenitors in Walsingham's account exposed potential conflicts between legal definitions of treason and more flexible cultural interpretations. This created possibilities for men to use the latter to deny or deflect allegations brought under the former.

Henry's second intervention in treason law also encapsulated the tensions between statutory, customary and chivalric understandings of treason. The change came in response to a Commons' petition regarding the procedure and venue used for trying treason, with the Commons being particularly concerned to ensure that the new king would not resort to judgments in parliament or in the Court of Chivalry. The petition asked that in future, no appeals of treason should be heard in parliament 'but rather in other courts within your realm, provided that it can be concluded in your said courts'.[20] It went on to request that any man accused of treason should be allowed to speak in his own defence, and would then be tried and judged according to ancient custom and the laws of the realm. Henry responded with a new enactment stating that any action relating to things done within the realm would be heard according to 'the good laws' of his ancestors, while anything done outside the realm would be determined by delegation to the Constable and Marshal in the

[19] Thornley, 'Treason by Words'; Rezneck, 'Constructive Treason by Words'; Bellamy, *Law of Treason*, pp. 114, 122–3.

[20] *PROME*, 'Henry IV: October 1399', Part One, Roll, Item 144.

Court of Chivalry.[21] This appeared to restore the situation to the pre-Ricardian status quo but in doing so, it removed none of the ambiguities surrounding either the scope of treason or the procedures by which it could be tried. The 1352 statute allowed uncertain matters to be referred to parliament and this left the new king ample room to manoeuvre, as did the reference to using the king's 'courts' in general rather than the common law court of King's Bench. In combination with Commons' requests to return to customary practices, the wording of Henry's new statute meant that treason accusations that raised matters of masculine honour between knights and noblemen could still be referred to the Court of Chivalry. Moreover, the king's enactments ignored altogether the request that in future, no one accused of treason should be deprived of a defence or of an opportunity to speak on his own behalf.

It was not left to the legal theorists to debate in the abstract these lingering questions about the meanings of treason and how it could be tried. Instead, the political community sitting in parliament was forced immediately to grapple with the problem when the Counter-Appellants and other ringleaders of 1397 were accused of treason. The treason proceedings of the 1399 parliament have attracted less interest from historians than the accounts of Richard's deposition and Henry's accession that preceded them. However, from a constitutional perspective the events were closely related because the exercise of royal justice gave Henry IV an immediate opportunity to perform legitimate kingship and to assert his right to supreme judicial authority. The trial narratives captured Henry enacting his relationship with his new subjects through the language of the law but also through his performance of knightly manhood as the judgments joined his own manly body to the political body of the crown. Through processes of association and abstraction, the legal narratives implicitly gendered as masculine the public political entity represented by ideas of the realm, the state and the nation.

The parliament roll presented a full but neutral and legalistic account of the 1399 trials, giving little indication of the frenetic recriminations and sensational revelations that characterised the session. The *St Albans Chronicle* and *The Great Chronicle of London* supply many of the deficiencies and were based on inside knowledge.[22] On 16 October, Sir William Bagot, a close associate of Richard, was brought before parliament to answer questions about a document in which he had accused the duke of Aumale (formerly the earl of Rutland) and others of 'evil counsel' and of conspiring in the murder of Gloucester.[23] When Richard fell, Bagot had escaped to Ireland but he was captured and was a prisoner in the Tower when he produced this testimony,

21 *Statutes*, II, p. 116, c. xiv.

22 Walsingham's detailed account was probably based in part on information from the bishop of Carlisle, who stayed at St Albans before and after the session: *Chronicles of the Revolution*, p. 200.

23 Given-Wilson, *Henry IV*, pp. 157–9. The editors of the *St Albans Chronicle* note that

which was then read out before parliament. Copies of the text were also almost certainly circulating in London during and after the parliament, as attested by its preservation in the *Great Chronicle*.[24] Like Gloucester's 1397 letter of confession, Bagot's text is in first-person English and he named it as a 'bille'. He was already under arrest for his actions during Richard's reign so it probably took the form of an approver's appeal, extracted in exchange for a lesser punishment. In this text, Bagot presented himself as an eyewitness to Richard's tyranny as the king violently forced the men about him to do his bidding, claiming that he:

> Hadde herde the kyng sey in diverse parliamentes and to diverse knyghtes that he wolde have his purpos and his luste [desire] of diverse maters … or ellis he wolde dissolvyn his parliament And when it were dissolvyd he made stryke of here hedes that were letters of his parliament and of is purpos [he would behead anyone who opposed his parliament and his will].[25]

Bagot portrayed Richard's actions in 1397 as a constitutional corrective to the events of 1387–8, when the young king had been cowed and humiliated by the Appellant lords and made subject to the Continual Council that constrained his power. He described Richard saying that he desired to see the crown of England once again held in the highest reverence and humbly obeyed by all his lieges, 'so that it myght be Cronycled perpetuelly that with witte and wysdome and Manhode he hadde recovered his dignyte Regalye and his honourable astate'.[26] Bagot then recounted a scene in which Thomas Mowbray, who in 1397 was still duke of Norfolk, asked him about the fate of Gloucester. Bagot said he knew nothing 'by my trouthe But the peple saithe ye have murdered hym'.[27] According to Bagot, Mowbray denied this and claimed that in fact, the arrival of Richard's writ during the 1397 parliament put him in fear of his life because Gloucester was not yet dead. Bagot continued by saying Mowbray had pointed the finger at Aumale and 'men of othir certein lordes', implying that they had murdered Gloucester on Richard's orders and adding that Mowbray told him:

> Ther was no man in the Reaume of Englond that the kyng was somuch holde to as to the Duke of Aumarle For he sette hym on the first purpos of takyng of the lordes and of the parliament and all the forfetours and of alle other thinges.[28]

Unsurprisingly, Bagot's shocking allegations provoked a storm of protest from

---

Bagot's trial does not appear in the surviving rolls of parliament and that the chronicle is the best source for it: *St Albans Chronicle II*, p. 246, n. 342.

24 *Great Chronicle*, pp. 76–7.

25 *Great Chronicle*, p. 76.

26 Ibid.

27 Ibid.

28 *Great Chronicle*, pp. 76–7.

Aumale and the other Counter-Appellants, which was expressed through dramatic performances of chivalric manhood. Aumale refused to accept Bagot's charges 'but rose to his feet and threw his hood into the middle, challenging him to a combat, saying that he would prove his innocence in a duel'.[29] This ritual gesture was followed by challenges from the dukes of Surrey and Exeter, who offered bodily combat against anyone who accused them of conspiring in Gloucester's murder or of giving 'evil counsel' to Richard.[30] The parliament roll was less dramatic in its narrative than the chroniclers but it records the lords' defensive posturing, including that Surrey 'was ready to defend himself and to acquit himself as a loyal knight'.[31] The throwing of hoods and the challenge to battle anchored the lords' words and gestures within the performative sphere of chivalric combats over insults to manly honour.

Henry IV was able to calm the waters on this occasion and he made the lords withdraw their challenges by retrieving their hoods. However, almost immediately, Walter, Lord FitzWalter and Thomas Lord Morley 'offered to fight a duel with anyone who wished to declare that the duke [of Gloucester] had been a traitor'.[32] FitzWalter and Morley had both served under Gloucester and been knighted by him in 1380, and Morley maintained a fierce loyalty to the dead duke.[33] Their challenges were still standing when Mowbray's servant John Halle was brought into parliament to answer for his part in the murder of Gloucester, to which he had confessed while being held prisoner in the Constable's chamber within the palace of Westminster.[34] As was the standard pattern for verbal interrogations transformed into written testimony, Halle's confession was recorded in third-person French and it features a question-and-answer pattern typical of legal questioning under duress. It confirmed the grim details of the duke's death, revealing that Halle and several other men had slipped into the duke's chamber while he was sleeping, held him down and smothered him with a featherbed.[35] Halle said the deed had been done on the orders of Mowbray and Aumale, and that Mowbray had told him 'the said former king had commanded him [Mowbray] to murder the said duke of Gloucester'.[36] Halle claimed he had at first stoutly refused to have any part in the deed but had been forced to participate after Mowbray 'gave him a great blow on the head' and threatened his life if he did not do

29 *St Albans Chronicle II*, p. 249.

30 Ibid., pp. 250–1.

31 *PROME*, 'Henry IV: October 1399', Part Two, Pleas, Item Four.

32 *St Albans Chronicle II*, p. 255.

33 Ibid., p. 254, n. 353; Goodman, *Loyal Conspiracy*, p. 124.

34 The confession was recorded before Henry Percy, earl of Northumberland, newly appointed Constable of England.

35 *PROME*, 'Henry IV: October 1399', Part Two, Pleas, Items Eleven–Sixteen.

36 Ibid., Item Eleven.

as commanded.[37] Having confessed, Halle was immediately executed. The punishment inflicted on him marked him not simply as a murderer, for which the penalty was hanging, but also as a traitor, which brought the more extreme penalties of dismemberment. He was dragged from the Tower through the city of London and out to Tyburn, where he was disembowelled and his entrails burned before him. He was then hanged, beheaded and quartered, and his head was sent for public display at the castle of Calais, the site of Gloucester's iniquitous murder.[38]

The parliament roll preserved only the details of Halle's confession and death sentence, but Walsingham also described the reactions of the nobles.[39] Again, accusations of treason flew, with FitzWalter, Morley and 'almost all the earls and barons' throwing down their hoods in challenge to Aumale.[40] Once more, Henry restored order, insisting that all the charges must be addressed with proper deliberation. Accordingly, on 29 October formal charges against Aumale, Surrey, Exeter, the marquis of Dorset, the earl of Salisbury and the earl of Gloucester (Thomas, Lord Despenser, elevated to the earldom by Richard in 1397) were read out in parliament. FitzWalter then repeated his challenge to Aumale and this was followed by a challenge from Lord Morley against the earl of Salisbury. Morley accused Salisbury of having 'acted falsely and equivocally, and so betrayed the confidences of [Gloucester] to the king, and the king's confidences to the duke. Although the duke had great trust in your loyalty, you cunningly arranged for him to be indicted'.[41] This condemnation captured in vivid terms the chivalric interpretation of treason as a personal betrayal of homosocial bonds. Morley's challenge was not withdrawn on this occasion; instead, as this was a matter of masculine honour between two noblemen, Henry referred the case to his Court of Chivalry.

I will return to the action between Morley and Salisbury in the Court of Chivalry below but first, I turn to the closing acts of the 1399 parliament. Judgment against Aumale and the other lords was given on 3 November and it obliquely confirmed Walsingham's account of the flurry of knightly challenges when it noted that no one said anything in reply, 'except Lord Morley to the earl of Salisbury, and Lord FitzWalter to the duke of Aumale'.[42] The judgment, read out by Chief Justice Sir William Thirning, is highly unusual for it was written in the parliament roll not in Latin or French, but in English. According to later fourteenth-century norms, formal judgments in the criminal court of King's Bench were recorded in the authoritative Latin,

37 Ibid.

38 Ibid., Item Sixteen.

39 *St Albans Chronicle II*, pp. 258–61.

40 Ibid., p. 261

41 Ibid., p. 267.

42 *PROME*, 'Henry IV: October 1399', Part Two, Pleas, Item Nine. The full text of the judgment comprises Items Nine and Ten.

with witness testimony and confessions usually recorded in third-person French. Similar conventions held in the parliament roll, where English was used very rarely in this period. Although Bagot's bill did not survive as part of the parliament roll, it can be considered another instance of this linguistic usage. In these cases, the vernacular worked to authenticate the veracity of the textual record by mimicking the linguistic authority of oral English in common law courts. Commenting on the use of English in the parliament roll to record Gloucester's 1397 confession and the formal renunciation of homage delivered to Richard in 1399, Giancarlo notes that these texts 'stand out in the record as small islands of the vernacular in a specific linguistic environment that was itself something of an island. Thus we might fairly ask what they are doing there and what purposes they serve'.[43] The judgment against the Counter-Appellants is another such island. It is unlikely that the use of English for this document was simply linguistic pragmatism, for it is bracketed on either side in the roll by the formal charges against the lords and by Halle's trial, both of which were recorded in French. When Justice Thirning recited the judgment before the political community in the aural vernacular of royal courtrooms and English was used to authenticate the written record of his oral performance, it placed the judgment and therefore the king's actions in rendering it within the framework of common law. Thus it actively helped Henry to negotiate his delicate relationship with his new subjects. On the one hand, it presented him as a king who would rule according to law rather than considering himself above it, as Richard had allegedly done. On the other hand, it took great care to delineate and preserve his prerogative powers as sovereign.

It is significant that Henry engaged directly in the judicial process. He personally questioned each of the Counter-Appellants 'and ordered each of them individually, without being aware of or hearing the others, on the faith and the allegiance that they owed to him, to tell him the truth' about 1397.[44] Having conducted these inquiries, Henry said he would take counsel with his nobles and senior officials, and would then 'proceed as he thought best, according to their advice'.[45] At this point, Henry had been king for a little over two weeks and he was no doubt sensitive to his still-tenuous position. The judgment exploited the rhetorical and linguistic authority of the common law to construct him as a king who accepted the expectations of the political community that he would be limited by law and guided by counsel. However, in practice it left Henry considerable freedom of action by also stressing his sovereign embodiment of justice and grace. The text states that because the Counter-Appellants' actions had been 'contrary to the course of the common

43 Giancarlo, 'Murder, Lies, and Storytelling', p. 79.

44 *PROME*, 'Henry IV: October 1399', Part Two, Pleas, Item Nine.

45 Ibid.

law', they could not be punished through the common law 'but only by the king and his lords, peers of his realm, in the high court of parliament'.[46] Then, although he said he would take the advice of his lords, Henry asserted his prerogative by saying he would make his final judgments by his own discretion. Further, he reserved 'always to himself the dignity of his grace and mercy as it belongs to his royal estate, and to which no man gives him the title', stressing that the power to pardon belonged 'only to himself, above all other estates, on account of his regality'.[47]

While the judgment carried a constitutional gloss of counsel and consent, Henry used it to reserve to himself the sovereign power to convict or to pardon. The parliament of 1399 had undone the events of 1397 and restored the judgments of 1388. Legislation passed in 1388 had declared that anyone who tried to reverse those convictions should themselves be executed as traitors, leaving the Counter-Appellants in a very exposed position.[48] The judgment of 1399 argued that if the 1388 legislation were to be applied, not only the Counter-Appellants but also many others could be branded as traitors. Therefore, Henry declared that the fate of the Counter-Appellants should not be decided by trial but that he would exercise his royal prerogative to judge them 'with mercy and grace, according to his discretion'.[49] He then decreed that Aumale and the others would not immediately be executed as traitors but would instead be degraded from the titles bestowed upon them by Richard in 1397 and would forfeit all the lands and possessions they had thereby gained. If in future they were found to be agitating on behalf of the deposed king, who was now Henry's prisoner, they would be summarily executed as traitors.[50]

The sentence against the lords can be viewed as realpolitik, a tactic that gave Henry a way to end the bloodletting of the final years of Richard's reign. From a pragmatic perspective, ending violent division amongst the political elite was an essential prerequisite to enable Henry to secure his grip on the throne. This was acknowledged in the judgment, which stressed that the sentence against the lords had to 'guarantee safety and security primarily to the king's high estate'.[51] However, the text also did strategic political work to negotiate the relationship between the new king and his political subjects. It made direct rhetorical and linguistic connections between Henry's 'challenge' for the throne and his promise to rule according to law and for the common profit of the realm, and his first judicial acts as a crowned king. In doing so, it legitimised the union between his usurping body and the body politic of the

46 Ibid.
47 Ibid.
48 *PROME*, 'Richard II: February 1388', Part One, Roll, Item Forty.
49 *PROME*, 'Henry IV: October 1399', Part Two, Pleas, Item Nine.
50 Ibid., Item Ten.
51 Ibid., Item Nine.

crown and, by drawing on the association already established between Henry's chivalric manhood and his virtues as a king, it gendered both bodies as masculine. Moreover, by positioning Henry as a king who ruled according to law, the judgment affirmed that Henry embodied in his person the sovereign powers of justice and mercy, giving him the freedom to intervene in future cases of treason in ways that redefined the meaning and scope of the crime as well as the nature of loyal political subjecthood.

PERSONAL BETRAYAL OR CRIME AGAINST THE STATE? TREASON IN THE COURT OF CHIVALRY

The challenge between Morley and Salisbury, which was assigned to the Court of Chivalry, provides more evidence of Henry exploiting the opportunities afforded by noble conflicts over treason to reinforce his claim to kingship. Henry's new treason statute had stated that in future, the Court of Chivalry would only be used for addressing matters of treason arising outside the realm. Nevertheless, in the dispute between Morley and Salisbury a nobleman's manly honour was being traduced. By knightly custom and the law of arms, the Court of Chivalry could deal with such matters of honour regardless of the specific context in which they had arisen. In parliament, Morley had accused Salisbury of betraying the duke of Gloucester by revealing his secret counsel to Richard and then by falsely appealing him of treason, thereby contributing to Gloucester's wrongful death. This understanding of treason was shaped by customary ideas about manly loyalty that converged in Morley's repeated allegation that Salisbury was a *faux chivaler*.[52] However, when the Court of Chivalry was called into session on 11 November, Morley introduced an *addicion* that transformed the nature of Salisbury's crime by incorporating new charges: that Salisbury had advised and assisted Richard II to destroy 'the lords and the *communalté* of the realm' and had engaged in other actions 'against the *chose public* [*sic*] and common profit of the realm'.[53] The term *chose publique* was a direct translation of the Latin term *res publica* and it expressed an abstract notion of statehood and public authority. In the early fifteenth century, the term *communalté* likewise invoked ideas of an inclusive and broadly representative national political community.[54]

The Court's treatment of these additional charges shows how constitutional issues were being negotiated through the laws of treason in the period immediately following Henry's seizure of the throne, with interpretations of treason covering the spectrum from a personal betrayal of homosocial bonds

52 *Morley v. Salisbury*. This terminology appears throughout the trial record.

53 *Morley v. Salisbury*, p. 173.

54 John Watts, 'Public or Plebs: The Changing Meaning of "the Commons", 1381–1549', *Power and Identity in the Middle Ages: Essays in Memory of Rees Davies*, ed. Huw Pryce and John Watts (Oxford, 2007), pp. 242–60.

to a crime against the state. At the same time, the trial reveals how a man facing charges of treason mounted under one construction of treason could evade or contest these by taking refuge in another. Throughout the proceedings, both men engaged in elaborate textual and gestural performances of knighthood that framed treason as a crime epitomised by false speech and oath-breaking, and therefore as a violation of manly trueness. However, Morley complicated this customary construction of treason by alleging Salisbury had treasonously attacked the public authority of the state. This abstract public entity was in turn implicitly masculinised when it was incorporated into a treason trial that turned upon determinations of true and false manhood.

On 11 November, the court session opened with the airing of Morley's original appeal. This alleged that Salisbury:

> Was of the counsel of Thomas, duke of Gloucester, and rode between Richard, late king of England, and the said duke as a spy and knew the plans of both parties, and then as a false knight, revealed his [Gloucester's] plans and traitorously deceived the duke.[55]

Morley re-enacted his earlier performance of knighthood in parliament by throwing down his gauntlet to back his words; Salisbury responded by throwing his own gauntlet in wager that Morley had falsely accused him and that he intended to defend his honour. After legal counsel had been assigned to both parties, Morley placed before the Court the second written testimony detailing new allegations he wished to make.[56] This *addicion* was written in the first person which, with the use of the French infinitive *dire* ('to say'), placed its contents into the context of spoken testimony in a royal court and thus pre-emptively authorised Morley's words as truth spoken under oath. Although the written record is in French, it is plausible to assume that oral proceedings were in English given the aural use of the vernacular in other royal courts including parliament. In his opening statement, Morley positioned himself as a loyal knight acting on behalf of the dead duke by describing himself as 'I, Thomas lord Morley, ally to Thomas, duke of Gloucester'.[57] He repeated his original charge that Salisbury had been a false knight to Gloucester but then expanded Salisbury's crimes well beyond a personal betrayal. He alleged that Salisbury, having been of the secret counsel ('conseil covigne') of Richard, had advised him to destroy the lords and communalty of the realm ('la comunalté de roialme'); and abetted him in many other evil and false plans against the *chose publique* and common profit.[58] It was these deeds that made Salisbury a traitor. After Morley presented the *addicion*, he again threw down his gauntlet

55 *Morley v. Salisbury*, p. 170.

56 Ibid., p. 171.

57 Ibid., p. 173.

58 Ibid.

as endorsement of the truth of his words. Salisbury made a personal rejoinder, stating in his own voice ('par parole de sa bouche propre') that Morley was a liar. He, too, then threw down his glove and declared he was ready to defend his words according to the law and custom of arms. That each party spoke in person rather than through his lawyer stresses that in this judicial arena, both ethical truth and legal proof ultimately rested in the words of the individual man.

Between the opening statements on 11 November and the final judgment delivered in early December, the Court convened several times to debate whether Morley's new charges could be considered. Salisbury argued that the *addicion* should be excluded because it was unrelated to Morley's original challenge in parliament, adding that Morley had failed to show his interest, in a legal sense, in an appeal of treason that did not involve him personally (the original allegation having concerned only Salisbury's betrayal of Gloucester). Salisbury concluded by demanding that the case be thrown out altogether. While the lawyers' influence can be discerned in debates over technicalities, these advocates were named only once.[59] By contrast, the trial record privileged the voices of Morley and Salisbury, describing in detail their verbal and gestural performances and repeatedly using the phrase 'par parole de sa propre bouche' to stress that what was at issue was the veracity of their own spoken words, and therefore their masculine honour and identities as true men.

For Morley's appeal to progress despite Salisbury's objections, he had to show why his original allegations regarding the betrayal of Gloucester should be considered treason and how the charges in the *addicion* related to that original crime. His strategy demonstrates that understandings of treason as a personal betrayal of one man by another could complement more abstract conceptions of treason as a crime against the state or community of the realm. Morley began by drawing the Court's attention to masculine virtues of loyalty, service and honour that were fundamental to the performance of knighthood. As evidence for Salisbury being 'of the counsel' of Gloucester, he described how in a previous action in the Court of Chivalry involving Salisbury's father, Salisbury had enjoyed Gloucester's support and had offered Gloucester his service in gratitude.[60] This service moved from the social to the military sphere when Salisbury was retained by Gloucester as one of his knightly entourage and went with him on campaign to Prussia; from then on, he became a trusted member of the duke's inner circle ('et allors and aprés privé de son conseill').[61] Morley claimed that once Salisbury had gained Gloucester's trust, he abused this intimacy by spying on him for Richard and

59 Thomas Stokes acting for Morley and Laurence de Stapilton for Salisbury.

60 *Morley v. Salisbury*, p. 182. This had been a dispute over armorial bearings.

61 Ibid., pp. 182, 186.

ultimately by lending his voice to the false appeal of treason of 1397. Finally, Morley countered Salisbury's objection that the matters in the *addicion* were unrelated to the original appeal and therefore inadmissible by arguing that it was precisely *because* Salisbury was of the trusted counsel of both Gloucester and Richard that he had been able to incite the king to destroy the leading nobles of the realm on false grounds, and to take other actions against the *communalté, chose publique* and common profit.

Morley's challenge in parliament had depicted Salisbury's treason purely in chivalric terms and by claiming to speak on behalf of Gloucester, he represented himself as a loyal knight who was willing to put his own body on the line to defend the honour of the dead duke. This was eminently appropriate considering that it was Gloucester who had elevated Morley to the status of knighthood in 1380 and Morley had been part of his homosocial affinity from that time onwards.[62] Morley reinforced this chivalric narrative by pointing out Salisbury's own violations of knightly fidelity. However, the *addicion* altered the terms of engagement by introducing a more potent construction of treason as a crime against the public authority of the state. Why this change in tactics? Firstly, Morley had his own reasons to deter the Court from focusing too intently on matters of chivalric betrayal. He was closely allied with Gloucester and seemed genuinely horrified at his murder. Yet, his own hands were not clean because in 1397, as lieutenant to the Marshal of England, it had been he who had wielded the executioner's axe against the earl of Arundel. Chronicle accounts of Arundel's death suggest he was widely seen as a martyr to Richard's tyranny and a short-lived saint's cult even sprang up at the site of his interment.[63] The Court of Chivalry no doubt took a more pragmatic view of Morley's grim duties as lieutenant. Nevertheless, considering the prominent place given to Arundel's unjust trial and wrongful execution in the articles of Richard's deposition, it is plausible to assume that any man who had helped to bring about the earl's death might be considered already tainted when it came to questions of manly honour. Notably, by moving from a notion of treason as a personal betrayal to the abstract conception of treason as an assault on the *chose publique* and the community of the realm, Morley's *addicion* elevated this case from a personal grievance involving the breaking of homosocial bonds between knights to a crime that touched the king himself as the embodiment of sovereign authority. If Morley's motivation in pursuing this case was personal revenge (as seems likely given its roots in the 1397 and 1399 parliaments), then the likelihood of success was increased if he could convince Henry that as king, he had a stake in the outcome. It is no coincidence that just weeks after Richard's deposition and Henry IV's coronation,

62 Goodman, *Loyal Conspiracy*, p. 124.

63 Simon Walker, 'Political Saints in Later Medieval England', *The McFarlane Legacy: Studies in Late Medieval Politics and Society*, ed. R. H. Britnell and A. J. Pollard (New York, 1995), pp. 77–106 (p. 81).

the language of the *addicion* mirrored that of the Record and Process as well as Henry's own words to parliament on claiming the throne. Morley accused Salisbury of aiding and abetting Richard's tyranny and helping him to destroy the community of the realm by extracting enormous ransoms and extorting his subjects, a reference to the blank charters and forced loans of 1397–8. When Morley characterised Salisbury's treason as an attack on the common profit of the realm, this echoed Henry's promise that he would not punish any of his subjects, excepting those persons who had acted against 'the gude purpose and the commune profyt of the rewme'.[64] By portraying Salisbury's actions as a crime against the entire political community and not just a knight's dishonourable betrayal of his lord, Morley gave his new monarch an opportune opening to perform legitimate kingship before his most powerful noble subjects, with the public authority he claimed to embody most clearly represented by his sovereign authority to execute justice.

Salisbury was given several days to respond to Morley's new allegations and on 2 December, he presented the court with a bill in which he mounted a vigorous defence on all points. He declared that Morley had failed to show how Gloucester had been falsely appealed of treason, before what judge or in what court, or how this had been the cause of his death. (This was clearly obfuscation, given that everyone present knew the circumstances of Gloucester's murder and his post-mortem conviction as a traitor.) As to the charges regarding Salisbury's knightly service with Gloucester, his betrayal of the duke by spying on him, and his false appeal of treason, Salisbury baldly denied each of these without explanations or excuses.[65] He concluded with a deft strategic manoeuvre in which he stated:

> And since the matter of the first appeal concerns the claim of an injury inflicted on an individual person, [and] the matter claimed in the *addicion* concerns allegations about the destruction of the *communalté* against the *chose public* [*sic*], the said two matters cannot by any law be assumed to be related or brought together as they are in the *addicion*, nor are they able to be so conjoined, but are at all times separate.[66]

Salisbury's defence was that there were two types of treason, one against 'un singuler persone' and another against the *chose publique*. These, he declared, could not be treated as the same category of offence. His strategy was to drive a wedge between traditional conceptions of treason, including those encompassed by the 1352 statute, and newer political imperatives to construct treason as a crime against the state. His defensive strategy failed and a shift towards the more expansive definition of treason was made clear in the Court's

64 *PROME*, 'Henry IV: October 1399', Part One, Roll, Item Fifty-six.

65 *Morley v. Salisbury*, pp. 186–7.

66 Ibid., p. 188.

final decision on 5 December. The parties had assembled in the king's privy chamber ('au cost du lit du roy') at the royal manor of Kennington, spatial symbolism that stressed Henry's position as the ultimate authority in this court.[67] Speaking for the king, the Constable declared that the parties should engage in a trial by combat to prove the charge that Salisbury had conspired to destroy the 'chose publique et comune profit du roialme'.[68] All other matters were to be left in abeyance.

The case had been boiled down to two competing first-person testimonies, contained in bills that were now signed by Morley and Salisbury. The Constable then inserted these bills into the two men's respective gauntlets and twisted the gauntlets together, declaring by the authority vested in him by the king that the case would be decided by combat. This ritual signified that it was the truth of the words contained in these bills that would be tested upon the bodies of the two men. This implicitly supported the continuing validity of judicial constructions of treason shaped by the values of chivalry and masculine honour (the 'corage et honesté de chivalrie' as the Constable put it).[69] However, the combat was to be fought not over an insult to the honour of an individual nobleman or even an attack on the person of the king, but over injuries to the *chose publique*. Henry's influence on this decision can be inferred from his personal presence and it served more than one purpose for a usurping king eager to validate his legitimacy. Certainly, it marked a formal recognition of his right to adjudicate disputes between his most powerful subjects. Of greater long-term significance, though, were the constitutional implications of constructions of treason as attacks against the *chose publique* and the common profit, entities that were themselves masculinised through their strategic deployment in a legal battle over manly honour. In the short term, this case helped to bolster Henry's claim to exercise sovereign power as the embodiment of both virtuous masculine kingship and a more abstract sense of public authority. However, by refiguring treason as a crime against the national community of the realm and not simply against the individual person of the king, it also signalled a more enduring shift in the relationship between the English state and its political subjects.

THE EPIPHANY RISING AND ITS AFTERMATH

The combat between Morley and Salisbury was scheduled for 14 February 1400 at Newcastle-on-Tyne, in the presence of the king. However, the battle was never fought because Salisbury was killed in early January during the Epiphany Rising. This was the name given to a plot organised by the Counter-Appellants

67 Ibid., p. 189.

68 Ibid., p. 190.

69 Ibid., p. 180.

including Salisbury, the earl of Kent, the earl of Huntingdon and Thomas Lord Despenser, with the support of other disaffected members of Richard's inner circle.[70] Their plan was to break Richard out of prison in the Tower, where he had been held since his deposition, and restore him to the throne.[71] Although their intentions for the redundant Henry were not as clear, Walsingham was not alone in believing that the conspirators had something more heinous than a restoration in mind. He claimed that they planned:

> To make a sudden attack upon the king at Windsor Castle, under the pretext of taking part in the Christmas games and tournaments, and to kill him cruelly with all his children.[72]

Although Richard's intimates had been degraded from their new 1397 titles in 1399, Henry had allowed them to keep their earlier titles and noble privileges, including attendance at court festivities such as the Christmas celebrations. Walsingham described them violating the king's trust by exploiting this opportunity of personal intimacy in order to murder him and his family in his own home. The *Continuatio Eulogii* told a similar story of intimate betrayals, adding that the nobles' plot was short-circuited when a London prostitute revealed their secrets to a member of the king's household with whom she had spent the night.[73] These were vivid portrayals of the customary idea of treason as a violation of homosocial trust and masculine bonds. The second account added a further gendered layer, with its triangulated relationship in which a woman served as the conduit between men. Kent's uncle Thomas Arundel, the archbishop of Canterbury, also saw the traitors primarily as destroyers of natural bonds of kinship and affinity between men. In a letter to the Convent of Canterbury Cathedral dated 10 January, he described his own narrow escape from the 'abominable ambush'. According to Arundel, '[a]bominable indeed is the word for an ambush of this sort, in which a nephew, with the calculated villainy of a traitor, attempts an armed attack against his uncle, like a son against his father' and he went on to excoriate the offenders as 'this would-be parricide, this foul ingrate'.[74]

With Henry forewarned of the move against him, the rising was stillborn and the main conspirators were forced to flee. The judgment against the

70 They had by this time been degraded from the titles awarded them by Richard II in 1397.

71 After this rising, Richard was moved to more secure custody at Pontefract. It was there that he died, probably murdered on Henry IV's orders, sometime in February. For general accounts of the rising and Richard's death: Given-Wilson, *Henry IV*, pp. 160–5; John Lavan Kirby, *Henry IV of England* (London, 1970), pp. 86–90.

72 *St Albans Chronicle II*, p. 285.

73 *Continuatio Eulogii*, pp. 385–6.

74 *Chronicles of the Revolution*, pp. 236–7 (p. 237). The earl of Kent was the son of Arundel's sister.

Counter-Appellants delivered in the 1399 parliament had clearly stated that if they did anything in support of the deposed king, this would be incontrovertible proof of their treason and they would be executed without trial. When they went on the run in early 1400, Salisbury and the other nobles were already effectively dead men. However, it was not the king who hunted them down and exercised justice against them but mobs of commoners. Usurper became usurped as Adam Usk graphically described the king's lowliest subjects taking upon themselves his royal prerogative to divide and display the bodies of traitors. The earls of Kent and Salisbury managed to get as far as Cirencester where:

> They were beheaded in an uprising of the common folk … I saw their bodies, chopped up like the carcasses of beasts killed in the chase, being carried to London, partly in sacks and partly on poles slung across pairs of men's shoulders, where they were later salted to preserve them. The earl of Huntingdon … was also captured by the local people, and beheaded by common folk and workmen … Lord Despenser …who was also a party to this conspiracy, was most despicably beheaded by workmen at Bristol; and the heads of those who had thus been brought to ruin were stuck on poles and displayed for a time on the far side of London bridge.[75]

The chroniclers had no sympathy for the traitors, but they were dismayed by the manner of their demise. The king had dispatched Lord Berkeley to arrest the nobles and bring them to him for judgment. This orderly legal process was upended when the townspeople of Cirencester demanded that the captured earls of Kent and Salisbury be handed over to them, and 'they even threatened Lord Berkeley with death' if he did not comply.[76] There was a similar turn of events in the case of the earl of Huntingdon. Sir Gerard Braybroke was holding him captive under orders to 'keep him safe until the king had had a word with him'.[77] However, the king's authority was over-ruled when 'the commons … immediately swore that unless [Braybroke] produced the earl … he would himself die in place of him. The knight, fearing the anger of the mob, promised to produce the earl'.[78] The author of the *Vita Ricardi Secundi* was equally horrified when Lord Despenser was murdered by Bristol workmen:

> Although the mayor tried hard to save him … there was nothing he could do about it, and finally they dragged him out to the cross which stands in the marketplace and beheaded him. Then they took his head away and placed it on top of London bridge.[79]

75 *Adam Usk*, pp. 89, 91. The executions took place on or around 8 January.

76 *St Alban's Chronicle II*, p. 291.

77 Ibid., p. 293.

78 Ibid.

79 *HVRS*, p. 165.

The locals of Cirencester and Bristol saw their actions through a customary lens in which treason was restricted to direct attacks on the king's person or his immediate family. They did not consider that making dire threats against the king's representatives or murdering and dismembering his enemies fell into the same category of treasonous offence as the actions of the noble conspirators. Nevertheless, when these events are considered in light of statutory definitions of treason, the commoners' actions could certainly qualify as treason because they had prevented the king's judicial representatives from carrying out his orders and had even threatened to kill them. Moreover, their temerity in appropriating the king's power to execute justice could be interpreted as accroachment. Henry had only recently usurped the throne of the still-living Richard and he needed to ensure that the political community accepted him as the unrivalled embodiment of sovereignty in the realm. The commoners' blithe disregard for Henry's status and even for his direct orders signalled the terrifying inversion of natural political and social order, and it threatened to subvert both his kingship and his manhood. After several weeks of chaos, Henry had to re-assert his control over events and define treason on his own terms rather than those of his unruly subjects.

The king achieved this by publicly exercising his royal prerogatives to pardon and to condemn. On 9 February, Henry summoned his leading subjects to a Great Council designed to restore peace and order. At this Council, he established special commissions staffed by sheriffs and justices of the peace and tasked them with rounding up and punishing any malefactors still at large. Henry astutely recognised the potential for these proceedings to get out of hand as people used them 'per malice' to settle grudges by falsely accusing each other, so he paired the commissions with a general pardon that excluded only 'certain principal persons according to the good and gracious discretion of the king'.[80] The peace commissions and general pardon were described as being 'for the quiet and tranquillity of the realm and the security of the people likewise in this new world' ('en ceste novelle monde'), an oblique acknowledgement of Henry's need to rapidly consolidate his regnal authority in the wake of his unprecedented seizure of power.[81]

Like the chroniclers, the king and his officials were perturbed by the way ordinary people had so violently appropriated royal judicial authority in the wake of the nobles' Rising. While agreeing that they had executed known traitors, the king's council described his subjects as having 'become so wild that they cruelly and wilfully destroy many liegemen of the king with no process of law'; this was a dangerous precedent that, if allowed to go unpunished, threatened peril to the realm by derogating from the estate of the king.[82]

80 'Minutes of Council, February, 1 Henry IV', in *PPC*, pp. 107, 109, quote at p. 107.

81 Ibid., p. 107.

82 Ibid.

Henry therefore commanded that in future, anyone who presumed to behead, kill or destroy his lieges should be adjudged as traitors themselves and be punished as such as an example to others.[83] These measures stressed that it was the king, acting through the processes and institutions of royal justice, who had the sole authority to determine an alleged traitor's guilt or innocence; by their violent and illegitimate interference in this process, the commons had demonstrated a defiant resistance to being governed. The implications were clear: even if his subjects claimed to be protecting their king from known traitors, their appropriation of his power to punish would not be tolerated because this undermined rather than strengthened Henry's claim to be their lawful king and the fount of justice in the realm. The Privy Council minutes for February 1400 reveal one final measure by which Henry reinscribed his own authority over that of his wayward subjects: he took into his own hands the lands and revenues of the dead noblemen. This, it was said, would enable him to better defend himself and his realm from enemies and sustain himself honourably without burdening his people. In other words, forfeitures from treason would provide the wherewithal for Henry to keep his promises to live of his own and avoid excessive taxation.

Twelve months later, the parliament held in January and February of 1401 offered Henry another opportunity to stamp the violent deaths of his rebellious nobles with his own judicial authority by re-enacting their convictions before the assembled political community. Why did Henry find it necessary to revisit the events of the previous year, given that the suppression of the Epiphany Rising, the deaths of the main conspirators and Richard's subsequent death in captivity appeared to have neutralised any serious opposition to his rule? Despite the narratives that lauded Henry as England's saviour from tyranny in 1399, the honeymoon period was startlingly brief. Within the first year of his reign, questions were already being asked about Henry's ability to defend the realm and his willingness to keep his promises about finance and taxation. On the military front, the king led an expensive but largely fruitless expedition into Scotland that succeeded only in provoking a Scottish raid into Northumberland. This was not only a military miscalculation but held the potential to call Henry's martial and chivalric reputation into question – a reputation that had been so critical to staging his claim to the throne. At the same time, a combination of falling revenues and mismanagement saw royal finances increasingly strained, and by the winter of 1400 people were publicly complaining about burdensome taxes and the extravagance of the royal household.[84] Shadowing these gripes about Lancastrian government, darker tales were starting to circulate alleging that Henry had murdered Richard.

Although the Epiphany Rising had been suppressed, bold challenges

83 Ibid., pp. 107–8, 113.

84 Given-Wilson, *Henry IV*, pp. 174–88; Bennett, *Richard II and the Revolution of 1399*, pp. 202–4.

to Henry's kingship had emerged from other quarters. The most pressing problem was the outbreak of the Welsh rebellion led by Owain Glyn Dŵr, who claimed to be the prince of Wales.[85] This was an audacious affront to Henry who, as part of his strategy of legitimation, had arranged for his eldest son to be formally invested as prince of Wales shortly after his own coronation.[86] The Welsh war would sap Henry's military and financial resources for years and it was a persistent source of grievance for his subjects. Meanwhile, the Scots and French stubbornly refused to recognise Henry as anything more than the duke of Lancaster. While Henry had been preparing his army in York in July 1400, he was challenged to combat by a French knight who sought to disprove his claim to the royal title in a trial by battle. This threatened to expose Henry to an unpredictable test of his manhood and legitimacy. Crisis was averted on that occasion because Henry's champion was the victor, but subsequent French challenges were linked to repeated accusations that Henry had murdered Richard and was no true king.[87] Several of these chivalric challenges were in play at the time of the 1401 parliament, for the roll records that 'the said commons told our lord the king that they had heard that certain lords … of this kingdom had been challenged by the French'.[88] The Commons were, however, careful to avoid any awkward references to the specific reasons the French had given for their challenges.

In this charged political climate, Henry was bound to be sensitive to criticisms of his kingship and therefore eager to exploit any opportunity to reiterate his legitimacy. The post-mortem condemnation of the Epiphany conspirators in parliament achieved this through several rhetorical steps. First, their plot on behalf of Richard was brought within the 1352 statutory definition of treason with the description that they 'rode in warlike manner, treacherously, against our lord the king, contrary to their allegiance'.[89] The record then described them being 'seized and beheaded in their armed uprising by the loyal lieges of our said lord the king', but while it was acknowledged that this was done without due process of law, nevertheless 'the lords temporal present in parliament, by the assent of the king' declared them traitors and confirmed the forfeiture of their lands.[90] This enabled Henry to render the murders lawful and bring them within the scope of his own royal judicial authority.

85 For a general account of the Welsh rebellion: R. R. Davies, *The Revolt of Owain Glyn Dŵr* (New York, 1997).

86 The political implications of this move are discussed further in Chapter Five.

87 Anthony Tuck, 'Henry IV and Europe: A Dynasty's Search for Recognition', *The McFarlane Legacy*, ed. Britnell and Pollard, pp. 107–11; Simon Walker, 'Janico Dartasso: Chivalry, Nationality and the Man-at-Arms', *History* 84 (1999), 31–51 (pp. 41–2 on the challenge at York).

88 *PROME*, 'Henry IV: January 1401', Item Twelve.

89 Ibid., Item Thirty.

90 Ibid.

The sentence made a final significant move when it asserted that the traitors not only planned to kill Henry, they also planned to destroy 'other great men of the realm, and to populate the said realm with people of another tongue' ('et le dit roialme de gentz d'autre lange enhabiter').[91] This expanded the scope of treason to encompass actions against the English political community and the abstract entity of the nation, represented here in the idea of language. In doing so, it gendered these constitutional abstractions by locating treason equally in attacks on the manly human body of the king and on the political community of the realm.

WOMEN TRAITORS: AN IMPOSSIBLE CONTRADICTION?

It was not only the body politic that was gendered masculine through the rhetoric of treason prosecutions. Traitors were also viewed in distinctly gendered terms and treason – whether this was represented as an act against the king's person, the community of the realm or the nation – was imagined as an exclusively masculine crime. This explains the pivotal role played by cultural values of homosocial loyalty, chivalric honour and masculine trueness in shaping accusations, convictions and the ritual of execution. The gendering of treason was also defined in negative terms through the exclusion of women from formal treason proceedings. It is not often that we find women engaged in treason plots, but in those cases their activities were transferred onto men while they 'disappeared' behind male relatives or accomplices. In short, if the traitor was the embodiment of false manhood, then women traitors were an impossible contradiction.

This patterning is prominent in the reactions to a curious conspiracy staged a few years after the Epiphany Rising, in which Lady Constance Despenser was the prime mover. Constance was the widow of the unfortunate Thomas Lord Despenser, who had been so ruthlessly dispatched by a mob of Bristol labourers. In early 1405, she rose briefly to prominence as the mind behind a conspiracy to abduct the young earl of March and his brother from the royal residence of Windsor and to take them into Wales.[92] When Richard was deposed, the earl of March was left as the royal heir with the most direct blood claim, so Henry IV had been keeping him safely out of the way under comfortable house arrest at Windsor. Constance's plan was that the boys would be used to rally support for the rebellion of their uncle Sir Edmund Mortimer, who had thrown in his lot with Owain Glyn Dŵr. Like the Epiphany Rising, this plot violated the king's trust in the most intimate space of his household because while Constance was staying at Windsor in December 1404, she had taken advantage of royal hospitality by having a locksmith make duplicate

[91] Ibid.

[92] *St Albans Chronicle II*, pp. 431–3; T. B. Pugh, *Henry V and the Southampton Plot of 1415* (Gloucester, 1988), pp. 78–9.

keys to the door of the boys' chamber. In early February, she succeeded in having the children smuggled out of the castle under cover of night but was stopped with her young charges at Cheltenham and taken to London.

Although it was Constance who had broken the king's trust, her treasonous plotting was quickly refigured as the violation of bonds between men. In late February, she was brought before the king's council at Westminster but was side-lined as the conspiracy's leader.[93] Instead, it was her brother Edward, now duke of York (Henry's cousin), who was saddled with the blame although there is little evidence he had any knowledge of Constance's plans. Consistent with earlier cases, this blame shifting placed masculine betrayals at the heart of the crime of treason. Walsingham presented the transference of culpability in the most direct way as he described Constance coming before the king to accuse her brother to his face.[94] She asked if any man present was willing to fight a combat with York to prove her charges and agreed that she 'would surrender herself to be burnt if her contender were defeated'.[95] One of her servants threw down his hood in wager of battle and York responded in kind, 'being prepared to affirm his innocence in a duel'.[96] The king did not allow this battle to take place. Instead, on 27 February (most likely the same day as the confrontation in council) he had York arrested and taken first to the Tower and then to Pevensey Castle.[97] In March, the duke's lands and goods were confiscated and several months later, York was writing to the council begging them to intervene for him with Henry, for 'he had suffered 17 weeks and more' incarcerated.[98] Constance, meanwhile, disappeared into a brief and informal confinement at Kenilworth and although her goods and lands were seized, they were restored to her the following year.[99] One man did end up paying the full price for the plot – the locksmith was executed as a traitor.

What of Constance's purported offer to suffer burning if her champion lost? Burning was a characteristically feminised punishment used against women convicted of 'petty treason', a crime that can be understood as domestic rather than political treason. In the 1352 statute, following the primary clauses describing acts of treason against the king, his family and his senior officials, a secondary clause added 'and in addition there is another kind of treason ... when a servant kills his master [or] a woman kills her husband [*baron*]'.[100] Such cases were vanishingly rare but there is one telling example of a woman

93 *St Albans Chronicle II*, p. 432, n. 613.

94 Ibid., pp. 431–3.

95 Ibid., p. 433.

96 Ibid.

97 *CCR, Henry IV: 1402–5*, pp. 426, 435–6.

98 *Rymer's Foedera*, VIII, p. 387: 'il ad souffert par xvij Semaigns & plus'.

99 York had also been restored to royal favour by December 1405.

100 *Statutes*, I, p. 320. This clause also included the murder of a prelate by a member of the secular or regular clergy. Cf. Bellamy, *Law of Treason*, pp. 225–31.

burned for petty treason in London on 17 April, 1388, at the same time the trials in the Merciless Parliament were racing to their bloody conclusions. The woman, Elizabeth Wauton, was engaged in a sexual affair with a priest while her husband Andrew was overseas.[101] On Andrew's return, 'the besotted priest was persuaded by the woman to kill him as he lay in bed'.[102] The monstrous pair of murderers was captured as they slept together and the priest was sentenced to the standard punishment for male traitors, 'while the woman was burned at the stake near Bermondsey'.[103] The description in the 1352 statute shows that this type of treason was considered a sinful inversion of divinely ordained patriarchal order, whereby the male head of household was lord over his servants, his wife and other female relatives. The shifting of culpability in Constance's case suggests that whereas men's treasonous acts were viewed as inherently political, entwined as they were within homosocial relationships between the king and his male subjects, women traitors in this political sense were unthinkable. The gendered nature of treason meant that women could only be imagined as perpetrators of domestic, not political, betrayals. This is a conclusion that is supported by the treatment of the few other women caught up in treason trials in the early years of Lancastrian rule and their cases will be explored in the next chapter.

In the turbulent climate created by Richard's deposition, the Lancastrian regime used the laws of treason to resolve the constitutional conundrum posed by usurpation, as well as to renegotiate the balance of power between the king, the law and the political community. In his first parliament, Henry IV had exploited noble acrimony and recriminations to bolster his own claim to embody sovereign political authority by exercising the royal prerogatives of justice and mercy upon the realm's greatest subjects. Although Henry promised to reverse Richard's expansions to treason law, the statutory enactments of 1399 left considerable room to manoeuvre. Henry made full use of this space to pursue as treason an array of offences not explicitly covered by the 1352 statute or encompassed by customary ideas. In parliament and the Court of Chivalry, interpretations of treason that included attacks on the *chose publique*, the *communalté* of the realm and the nation were redefining treason in more expansive terms as a crime against the public authority of the state. These proceedings served immediate political ends by defining threats against Henry's person or his family as treason, thus offering a means by which Henry's usurping body and that of his patrilineage could be joined more securely to the body politic of the crown. But while improvised solutions solved Henry's immediate problems, these legal constructions of treason would also have lasting effects.

101 *Westminster Chronicle*, p. 323. For a detailed examination of this case, see Strohm, 'Treason in the Household', *Hochon's Arrow*.

102 *Westminster Chronicle*, p. 323.

103 Ibid.

As has been seen, chivalric notions of treason remained powerful and the perception of treason as a personal betrayal of masculine loyalties influenced the way the crime was constructed by accusers as well as the defensive strategies of the accused. Nevertheless, the innovative definitions of treason that were deployed in parliament and in the Court of Chivalry to address challenges from a small group of malcontent nobles soon began to influence interpretations in the court of King's Bench and so to have much wider import. There, new common law precedents defined treason as an insult to the public authority of the state and a crime against the nation. While 'state' and 'nation' might appear neutral and un-gendered constructs, King's Bench treason indictments that were structured in these terms were underpinned by shared cultural understandings of true and false manhood. Through these expanding definitions of treason, the body politic – even when disarticulated from the manly body of the king – was being imagined as a masculine entity, with significant implications for the constitutional relationship between the state and political subjects.

4

FROM PUBLIC SPEECH TO TREASONOUS DEED

In the wake of Richard's deposition, Lancastrian propaganda had painted a picture of near-universal approbation for Henry's accession to the throne, but the reality was more sobering. Between 1400 and 1405, people from all walks of life were charged with treason for criticising Henry's kingship and for voicing in public dangerous questions about his dynastic legitimacy and right to rule. Although Richard had perished in captivity in early 1400, in taverns, streets and marketplaces around England people were saying that he was still alive, living in exile in Scotland or elsewhere, and that he would soon return to reclaim his rightful throne.[1] Some added that if Richard were indeed dead, then it was not Henry but Edmund Mortimer, the earl of March, who was the true king.[2] Henry was also called false and dishonest because by imposing heavy taxes on his new subjects, he had broken his promises to 'live of his own' and to rule for the common good.[3] The money was sorely needed to fight Welsh rebels and Scots aggression, but early military setbacks threatened to expose Henry as a weak king who could not protect his subjects. Disillusion was further fuelled by accusations that taxes were being frittered away on lavish living in the royal household. Philip Repingdon, Henry's confessor, even rebuked the king in a public letter lamenting that the people's early euphoria had been replaced by despair because 'in the place of the law, *tirannica voluntas* now suffices'.[4]

In 1399, as part of the process of reconciling a fractured political community

1 Peter McNiven, 'Rebellion, Sedition and the Legend of Richard II's Survival in the Reigns of Henry IV and Henry V', *Bulletin of the John Rylands Library* 76 (1994), 93–117; Philip Morgan, 'Henry IV and the Shadow of Richard II', *Crown, Government and People in the Fifteenth Century*, ed. Rowena E. Archer (New York, 1995), pp. 1–31; Simon Walker, 'Rumour, Sedition and Popular Protest in the Reign of Henry IV', *Past & Present* 166 (2000), 31–65; Paul Strohm, *England's Empty Throne: Usurpation and the Language of Legitimation, 1399–1422* (New Haven, 1998), pp. 101–27.

2 On the issues surrounding Henry IV's dynastic claim: McNiven, 'Legitimacy and Consent'; Michael Bennett, 'Henry IV, the Royal Succession and the Crisis of 1406', *The Reign of Henry IV: Rebellion and Survival, 1403–1413*, ed. Gwilym Dodd and Douglas Biggs (York, 2008), pp. 9–27.

3 Bennett, 'Henry of Bolingbroke and the Revolution of 1399'; Given-Wilson, *Henry IV*, pp. 205–9.

4 Quoted in Bennett, 'Henry of Bolingbroke and the Revolution of 1399', p. 29.

and establishing himself as a just sovereign, Henry had vowed that he would not treat verbal criticism as treason in the way that Richard had done. This promise was soon sacrificed at the altar of political necessity as Henry's need to defend his regality and manly honour led him to take measures designed to stop the mouths of his detractors by whatever means were necessary. This included using the jurisdiction of the Court of Chivalry to deal with purely domestic matters, contrary to Henry's earlier promises and the new treason statute passed in the 1399 parliament. Accordingly, on 1 February 1401 a writ sealed with the king's personal signet was issued to Henry Percy, earl of Northumberland and Constable of England since 1399. This writ charged Percy 'to hear and determine divers unaccustomed cases and businesses concerning the estate, fame and condition of the king's person and the dignity of the crown'.[5] The strategy seems to have quickly borne fruit for in the same month, Adam Usk reported the death at Shrovetide of a scribe:

> Condemned by judgment of the court of chivalry firstly to have his tongue cut out, because he had spoken disrespectfully of the king ... secondly, to have his right hand cut off, because he had written these things down, and thirdly, by penalty of *talion*, to be beheaded at the Tower, because he had not been able to prove his false allegations.[6]

Talion was a civil law term that meant roughly 'an eye for an eye'. In the case of the scribe, his false words were deemed to be a deadly attack on the person of the king and so were expiated through the destruction of his body. Beyond the Court of Chivalry, a series of treason prosecutions pursued in King's Bench in the early 1400s also hinged upon men's false words, in the form of verbal rumours and vernacular texts that undermined Henry's kingship or denied his right to rule. These cases had enduring effects on the treatment of treason in the English legal system and the narratives they generated also underscore the ways treason was gendered through political and cultural norms. Firstly, they exposed the extent to which the potent notion of chivalric manhood that had bolstered Henry's claim to the throne could also be deployed to justify opposition to his rule. Secondly, close analysis of the trial records reveals that gendered conceptions of public speech were central to the way the crime of treason was being defined. This enabled the king and his judicial officers to establish common law precedents for treating dissenting political speech as an act of treason, but it also created new means by which accused men could evade or resist royal justice. Thirdly, the legal records bring to light gendered discourses of treason that helped to bond Henry's own usurping body to the masculine body politic of the realm. By explicitly detailing the ways traitors threatened both the king and his sons, prosecution narratives stressed Henry's

5 *CPR, Henry IV: Vol. I: 1401–1405*, p. 458.

6 *Adam Usk*, p. 123.

legitimacy by locating him at the centre of a royal patrilineage that reached forward but also, implicitly, into the past.[7] At the same time, this legal rhetoric fed into an idealised image of masculine kingship that highlighted Henry's sexual and reproductive capacity in contrast to the childless and 'unmanly' Richard II.[8] Finally, through these trials the English language itself took on a new and complex role in gendered discourses of treason. Used by prosecutors as a marker of nationhood, it worked to unite Henry as king with the realm of England and in the process, contributed to an evolving strand of legal reasoning that defined treason as a crime not only against the king and his sons, but also against the people and nation of England. However, the vernacular could also exert subversive power by verifying the resistant claims of men accused of treason to be loyal subjects and true men.

The value of homosocial bonds forged through chivalric brotherhood had been made abundantly clear to Henry when in the weeks leading up to Richard's deposition, English knights and noblemen had strapped on their armour and rallied to his cause. Henry's own manly reputation could only be burnished by the early support of men like Sir Henry Percy, whose sobriquet 'Hotspur' neatly encapsulated his chivalric renown and honour.[9] But beneath the many political, intellectual and legal justifications for replacing Richard with his cousin there remained an unsettling awareness that Henry's journey to the throne could be read, essentially, as an argument for 'might makes right'. The dangerous potential of such a position was not lost on Henry's advisers. In his account of Richard's deposition, Thomas Walsingham included a dialogue in which Chief Justice Sir William Thirning had 'utterly forbidden' Henry from making a claim by conquest because 'if he claimed the kingdom on those grounds, he could have disinherited anyone he liked'.[10] Thirning's words may well have been apocryphal but the underlying sentiment was real. The precedent of conquest was not only a threat to the king's subjects, it could be a threat to the king himself because a ruler who overthrew his predecessor by force could not be surprised if the same tactic was later used against him. This stoked fears that positive homosocial bonds of knightly loyalty and brotherhood could be perverted into dark conspiracies against the king.

The case of a servant called Thomas Samford provides early evidence for

[7] Although Henry also had two daughters, they were never referred to in the records of treason trials or in related legislation from his reign.

[8] On sexual and reproductive capacity as a marker of masculine political authority: Broomhall and Van Gent, 'Introduction', *Governing Masculinities*. Richard's strategy for addressing his problematic childless status after the death of his first wife is discussed in Katherine J. Lewis, 'Becoming a Virgin King: Richard II and Edward the Confessor', *Gender and Holiness: Men, Women, and Saints in Late Medieval Europe*, ed. Sam Riches and Sarah Salih (London, 2002), pp. 86–100.

[9] This Percy was the eldest son of Henry Percy, earl of Northumberland and Constable of England.

[10] *St Albans Chronicle II*, p. 209.

these dynamics. In November 1400, Samford was a prisoner in the Fleet when he confessed to being party to an eye-popping plot in which necromancy and poisoning were merely the opening acts. The Latin text that opens the King's Bench record stated that Samford was already in custody 'for certain reasons touching the king's estate' when he told his story.[11] The confession that follows represents Samford's oral testimony, given in first-person English but translated into the French of formal legal record as third-person reported speech. The record framed this confession as entirely voluntary by asserting that the king's clerks were sent 'to hear what he wished to say, and he was sworn on a book to speak the truth in all he would say'.[12] This act of swearing truth placed Samford's 'voluntary' speech within the ambit of men's oaths as proof, eliding the power differential involved in making a prisoner talk and then transforming his speech into the authorising written language of the common law.

Under questioning, Samford confessed that in January 1400 he had carried letters between his master John Inglewood and a number of other men who were collecting money to fund a rising against Henry. Thomas and his master had also visited the house of John Salerne of Rye, where they met a merchant called Bernard who stood ready to contribute 500 Flemish men-at-arms to the cause. The conspiracy darkened further with the revelation that Inglewood was plotting with Robert Marner, a canon, and with a friar, 'late confessor to King Richard so he said', to 'arrange by necromancy and spell to make an ointment with which to secretly and cunningly anoint the saddle of our said lord the king'.[13] Before riding more than ten miles exposed to this poison, the king was expected to swell up and die suddenly, 'sitting up in his saddle'. Samford said he had witnessed the conspirators engaged in clandestine conversations in various places including a graveyard – a detail that reinforced the sinister character of the plotting – and to assisting them by carrying letters between them. Several times, Samford stated that he had been made 'to be sworn on a book that he would be loyal' to the plot's leaders and he described other conspirators being made to swear likewise.[14] The impression given in the record (and no doubt intended for a trial jury) was of homosocial brotherhood gone drastically wrong, as this network of men bound themselves to one another by evil oaths that violated their most fundamental bonds of loyalty and obligation to their rightful lord.

The references to necromancy and poison were dramatic, but at first glance this plan appears to be an exemplar of treason in the customary sense, with the intent being to destroy Henry's physical person. From the timing and the fact that Richard's former confessor was implicated, it can be assumed that it was directly related to the suppression of the Epiphany Rising and so was one of the

11 TNA KB 27/560 Rex m. 9. Cf. *Select Cases*, pp. 111–14.

12 TNA KB 27/560 Rex m. 9.

13 Ibid.

14 Ibid.

first cases in King's Bench that featured the 'returning king' theme. However, a closer look reveals these conspirators had something far more radical in mind. In a scheme that seems inspired by Henry's own forceful usurpation of power and the textual processes used to legitimise it, their plan was that once the king had been killed, they would use armed might to establish a regime of their own. According to Samford, Sir Thomas West would capture the Isle of Wight and its royal castle with the help of men gathered by the rector of Ashridge and 'the men named Thornes'.[15] Eschewing any reference to restoring Richard, Samford claimed they would then bring Sir Edmund Mortimer (uncle to the earl of March) to the Isle of Wight by force, 'and there they would cause him to take an oath that he would be ruled by them and, if he refused, they would put him to death'.[16] With Mortimer in their grasp, they would 'take his seal from him and send letters under his name' to raise men in Chester and elsewhere who would join them and fight for their cause.[17] Just as Henry had done, the ringleaders promised to reward their supporters with offices and prestige, granting them the ability to establish their own knightly dynasties. For example, John Salerne was told that if he served the conspirators well, 'he would have the castle of Lewes for himself and his heirs' and be made Constable of Pevensey for life. This was a vision in which men constructed an alternative masculine body politic wherein no king would be recognised as having sovereign authority that outweighed their own right to power by conquest.

Samford concluded his confession by saying that his master Inglewood had told him that a clerk called Thomas Yokflete had consented to this plan and it was because of this final allegation that the contents of Samford's confession were being heard before the court of King's Bench in the Easter term of 1401. The next part of the record, which returns to the formal Latin of legal rhetoric, reported that Yokflete voluntarily 'came in his own person before the king at Westminster' with the intention of clearing himself and was committed to the custody of the Marshal to await a hearing on 12 March, 1401.[18] Yokflete's defence rested in the fact that Samford's testimony 'establishes nothing in fact against the aforesaid Thomas Yokflete with respect to the aforesaid acts of treason but only the verbal statement of the said Thomas Samford of what John Inglewood said'.[19] In other words, the only evidence of treason against Yokflete was a story told at second hand, a verbal rumour. This was deemed insufficient proof against Yokflete and he was not sent to trial.[20] However, given the government's growing anxieties about dissenting

15 Ibid.
16 Ibid.
17 Ibid.
18 Ibid.
19 Ibid.
20 Ibid.

and deviant speech, the record closes by putting forward a different reason for Yokflete's discharge. This was that Samford had already confessed 'at another time' to various felonies and had abjured the realm, 'as fully appears on record by the said abjuration which the present king for certain reasons caused to come before him for determination'.[21] Therefore, the court declared, Samford's evidence against Yokflete was inadmissible.

These legal machinations show the king and his judicial officials were at a legal crossroads. We recall that in 1399, Henry had backed up his verbal undertakings to restore royal justice and to rule according to law by promising to repeal Richard II's 1397 extensions to the 1352 treason statute.[22] These had been viewed as emblematic of the deposed king's tyranny because they made mere talk against the king grounds for a treason prosecution even in the absence of any overt acts. However, by the time Samford's confession was brought into King's Bench, dissatisfaction with Henry's rule was regularly and loudly being voiced in public and his government was increasingly sensitive to the role of rumours and 'murmurings' in the incitement and organisation of anti-Lancastrian (or pro-Ricardian) plots. The problem, though, was that when Samford made his accusations against Yokflete, no definitive legal formula existed in common law to treat a verbal statement alone as sufficient proof of treason. Yokflete was therefore allowed to 'go quit' of the charges. Yet by stating that this was because Samford was not able to bring a legal case against anyone because he had already been outlawed, rather than by declaring his evidence inadmissible because it was only hearsay, the government left itself a loophole for treating such hearsay as tantamount to proof of treason through the explicit interpretation in case law of words as deeds.

This legal reasoning drew on an underlying late medieval cultural intersection between gender and particular types of deviant and harmful speech. Several of the cases from the early 1400s have provided the fuel for a long-running debate over whether treason by words was an offence that fell within the 1352 statute's definition of compassing or imagining the death of the king or, alternatively, whether the common law scope of treason was being stretched to new limits through ad hoc judicial construction in individual cases.[23] However, legal historians have not contextualised the shift in the interpretation of treason within a wider cultural context in which speech was

21 Ibid.

22 *PROME*, 'Henry IV: October 1399', Part One, Roll, Item Seventy. However, as noted in Chapter Three, Henry IV's new statutory enactments incorporated only a general undertaking to adjudge treason by the terms of 1352, leaving considerable ambiguity as to the scope of treason and the procedures by which it could be prosecuted: *Statutes*, II, pp. 114 (c. x), 116 (c. xiv).

23 Thornley, 'Treason by Words'; Rezneck, 'Constructive Treason by Words'; Bellamy, *Law of Treason*, pp. 102–37; C. A. F. Meekings, 'Thomas Kerver's Case, 1444', *The English Historical Review* 90 (1975), 331–46; Powell, 'The Strange Death of Sir John Mortimer', pp. 93–4.

integral to masculine social embodiment; the distinction between 'words' and 'acts' begins to appear too narrow when allegations of treasonous speech are assessed against a background in which a man's words *were*, innately, material acts.[24] The trial records themselves alert us to the importance of this context by putting particular weight on the traitor's sworn words in combination with their public performance.

The belief that words alone could do tangible harm was central to theological doctrine concerning blasphemy and under canon law, blasphemous speech was deemed an act that harmed the physical body of Christ.[25] In continental treason laws deriving from Roman civil law, discussing or predicting the king's death was also deemed blasphemy because it subverted divine order; such words were in turn construed as material acts of treason.[26] Although the 1352 statute did not explicitly equate treason with blasphemy, the idea that words alone could do physical damage was equally familiar in late medieval England. Blasphemy and other 'sins of the tongue' such as lying and slander were popular topics of preaching and for clerical and secular authorities alike, 'speech and its instrument the tongue were powerful agents'.[27] Once sins of the tongue became a target of spiritual and social vigilance, gender emerged as a key determinant in categorising particular speech acts as harmful deeds rather than merely words. Men's words could have positive instrumental effects when they enacted homosocial bonds and contracts, but the incarnate qualities of masculine speech also had negative potential, so that men's words were considered capable of causing tangible harm. While women's deviant speech was dismissed or punished relatively lightly as gossip or 'scolding', men's unruly speech was more severely punished as blasphemy or defamation and therefore as an action that caused physical injury, particularly when their words assaulted the honour and worship of other men.[28] The legal nuances surrounding treasonous speech cannot therefore be fully understood without recognising that these trials took place in a judicial culture in which

24 I examine the historiography in McVitty, '"My Name of a Trewe Man"'.

25 Sandy Bardsley, *Venomous Tongues: Speech and Gender in Late Medieval England* (Philadelphia, 2006), pp. 95–9. For an extended examination of the intersections between blasphemy, treason and heresy in medieval theology and political theory, see Leonard W. Levy, *Treason against God: A History of the Offense of Blasphemy* (New York, 1981).

26 Billoré, 'Introduction', *La Trahison au Moyen Age*, pp. 17–21; Cuttler, *The Law of Treason and Treason Trials in Later Medieval France*, pp. 1–54.

27 Edwin D. Craun, *Lies, Slander, and Obscenity in Medieval English Literature: Pastoral Rhetoric and the Deviant Speaker* (Cambridge, 1997), p. 1. See also Bardsley, *Venomous Tongues*, pp. 26–7.

28 Bardsley, *Venomous Tongues*, pp. 1–34, 90–105; Sandy Bardsley, 'Sin, Speech, and Scolding in Late Medieval England', *Fama: The Politics of Talk and Reputation in Medieval Europe*, ed. Thelma Fenster and Daniel Lord Smail (Ithaca, 2003), pp. 145–64; Neal, *Masculine Self*, pp. 175–82.

'the distinction between words-as-words and words-as-deeds was heavily gendered, especially from the late fourteenth century onward'.[29]

TREASONOUS SPEECH AND MASCULINE PERFORMANCE

The crucial move from cultural norm to legal precedent can first be seen in the case of John Sperhauk, which came before King's Bench in April 1402. Sperhauk was described in the indictment against him as a vagrant ('vagant home') and the record of his trial opens with a passage in French stating that what followed was his confession taken on 13 April 1402 before the king, Constable, Marshal and coroner of King's Bench.[30] As with Samford's confession, it represents a first-person oral confession made in English that was translated into the third-person French of legal record. Characteristic of the records in treason cases, it is richly informative about dates, times and places. In parts of the narrative, the evidence was shaped and presented as a dialogue that appears to convey the colloquial language and rhythms of informal speech. Capturing this level of detail was a practice that met the standards for legal evidence, but it also served a more subtle purpose by authenticating the text as an unmediated written representation of Sperhauk's oral speech.

The confession begins with a statement that while passing through a village near Baldock after breakfast on Palm Sunday 1402, Sperhauk 'came to the house there of a tailor unknown to him'.[31] Sperhauk then described a scorching diatribe against the king that was addressed to Sperhauk by the tailor's un-named wife. Amongst other things, she told him:

> That the present king was not the rightful king but that the earl of March is king by right, and that the present king was not son to the very noble prince John, duke of Lancaster ... but that he was the son of a butcher of Ghent, and that Owain Glyn Dŵr is the legal prince of Wales and of Cornwall, and that the pope sent a bull ... [declaring] that all who are willing to help the said earl and Owain in their aforesaid right are to have full indulgence and remission of all their sins ... And she also said that the king had not kept his covenant with his commons, for at his entry into England he promised them that they would be quit and discharged all kinds of payments and customs except those for his wars overseas, but in the meantime he has collected much wealth from his commons and done nothing with it to the profit of the realm but only for all his lords and many other gentlemen.[32]

29 Bardsley, *Venomous Tongues*, p. 99.

30 TNA KB 9/189/27 (indictment); KB 27/564 Rex m. 12 (plea roll record). For the latter, see also *Select Cases*, pp. 123–4.

31 TNA KB 27/564 Rex m. 12.

32 Ibid.

This outburst was more than generalised griping; it contained a series of specific, pointed political criticisms. First, the woman brought up the issue of dynastic legitimacy by saying that the earl of March was the true king. Then, she undermined Henry's legitimacy from another angle by saying that he was not the son of John of Gaunt but a butcher's bastard. The reference to this Ghent butcher was not simply a random titbit of salacious gossip. It directly recalled libellous vernacular handbills saying the same thing about Henry's father, which had been nailed up in prominent public sites across London at the time of the Good Parliament in 1376.[33] Complaints about Gaunt had centred on his perceived position as an over-mighty noble who had usurped the king's power for his own private gain and that of his adherents.[34] Given the circumstances of Henry's accession we can posit here a direct link to perceptions of Henry's own seizure of power, particularly as the woman went on to find in him the same faults of financial self-interest and favouritism that were attributed to his father. This element of the woman's critique is significant because it illustrates the long life that political ideas circulated in vernacular public bills could have in the minds of the populace, despite the ephemeral nature of the written bills themselves. It also testifies to the porous boundaries between written and aural forms of political speech.

The woman's statement that Owain Glyn Dŵr was the legal prince of Wales and Cornwall directly attacked Henry's title from another direction, one that displays a degree of political sophistication. On 15 October 1399, just two days after Henry's coronation, the men assembled in his first parliament were asked to assent to Henry's eldest son (the future Henry V) being invested with the titles prince of Wales and duke of Cornwall, and to recognise Prince Henry's right to succeed his father as king of England.[35] These were the actions of a king uneasy about the deficiencies of his own title and consequently anxious to secure public recognition of the place of his Lancastrian patrilineage as part of the legitimate royal bloodline. The purported papal bull in support of Glyn Dŵr's title as the legal prince of Wales and Cornwall must have raised further fears. Such a bull, if it existed or even if it was simply believed to exist, would give valuable moral and legal justification to the Welsh rebellion, which by 1402 was absorbing a great deal of the king's attention and resources.[36]

33 *The Anonimalle Chronicle, 1333 to 1381: From a MS Written at St Mary's*, ed. V. H. Galbraith (Manchester, 1970), p. 104. The incident is discussed in Scase, '"Strange and Wonderful Bills"', p. 240.

34 Anthony Goodman, *John of Gaunt: The Exercise of Princely Power in Fourteenth-Century Europe* (New York, 1992), pp. 55–8; Gwilym Dodd, 'A Parliament Full of Rats? *Piers Plowman* and the Good Parliament of 1376', *Historical Research* 79 (2006), 21–49 (pp. 27–9).

35 *PROME*, 'Henry IV: October 1399', Part One, Roll, Item Seventy-one.

36 I have been unable to trace the bull, although it is possible it was suppressed. This was the strategy used by Henry to defuse a bull of excommunication issued in 1405 after his execution of Richard Scrope, the archbishop of York: R. G. Davies, 'After the Execution

Finally, by complaining about Henry's burdensome taxation, Sperhauk's female interlocutor struck that potent vein of popular discontent that was already clearly visible by 1401. This took the form of suggestions that Henry was proving a dishonourable man and a false king because he had broken his word to his subjects and violated his coronation oath. Such an idea was particularly dangerous given that while the role of conquest had been played down in Henry's seizure of the throne, references to the consent of the estates in parliament had been integral to solidifying his claim.[37] This left Henry vulnerable to the possibility that consent given could also be withdrawn.

There is no evidence that the tailor's wife was herself particularly politically astute in constructing her critique; in fact Sperhauk claimed that she told him she had heard everything she repeated to him from another man who had recently been imprisoned at Westminster. Yet, despite the serious nature of her allegations against Henry, it was not she who was arrested and charged with treason for spreading these ideas, but Sperhauk. In his confession, he admitted:

> That on the Monday following the said Sunday after breakfast he openly recounted all the aforesaid matters of his own accord, knowledge and will [*de sa propre test, science et volunte*] at the village of Morden in the county of Cambridge to John Taylor and to a poor beggar and his wife and to many others of the said village, affirming and avowing the said words as true with the intention of inciting and arousing the people … against their aforesaid liege lord.[38]

It is telling that we do not have even the reported speech of what Sperhauk actually said to his audience of villagers, only his admission that he had repeated the woman's words. This was enough to get him hanged, drawn and quartered as a traitor. By contrast, although the tailor's wife had said things that were far more inflammatory and directly damaging to the king's honour and manly reputation, her speech appears to have been dismissed as inconsequential, as mere 'women's gossip', for there is no record of her being questioned let alone indicted. This was a classic instance of homosocial triangulation, whereby her independent political agency was erased, and she was reduced in the record to nothing more than a conduit for the much more damaging verbal performances of two men – the prisoner at Westminster and Sperhauk. It was Sperhauk's act of publicly repeating this political speech and of authenticating it by swearing to its truth that transformed deviant words into a material deed of treason.

---

of Archbishop Scrope: Henry IV, the Papacy and the English Episcopate, 1405–8', *Bulletin of the John Rylands University Library of Manchester* 59 (1976), 40–74.

37 McNiven, 'Legitimacy and Consent'; Bennett, 'Henry IV, the Royal Succession and the Crisis of 1406'.

38 TNA KB 27/564 Rex m. 12.

This transformation became evident in the clause that characterised Sperhauk's words as 'intent' to incite others to rise against the king. Early modernists argue that it was not until the Tudor period that seditious speech in the absence of overt acts came to be punished as treason, because in sixteenth-century jurisprudence the term 'imagine' in the 1352 statute was interpreted as 'intention'; intention then took on the status of a corporeal action.[39] Sperhauk's case and those that soon followed it demonstrate that the groundwork for this legal reasoning was laid down as early as Henry IV's reign, and this was precipitated by new cultural perceptions of the material impacts of masculine speech. Sperhauk's conviction marked the first time this interpretation of men's words as an *act* of treason was canvassed by the king and his justices in King's Bench and accepted as justification for imposing the death penalty.[40]

The evolution of this thinking can be pinpointed in the record at the site where it reverts to Latin, with the change in language anchoring Sperhauk's confession within an authorising framework of legal evidence, judicial reasoning and the determination of guilt. After his confession was read out in King's Bench on 13 April, Sperhauk was kept in custody until he was brought back into court on 20 April. In the intervening period, his judges examined the coroner's record of his confession and found themselves unsure how to treat his case.[41] When they asked Sperhauk if he could say anything in his own defence why he should not be convicted and condemned to death as a traitor, he replied that he could not. His confession stood in the record as an open admission of guilt. Not only that, but the trial records show that Sperhauk repeated his inflammatory statements without hesitation when he was questioned in person by the king.[42] Yet despite this seemingly incontrovertible proof, the judges spent some time deliberating with the king's council before pronouncing sentence. When they did, they emphasised several factors that transformed Sperhauk's words into treasonous acts according to common law: he had said them in public and of his own accord, knowledge and will; he had spoken, affirmed and avowed them as true; and he had said these things 'with the will and intention of inciting the said king's lieges to depart from the love and good will owed to their liege lord by the law of nature'.[43]

This last phrase was rendered in Latin in the record as 'ad intencionem et voluntatem excitandi ligeos ipsius regis de eorum bono zelo et voluntate contra

39 For example, Rebecca Lemon, *Treason by Words: Literature, Law, and Rebellion in Shakespeare's England* (Ithaca, 2006), pp. 6–10; Cunningham, *Imaginary Betrayals*, pp. 7–12.

40 Both Thornley and Bellamy see Sperhauk's case as a watershed in this regard: Thornley, 'Treason by Words', pp. 556–7; Bellamy, *Law of Treason*, pp. 116–17.

41 TNA KB 27/564 Rex m. 12.

42 TNA KB 9/189/27.

43 TNA KB 27/564 Rex m. 12.

dominum suum ligeum naturaliter debitis', and it signalled the appearance in King's Bench of a new common law category of treason: speaking with the intention of inciting others against the king.[44] The slippage from men's words to intention to act of treason affirms what Scase has described as the 'political agency of verbal acts' in the aural political culture of late medieval England.[45] However, the very different outcome experienced by the tailor's wife in contrast to Sperhauk confirms that in cases of treason, what was at issue was the political agency of *men's* verbal acts. In a masculine body politic, the tailor's wife lacked political power and agency by definition and she was therefore not perceived as any kind of real threat. It was only when her words were repeated by a man that they were put into public circulation as an act of dissenting political speech. Moreover, when Sperhauk avowed his words as true – a speech act that drew on the legal and ethical force of men's verbal oaths – he imbued them with the power to do material harm. The judgment declared that it was not only Henry as an individual man that Sperhauk had injured with his words but the realm of England. Henry's body natural and the body politic of the realm were conjoined as one masculine political body through the repeated assertion that Sperhauk was 'a traitor to the king and his realm of England in speaking and avowing such enormously wicked things', and the damage words did to one body inflicted damage by default upon the other.

WORDS AS DEEDS: CEMENTING A PRECEDENT

It was this insecure juncture between king and realm that was continually troubled by instances of treason, because men were able to argue that their words and actions against Henry were the very factors that made them loyal political subjects and true men. This pattern shaped the 1402 trial of Nicholas Louthe, where the extant evidence includes a third-person confession recorded by a court official but also the first-person English words of the accused man himself. These were transcribed into the record from a letter Louthe confessed to writing and which the prosecution accused him of circulating in Norfolk, Suffolk and other counties.[46] As cases like that of the duke of Gloucester in 1397 demonstrate, the English language had the potential to shape political identities in ways that could contest and subvert prosecution narratives. Louthe's letter provides a compelling example of this potential when he combined vernacular textual performance with the cultural model of true manhood to claim identity as a loyal subject to Richard II, his rightful king.

44 Ibid.

45 Scase, '"Strange and Wonderful Bills"', p. 234.

46 TNA KB 27/565 Rex m. 4d.

Louthe was one of a group of fourteen friars and other clerics executed for treason in June 1402 for conspiring to restore Richard to the throne.[47] It is not clear when Louthe was arrested but he was being held in the Tower when he confessed to the coroner of King's Bench. The charges against him, propped up by his verbal confession and the letter he was carrying when he was arrested, were presented in court on 9 June and the sentence of execution was pronounced. Louthe was to be hanged, drawn and quartered and he was dead by 18 June.[48] In the record that declared Louthe a traitor, the seemingly neutral Latin formula opening the text in fact actively framed the confession that followed it. Louthe's identity as traitor was predetermined even prior to his examination because the court was told he was already in the Tower for 'diverse treasons' and it was because of these 'aforesaid treasons' that he was questioned.[49] The coercive question-and-answer interrogation that produced Louthe's confession was signalled by the statement that when placed under examination, he had given up what he knew 'in these words'. The text then changed to French, transforming an English-language oral interrogation into the third person of legal testimony, and the purported veracity of this judicial narrative was supported by its exhaustive factual details of dates, times and places.

Louthe told his questioners that he had been visiting the village of Walkern when a local barber asked him for news. Louthe replied that King Richard was still alive and had recently been spotted in Westminster by some women who recognised him by a blemish on his face ('un signe dune werte en sa fauce') and by his distinctive white gown ('une blank drap de livere').[50] Initially it seems that Louthe, like Sperhauk, was to be declared a traitor for transforming women's gossip into the dangerous act of male political speech. However, Louthe went on to embellish the women's story with his own trenchant critique of Henry. He admitted telling the barber that 'the duke of Lancaster who named himself king of England was nothing more than the provost and bailiff for the said king Richard', and that Henry would soon be called to account for Richard's realm.[51] The use of the possessive form *son realme* rather than the neutral *le realme* in this clause unambiguously identified the realm as Richard's. This construction hit on the crux of Henry's problems in dividing the deposed king from his regality and crown, and his subsequent difficulties in joining himself to the latter. Henry's inability as a usurper to forge a true

47 A total of twenty clerics were charged: Robert L. Storey, 'Clergy and Common Law in the Reign of Henry IV', *Medieval Legal Records: Edited in Memory of C. A. F. Meekings*, ed. R. F. Hunnisett and J. B. Post (London, 1978), pp. 342–408 (pp. 353–61).

48 Storey, 'Clergy and Common Law', p. 356.

49 TNA KB 27/565 Rex m. 4d. A partial transcript is provided in Storey, 'Clergy and Common Law', p. 358.

50 TNA KB 27/565 Rex m. 4d.

51 Ibid.

union between his body natural and the body politic of the realm was also implicit in Louthe's claim that Henry had named himself as king rather than being born into the direct patrilineal line of royal succession that reached back to Edward III. This was reinforced by his dismissal of the 'duke of Lancaster' as a mere bailiff for the real king, a criticism that echoed alarming reproaches emanating from the French and Scottish courts, where kings and their diplomatic representatives continued to refer to Henry disparagingly as 'Henry of Lancaster, who calls himself king of England'.[52]

By incorporating men's political speech into judicial discourse through the process of confession, legal records could unintentionally give this speech textual authority and political agency by recognising its proof value and ethical weight as 'truth' voluntarily revealed. This was the case with Louthe's confession, which allowed a disturbing critique of Henry's legitimacy to leach into the official record and be voiced through a hearing in King's Bench. The paradoxical result was that a constellation of volatile political ideas was given a public airing in the very space that was the symbolic and material centre of Henry's claimed but disputed power to dispense the royal justice that was the wellspring of legitimate kingship. The insurgent potential of Louthe's words was increased by the inclusion at this point in the record of a direct English transcript, rather than a French translation, of Louthe's letter. The letter was presented as damning evidence against Louthe but when it was embedded virtually unmediated within the prosecution narrative, it voiced Louthe's own resistant vision of gendered political subjecthood, enacted through his vernacular self-representation as a true man to the deposed king. Calling Richard 'the most frend that we lovede', he promised an audience of potential allies that 'we shul come so stronge' in the deposed king's cause that Henry, 'the erl of Darby that now is the kyng' would not know how to defend himself.[53] This was an exemplary performance of homosocial love and fidelity to one's lord, and one that Louthe reinforced in his next statement that his readers (or listeners, assuming aural transmission of the letter's contents) should 'pray for yowre leeth [liege] lord kyng Rychard and for al his men'.[54]

Louthe's letter is intriguing not only for what he said, but also what he refused to say. The text in fact gave no details of any actual plans or plots, the most direct reference being the promise that Richard's 'friends' would 'come so strong' against Henry. However, Louthe's strategic silences hint at the disruptive political potential of the words of a true man. Louthe closed his letter by saying he had no more to tell at that time but nevertheless, 'Yhesu

52 Tuck, 'Henry IV and Europe', pp. 107–11. For example, instructions from the court of Charles VI to a French envoy being sent to England in September 1400 referred to 'celui qui se dit roy d'Engleterre' (quoted in Tuck, p. 107).

53 TNA KB 27/565 Rex m. 4d.

54 Ibid.

kepe wel yowre tonge and be stylle'.[55] This appeal to performative silence enacted in negative form the power of men's public speech, recognising that even this enigmatic account could have serious repercussions were it to be repeated to others. Louthe also actively refused to reveal his name, signing off his missive by promising, 'A nother day I schal telle yow my name for I was dredand to tel them what I was'.[56] By refusing to name himself immediately but promising to do so in future, Louthe implicitly invoked the material, ethical and legal weight that inhered in a man's 'name' and worship, the guarantor that his speech was the incarnation of his true manhood.

At the conclusion of this transcript, the record shifted back to the third-person French of Louthe's coerced confession, which abruptly concluded that it was for 'the cause he talked about in his letter' that Louthe had been travelling through various counties.[57] There was precious little hard evidence in Louthe's vaguely worded letter that the authorities could use. However, by embedding it between the two sections detailing the political criticisms Louthe voiced under interrogation, the record was carefully constructed so that his first-person vernacular speech modelled an oral plea in open court and thus could offer seemingly incontrovertible and concrete validation of the far more damning speech reported in the French of the third-person confession.

It was this validation the king and his justices used to establish a firm precedent for punishing men's dissenting political speech as treason. This becomes evident where the record reverted to the authoritative Latin to pronounce the verdict and sentence. First, the coercive process used to make Louthe talk and to transform his revelations into an evidentiary legal narrative that could be used against him was elided in the statement that 'the above said information' having been given freely, Louthe from his own testimony was declared a traitor to the king and realm of England.[58] The judgment continued in a formula patterned on the verdict against Sperhauk: by saying these words, Louthe intended to incite the king's people against the love and allegiance they owed him, to the final destruction of the realm of England.[59] In Louthe's case, there was one significant development on the Sperhauk verdict: in the sentencing clause, the 'realm of England' was now explicitly incorporated alongside the person of the king in the category of things damaged by the false speech of traitors. This connection was forged in the legal formula that said Louthe intended not only to disrupt the natural bonds of love and loyalty between the people and their king, but also to destroy the realm of England itself.

55 Ibid.
56 Ibid.
57 Ibid.
58 Ibid.
59 Ibid.

Louthe's vernacular identity as a loving liege man to the real king was awkwardly juxtaposed to the prosecution's claims that he was an enemy not only of the king but of the people and realm of England. The critical juncture between loyal subjecthood, vernacular language and gendered political identity as true man or traitor was also present in the case against twenty of Louthe's fellow clerics, who were arraigned in King's Bench on 14 June.[60] The men were charged with spreading 'false words' and 'murmurings' both in public and in private; 'conspiring and imagining' the death of king; and seeking to obliterate the language and the law of England 'to the final and total destruction of the whole realm'.[61] The threat was amplified by assertions that the accused men planned to ally with Wales and Scotland, and they were repeatedly described as enemies of the English nation, represented as an imagined community united by a common tongue and common law: the 'lingue regni et legis Anglicane'.[62] The growing cultural connection between the English language and English national identity had previously been exploited in parliament for political ends, but it was only in the early 1400s that this formulation began to seep into common law indictments. The clerics' case can, for example, be compared to a case from October 1400, when a group of men were charged with 'plotting, conspiring, and intending' the death of the king and his sons but also with planning 'the death, destruction and everlasting obliteration of the whole English language'.[63] This phrasing figured the body politic as the patrilineal unity of Henry and his male heirs, and then directly linked the death of this masculine social body to the death of a national political body that was defined by a shared tongue. In the 1402 trial, the reiteration of this rhetoric throughout the indictment achieved two ends. First, it represented the masculine bodies of the king and the nation as coterminous and interdependent through the unifying construction of 'our king Henry and his realm of England'. Secondly, by emphasising the threat to the nation through multiple references to the traitors' intent to destroy England's language and law, the record elided the real threat the accused men posed. This was that their words, spread publicly and 'in diverse places', turned a spotlight onto the problems Henry continued to have with legitimising his title and securing the throne for his male heirs. The evidence reveals that this, rather than any genuine threat from Wales or Scotland, was the king's chief concern in pursuing the case. Henry took an active role in the trial process and his anxieties were reflected directly in the record, which retold at some length the official story of Richard's 'voluntary' resignation and of his deposition, on the

60 TNA KB 27/565 Rex m. 11. For a transcript, see Storey, 'Clergy and Common Law', pp. 359–61.

61 TNA KB 27/565 Rex m. 11.

62 Ibid.

63 TNA, KB 27/560 Rex m. 18; *Select Cases*, pp. 114–15.

grounds of his inept and evil rule, for the common good of the realm.[64] Thus while the record was forcefully reiterating the conjunction between Henry as king and the realm of England – imagined now as a national community delineated by a common language and law – it simultaneously re-enacted the legal division of Richard from his crown.

By charging all twenty men under a single indictment, the prosecution created the impression that they were fomenting a widespread and well-organised conspiracy. The long list of names and occupations of the accused men, along with the list of eighteen different counties in which they were said to have been operating, met the administrative requirements of a correctly prepared indictment but when it was read out in court, it would also have had the effect of multiplying the perceived threat. Combined with the way the charges were framed, this multiplier effect was no doubt intended to convince a trial jury that the accused threatened not only their king but also their language and laws – in other words, their very identities as English men. By portraying the accused in this way, 'the indictment was so designed that a jury would be faced with the responsibility of defending the national interest'.[65]

Despite this careful preparation, the king and his judicial officials had difficulties convincing the political community of the threat. Men of London and Holborn refused to serve on a trial jury, and according to the *Continuatio Eulogii*, the jurors from Islington who eventually condemned the clerics later claimed they had reached this verdict only after the king threatened them with death.[66] Even in the face of royal pressure, when fourteen of those indicted stood trial on 20 June, three of them were acquitted; juries also acquitted three men who stood trial at a later date.[67] Acquittals were not all that unusual for offences carrying the death penalty because medieval juries were often reluctant to impose capital sentences.[68] Nevertheless, the chronicler's unsettling description of the king threatening reluctant jurors in order to secure convictions suggests that Henry's subjects harboured a more specific unease with the Lancastrian regime's expanding definitions of treason. This impression was heightened by the chronicler's description of public reactions to the executions of the convicted men. The sentence of drawing, hanging, beheading and public display of their heads, which remained on public display

64 TNA KB 27/565 Rex m. 11, where this narrative begins approximately one-quarter of the way down the recto membrane.

65 Storey, 'Clergy and Common Law', p. 356.

66 *Continuatio Eulogii*, pp. 383–4. On the *Eulogium* chronicle as an accurate account written at the time of the 1402 trials and corroborated by other sources: Storey, 'Clergy and Common Law', pp. 353, 357.

67 TNA KB 27/565 Rex m. 11, where the acquittals are noted by the word 'quietus' in the margin. The verdicts appear as interlined additions of 'cul[pabalis]' or 'non cul[pabilis]' in the original indictment: TNA KB 9/190/36.

68 Green, 'Societal Concepts of Criminal Liability'; James Masschaele, *Jury, State, and Society in Medieval England* (New York, 2008), pp. 84–5.

until November 1404, was intended to communicate the message that the destruction and division of their bodies was a fitting punishment for men who had tried to divide and destroy the political body of the nation.[69] However, this symbolic act of power backfired when the public instead interpreted the men's deaths as a political martyrdom.[70]

CONFESSION, TRUTH AND EVASION

In the 1402 indictments, Henry and his legal officials went to new lengths to secure convictions by asserting that traitors intended to destroy not only the king and his sons but also the nation, language, law and people of England. The prosecution made this claim more tangible by incorporating allegations of Welsh and Scots involvement in an invasion plot. This strategy was also deployed in response to a conspiracy instigated in late 1403 by Maud de Vere, the countess of Oxford, in concert with Geoffrey Storey, the abbot of St John's Colchester and in a more minor role, Thomas Cokke, the abbot of Beeleigh. At least twenty other men were involved, many of them servants or associates of De Vere and Storey. Contrasts between the government's treatment of Maud and the rest of these plotters lay bare medieval perceptions of treason as a masculine political and legal category. The trial records and related documents also show how treason prosecutions worked to gender the body politic against which traitors offended.

The details of the plot were publicly revealed when several of the conspirators came before King's Bench in February 1405.[71] The wheels had been set in motion in December 1403, when the countess sent her servant John Staunton to meet one William Blythe, who had boasted of participating in a rising led by Sir Henry Percy and his father the earl of Northumberland during the summer of 1403.[72] Maud's plan was for Staunton and Blythe to ride together

69 *CCR, Henry IV: 1402–1405*, pp. 388–9 records the grant of permission to remove the heads.

70 *Continuatio Eulogii*, pp. 391–3. Usk's account is more circumspect but he portrays the clerics as victims who had been 'betrayed to the king' and subsequently 'cruelly hanged': *Adam Usk*, p. 175. Dunn notes a number of similar cases where Henry IV's brutal executions managed to make martyrs of convicted traitors: A. H. Dunn, 'Henry IV and the Politics of Resistance in Early Lancastrian England, 1399–1413', *The Fifteenth Century III: Authority and Subversion*, ed. Linda Clark (Woodbridge, 2003), pp. 5–23 (pp. 13–14).

71 The main records in the case are TNA KB 27/575 Rex ms. 3, 4d, 5, and 5d; and TNA E 163/6/28 ms. 1–16. The latter is an Exchequer Miscellanea file containing confessions, writs and other documents relating to the case. For TNA KB 27/575, Rex m. 5 see also *Select Cases*, pp. 151–5. Partial transcriptions of some of the documents from the Exchequer Miscellanea file E 163/6/28 were included in Benjamin Williams, ed., *Chronicque de la Traïson et Mort de Richart Deux Roy Dengleterre* (London, 1846), pp. 267–77.

72 The Percys' desertion of Henry IV and their subsequent rebellion are examined in

along the south coast and extinguish the English warning beacons, allowing a French invasion force to land undetected at Ipswich and Orwell on 28 December. Staunton and Blythe would then guide the French army, headed by Richard II's former queen Isabelle, her cousin the duke of Orléans and the count of St Pol, towards Northampton. There, they would join forces with an army led by Richard himself, returned from exile with the support of the Scots and a Welsh force under Owain Glyn Dŵr.

Ross, whose 2003 article presented the only extended investigation of this conspiracy since Wylie's account in the 1880s, argued that it was a more significant threat to the king than has generally been acknowledged.[73] It was a high profile and well-resourced manifestation of the Ricardian survival story that could be directly linked to military activity by England's foreign enemies. Moreover, it coincided with the circulation of letters purporting to be from Richard and sealed by the king's own signet, making the threat of a returning king bent on vengeance appear that much more credible. In 1399, William Serle, a gentleman of the royal bedchamber, had taken advantage of the confusion surrounding Richard's capture to steal the king's signet seal, and he was using it to produce forged letters from Richard until he was caught and executed in July 1404.[74] The royal seal was a powerful authenticating device and it convinced at least some of the conspirators that Richard was indeed still alive; Abbot Geoffrey even sent a man to Scotland to confer with Richard and get his instructions.[75] The circulation of letters in Richard's name, calling upon his loyal subjects to take up arms against the man who had usurped his throne and presented in a form that carried his political body in the potent symbolic form of the king's signet, added fuel to fires of suspicion and unrest that were already well ablaze. When, for reasons that need not delay us here, Sir Henry Percy abandoned his Lancastrian loyalties, he had publicly accused the king of murdering Richard; this story was enthusiastically repeated in England and abroad by other detractors including the count of St Pol and the duke of Orléans.[76] Misgivings about Henry's part in his cousin's death were being voiced in other quarters, too. The *Continuatio Eulogii*'s account of the friars' 1402 treason trial featured Roger Frisby, Master of the Grey Friars, saying to

Chapter Six.

73 James Ross, 'Seditious Activities: The Conspiracy of Maud de Vere, Countess of Oxford, 1403–4', *The Fifteenth Century III: Authority and Subversion*, ed. Clark, pp. 25–41; James Hamilton Wylie, *History of England under Henry the Fourth. Vol. I, 1399–1404* (New York, 1884), pp. 417–28.

74 Walker, 'Rumour, Sedition and Popular Protest', pp. 38–9.

75 TNA E 163/6/28 m. 15.

76 McNiven, 'Rebellion, Sedition', pp. 104–5. Percy's strategy is explored in detail in Chapter Six.

Henry that if Richard were still alive then he was the true king but if he was dead, then Henry was his murderer.[77]

McNiven and Ross agreed that there was no substantive evidence for foreign involvement in any plot and that the account of a planned invasion in the indictments was a smokescreen, 'intended to distract those who heard it from the more important, and dangerous, issue, as far as the Lancastrians were concerned, [of] the restoration of Richard' and, by implication, Henry's dubious legitimacy.[78] By stressing the traitors' collaboration with the French and Scots, and describing them as 'public enemies' ('inimicis publicis') who had plotted together to 'destroy and annihilate our king and his people' ('populum'), the indictments identified Henry with the political abstraction of the *res publica*.[79] Further, by repeatedly and directly connecting the destruction of the king and his sons to the destruction of the realm, the legal rhetoric joined Henry's Lancastrian patrilineage to the masculine body politic represented by the people and nation of England.

We do not know exactly how or when Henry came to hear about the plot being hatched against him but in April 1404, he issued a commission to Sir William Coggeshale of Essex to inquire into treasons committed by Maud de Vere and the other named conspirators.[80] The ensuing legal process produced vernacular first-person written confessions from a number of the men involved. Although the process of legal confession is coercive by nature and these texts were produced in an atmosphere of psychological duress and veiled threat, the authorities had a vested interest in presenting them as entirely voluntary revelations of truth. The use of English and the first person was part of a deliberate prosecutorial strategy to ensure these confessions stood as direct proxies for oral testimony in a courtroom. They were intended to carry all the evidentiary weight of a man's words spoken on oath. As shall be seen, they were central to establishing the prosecution's case because there was precious little other hard evidence – as opposed to rumour and suspicion – against the conspirators. However, the first-person vernacular and personal endorsements that validated these texts as legal proof of treason were the same elements that enabled the accused men to contest the charges against them and to defend themselves through textual performances of true manhood.

John Staunton was the first of the conspirators to be taken into custody and questioned. The warrant for his arrest was issued on 17 April and his confession, dated 31 May, provided the evidence on which other men were implicated, with further arrest warrants being issued on 6 June. As a result, Abbot Thomas of Beeleigh presented himself before Coggeshale and on 22 June, he wrote out a full confession before Coggeshale and Thomas

77 *Continuatio Eulogii*, pp. 391–2.

78 Ross, 'Seditious Activities', p. 31. See also McNiven, 'Rebellion, Sedition', pp. 103–5.

79 TNA KB 27/575 Rex m. 5.

80 TNA E 163/6/28 m. 1.

Makwillem, the coroner of Essex. Written confessions were also secured from Sir John Pritewell and William Blythe, although the circumstances of their production are not as clear as in Abbot Thomas's case. Pritewell no doubt had more cause than the others to worry: he had barely escaped the fate of the conspirators involved in the 1400 Epiphany Rising when one of its ringleaders, Richard's half-brother John Holand (the earl of Huntingdon), had been discovered hiding in his home.

Staunton's confession was copied into the King's Bench record directly after the lengthy Latin indictment listing the charges, naming the accused, and describing their plans to ally with the French and Scots to 'destroy and annihilate our lord the king and his people'.[81] This Latin legal narrative painted a frightening picture of secret meetings and of preparations being made by the traitors 'with armed forces of diverse enemies'.[82] The plotters were also charged with:

> Stating, publishing and announcing … that Richard …was still alive and would come back from northern parts into England with a very great host of French, Scots, and Welsh people to regain his royal estate …

and with spreading rumours that:

> Our present lord the king was not the true king but nevertheless, so they said, he had made himself king and falsely and wickedly obtained the realm and crown of England.[83]

Adding to these offences, they were accused of distributing livery badges featuring Richard's device of the white hart to 'various persons of their covin[e]', with the intention of turning Henry's liege men against him.[84] The livery badges embodied in physical form the danger posed by corrupted homosociality, as this network of false men conspired through lies and deception to sunder the bonds of masculine fidelity between the king and his subjects.

This part of the prosecution narrative was long on hyperbole but short on specifics. Staunton's confession was copied in immediately afterwards and it was his testimony, straightforward in its first-person English and replete with details of times, days and places, that bolstered the Latin indictment with tangible proof that was verified through its characterisation as *cognicio* – that is, facts rather than speculation or hearsay. The impression that Staunton's confession was a statement of objective fact was enhanced by the concision of

81 TNA KB 27/575 Rex m. 5.

82 Ibid.

83 Ibid.

84 Ibid.

its language and the absence of any embellishment with excuses or appeals for mercy. Staunton described how:

> On Seterdaye to fore Crystemasse Boloygne cam to me in the halle of Benteleyghe and seyde that the countasse of Oxenford wolde that I schulde rydyn whit William Blythe to Gyppewych [Ipswich] to schewyn hym the countre and the coost. And I the forsayde Staunton went to my lady to wytyn [know] if hit were here wylle and sche seid ye and prayud for here love that [I] schulde goune whit hym and schewe hym the countre ... and schewyd hym qwat brygges [bridges] weren in the wey and ledde hym to Caldewelle Hyll and schewyd hym the comynge [route] from Harwich for rydynge and coming of Frenchmen and wen thys was do[ne] we rydyn to Colchestre on the nexte day ... and on the Mondaye Crystmasse evyn ... we comyn ageyn to Benteleyghe to evensong qwat William Blythe telde my lady aftur I can nought seyn and as touching the commynge by the wey [it] was for to kepyn [prepare for] Frenchemennes aryvyng and for to sawe the bekenes be the coost [saw down the coastal beacons] that the countre schulde not bewar of here aryvyng, for Isabelle that was qwene schulde aryven at Harwich.[85]

In the midst of this logistical report of the planned invasion, Staunton abruptly changed tack to name the countess as the person responsible for having the Ricardian livery badges made:

> And overmore I knewe of hertys weren made for qwyche the countesse leyde a sensure of selver and gylt to wedde [in pledge] to Neel Goldsmyth to qwyten ount [account for] the hertes that weren of kyng Richard lyvere.[86]

Staunton then returned to the story of his 'riding' with William Blythe, saying they continued to St John's abbey where Abbot Geoffrey welcomed them warmly and expressed his support for their plans. Finally, Staunton validated his confession with the endorsement: 'that this bylle is soth I have wrytyn hit whit my owyn hand'.[87] The term 'soth' invoked the potent notion of soothfastness, the idea of words as true in an objective, factual sense but also in the sense of a true man's verbal performance as a form of legal and ethical proof.

However, closer reading reveals that Staunton's confession was not in fact freely revealed truth but rather a carefully constructed narrative that the king's justices played no small part in fashioning. The written text was presented as a direct analogue of Staunton's verbal speech in its opening line 'I, John Staunton, knowleche and saye' but it was manipulated to fit into and support the damning Latin indictment that prefaced it.[88] The phrase 'I the forsayde Staunton' inserted before each substantial allegation or piece of information

85 Ibid.

86 Ibid.

87 Ibid.

88 Ibid.

was a formal legal construction that points towards an intensive question-and-answer interrogation. As a man already under arrest for treason, Staunton was no doubt coerced by threats or inducements to name the ringleaders and furnish concrete details that lent credibility to the dramatic account of England's three greatest enemies uniting for an imminent invasion. Staunton made no attempt to explain, excuse or deny his actions nor did he make a plea for mercy, so that his testimony appeared in the record as a dispassionate and objective report rather than an account produced under considerable duress. In fact, in its narrative structure, wording and content Staunton's confession looks more like an approver's appeal that was manipulated by the king's judicial officers to appear as a voluntary revelation. The function of Staunton's confession within the larger structure of the legal record, and the relationship between the text's Latin and English elements, makes it clear that it was this statement, authenticated by Staunton's first-person vernacular endorsement, which provided the ammunition for pursuing the conspiracy's more powerful ringleaders. It may have been in return for his damning testimony that Staunton was later pardoned, a trade-off that would be consistent with Staunton being coerced to turn approver.[89]

Staunton provided ample evidence of a nefarious anti-Lancastrian conspiracy, but he was able to evade responsibility and to minimise his own involvement by positioning himself as a loyal and loving servant who was simply carrying out his noble mistress's bidding. In other words, he was performing as a true man to his (female) lord. Abbot Thomas and Sir John Pritewell also pursued this strategy, which relied on shared customary expectations of manly loyalty and service. In their confessions, each man offered oblique but compelling evidence for thinking that Richard was still alive. Although they had to admit to some guilt as part of the supplicatory performance of petitioning for mercy, they never explicitly disowned their belief in Richard's survival. Their confessions, authorised as legal testimony through the use of first-person English and the endorsement of being written by their own hands, positioned them as true men and loyal subjects, but it was never entirely clear whether their loyalties lay with Henry or with Richard. These texts therefore demonstrate the subversive potential for self-claimed vernacular identity as a true man to legitimise resistance to the Lancastrian regime.

Abbot Thomas began his confession by denying that he had ever 'comunyd in this mater that I schal sey' except with Abbot Geoffrey of St John's and with William Blythe.[90] He then told a convoluted story of being tricked into engaging with the conspirators, having been summoned to St John's by Abbot Geoffrey to, as he thought, sing a mass 'and for this cause and for none othir

[89] *CPR, Henry IV: Volume I: 1401–1405*, p. 473.

[90] TNA E 163/6/28 m. 15.

I came thedir'.[91] When Thomas arrived at the abbey, Abbot Geoffrey drew him into conversation with Blythe by asking the latter for news. Thomas claimed Blythe promptly offered to read the two abbots a prophecy that was about to 'falle hastly, and with that he toke oute a litil quayer [out] of his bosim of papere and red theron diverse thyngis of the wich I have no meynde [memory] of'.[92] This prophecy was no doubt the widely circulated political prophecy of Richard's return and consequently, Henry of Lancaster's fall and the dismantling of his illegitimate regime.[93] Despite the prophecy's dramatic import, Thomas was quick to deny he could even recall what it was about. As his tale unfolded, Thomas painted Blythe as the active conspirator while portraying himself as the passive and unwilling victim of a wicked man's falsehoods and deception. He described how some days after his unnerving encounter at St John's, Blythe turned up at Thomas's own abbey and proceeded to tell him of a plan for a rising on behalf of Richard. Blythe then claimed to have 'a patent of King Richard ceele encelid to proclame as sone as yis pepil weryn come to knowyn that wich party wold hold with King Richard and wech nowt'.[94] Whether or not Thomas believed this letter really was from Richard (a belief that was certainly plausible given the symbolic authority of the signet seal), Blythe's last phrase worked in Thomas's account as a means of mitigation, for if the letter proved that Richard was alive then Thomas could explain himself on the grounds he thought he was acting as a true liege man should. Thomas could also position himself as fearing the subtle threat Blythe conveyed. Placed immediately after the description of a planned armed rebellion, Blythe's description of the letter being used to find out who would be loyal to Richard and who would abandon him could be read to imply reprisals against the latter.

Thomas's confession continued with a blend of justifications and excuses as he alternated between providing evidence that his belief in Richard's survival seemed reasonable at the time and claiming that he had been physically threatened to participate in the conspiracy. First he said Blythe had asked him for a horse, spear and other arms, which Thomas did not have and said he would not have given to Blythe in any case. He then said Blythe sent him letters asking for money, and 'swere so hindirly grete that al the maters afornsaide weryn soth'.[95] Williams glossed the term 'hinderly' as 'vulgarly' and interpreted this to mean that Blythe had shouted profanities at Thomas.[96] However, Thomas was referring to letters – at one point he explicitly said that

91 Ibid.

92 Ibid.

93 Such political prophecies had been circulating since Henry's usurpation: Morgan, 'Henry IV and the Shadow of Richard II', pp. 28–31.

94 TNA E 163/6/28 m. 15.

95 Ibid.

96 Williams, ed., *Traïson et Mort*, p. 275 n. 2.

Blythe 'swere inderly in his letter' – so it is more plausible that 'h/inderly' in this phrase meant 'in the vulgar tongue' or vernacular English. This would be consistent with the notion of 'soth' as a man's spoken word in English proving the truth of his testimony. Thomas's attempt to explain his actions on the grounds that he was given convincing evidence of Richard's imminent return continued when he went on to confess that Abbot Geoffrey had told him he had sent a man to Scotland to confirm the story, and on his return this man 'kame to him [Geoffrey] and browgt him word that King Richard was on lyve'.[97] On the one hand, Abbot Thomas's confession deflected suggestions he was a traitor by stressing his own fundamental manly loyalty: he had only acted as he had because several people, including another abbot, had given him convincing proof of Richard's survival and imminent return. On the other hand, Thomas implied he had been forced to participate by threats of violence. Describing Blythe as a 'perilouse' man, he claimed to fear 'he meygt have desesid [physically harmed] me and oure place' if Thomas did not hand over the money he demanded.[98] He then described being rousted from his bed at midnight by a servant and fleeing because a group of armed men had gathered outside, 'and for drede that I was ferid to have be take and desesid bodeli I voidede [left his abbey]'.

Abbot Thomas concluded his confession by asserting the full, voluntary and truthful nature of his speech, eliding the psychological duress implicit in its being articulated only after he had been named in an arrest warrant. He said he had presented himself willingly to the justices and swore before God 'I mente none evill in no weise ne non untrowth to my lege Lord'.[99] He then authenticated his text as the words of a true man by confirming 'this same bille with all the entirlinyg I Thomas Abbot of Bile wrot with my owyn hand'.[100] Finally, he admitted to being guilty of not speaking sooner, and 'for the conselment of this articlis beforsaide aske mercye grace and pardon, ywrete with myne owyn hand'. This last phrase restored right order, at least as the Lancastrian authorities would have it, because by admitting his guilt and throwing himself on Henry's mercy, Thomas recognised Henry's royal prerogative as the true king. This passage epitomised the tensions that inhered in vernacular first-person confessions. It served the prosecution's purpose to pressure or entice Thomas into admitting his own guilt because this provided sworn testimony that could be used against the other conspirators while also reinforcing Henry's regality. Yet, while Thomas participated in this process, he simultaneously resisted it by authenticating 'with his own hand' his claims to be a loyal subject and true man, rather than a traitor.

When Sir John Pritewell confessed, he staged a more overt textual

97 TNA E 163/6/28 m. 15.

98 Ibid.

99 Ibid.

100 Ibid.

performance of true manhood that was grounded in chivalric honour and his masculine identity as a knight. Pritewell began by characterising his actions as those of a loyal man called to serve his lord. He claimed that Blythe, posing as a knight himself, had sent for him in the name of their rightful king, conveying a message from Richard that thanked Pritewell for his continued loyalty:

> Ther was on [that is, Blythe] at Bylee in gyse of a knyghte and sente for me John Pritewelle to come to hym thyder and seyde to me John Sire youre mayster and myn and oure alder mayster our right ligelord Kyng Richard greteht you often tyme and derelithe [affectionately] wel and thanketh you hyeliche of youre grete trouthe that ye have contened you inne to hym ward sithen he parted fro you and sori is and often hath been for the desese [harm] that ye have so ofte tyme suffred for hym and for his brother of Huntyngdon that was taken at your hous.[101]

Pritewell added that Blythe claimed 'he hadde ihad thre lettres to hym self fro Kyng Richard fro the Cristemasse in to that Sonday', amounting to what seemed very recent proof of life. Further, Blythe told him that in these letters Richard:

> Prayeth ful hertely for you to God that he wil kepe you fro alle manner defeses [harm] and that so specialy that I trow that ye and alle that langeth to you faren right moche the betere for his prayere. And of that he [Blythe] sayde & swor … by the sacrament of bothe masses.[102]

Pritewell represented himself as a man confronted by a deeply personal appeal to his masculine truth and the enduring love and chivalric loyalty he owed to his rightful liege lord, Richard. The message was made more compelling by the reference to Pritewell's previous service in sheltering the king's half-brother Huntingdon during the Epiphany Rising. The repetition of Blythe's words in direct speech rendered them more urgent and authentic, with their truth value augmented by being sworn by the sacrament of not just one but two masses. Pritewell went on to repeat a story that Blythe had told him of how he had helped to spirit Richard out of prison at Pontefract and into safe exile in Scotland, from whence the king was about to return. Recalling the contemporaneous circulation of the forged letters under Richard's signet, Blythe's claim that he had recently received three letters from the king would have been another element that seemed to verify that Richard still lived.

In retelling this extraordinary story, Pritewell obliquely explained his involvement in the plot and tried to mitigate his culpability by emphasising his own honour and identity as a knight and true man. We cannot tell if Pritewell genuinely believed Blythe's tale about Richard's survival, although his reference to the king's letters and to Blythe swearing 'trowe' on the sacraments

101 TNA E 163/6/28 m. 12.

102 Ibid.

certainly presents plausible rationale for such a belief. Once caught in the net of a royal judicial inquiry, Pritewell attempted to defend himself by staging a textual performance of manly loyalty to Richard while not going quite so far as to openly declare Henry's illegitimacy. According to Pritewell, he initially told Blythe he did not believe that Richard was still alive, and it was this denial that had prompted Blythe to tell him about Richard's escape from Pontefract. However, later in the text, Pritewell admitted that when Blythe offered him a horse and armour to ride in Richard's defence, he did not refuse outright on the grounds Richard was dead but instead pleaded sickness and poverty, saying that even if Richard were alive, 'Ich ne myghte do no servise to hym'.[103] Towards the end of his confession, Pritewell swore it was illness, rather than unwillingness to serve Henry, that had prevented him from arresting Blythe or informing the king of the plot against him. Although it was in the prosecution's interests to get a definitive and damning confession out of Pritewell to back up the evidence already secured from Staunton, Pritewell's evasive tactics made this difficult as he repeatedly offered up plausible proofs for Richard's survival and then carefully distanced himself from them by putting them into another man's mouth.

An undercurrent ran throughout Pritewell's confession that juxtaposed his own true, if gullible, knighthood with the false knighthood of Blythe. When Pritewell described Blythe coming to him 'in gyse of a knyghte', this suggested both physical appearance and demeanour. In the context of the explanations and mitigations that followed, 'gyse' conveyed deliberate deception. Pritewell repeatedly accused Blythe of being a false man who had taken advantage of Pritewell's knightly truth and sense of honour, as well as his self-confessed 'unredy wyt'.[104] Pritewell stressed this explanation again near the end of his account. Denying that he had ever agreed to help the countess and the other conspirators, he argued 'by the feyth that I owe to God and to the Kyng … Ich ne herde haver this matere imoved but hit were of him so feyned hym knyght'.[105] He then backed his own claim to be the true man by saying he would prove all that he had said in court. He put himself in the king's grace for the single act of failing to arrest Blythe or inform the king about his activities, but as to everything else he had been accused of, he asserted more than once that he would acquit himself by having a jury attest to the truth of his account.

Given the gendered discourses of true and false manhood that conditioned all these narratives, what of the ultimate instigator of this conspiracy, Maud de Vere? Unlike the anonymous women implicated in the cases of John Sperhauk and Nicholas Louthe, Maud de Vere was not only identified by name; she also took a much more prominent and active role in events. John Staunton

[103] Ibid.

[104] Ibid.

[105] Ibid.

had directly implicated her, describing how she gave detailed instructions to William Blythe and arranged for the making of the Ricardian livery badges, among other things. Despite the weight of that evidence, she was never even questioned, let alone charged with any crimes. She escaped with the minor penalty of temporary confiscation of her estates, something that did not in the end cost her greatly even in monetary terms.[106] One possible explanation for this treatment is the countess's high status but although her son Robert de Vere had been central to national politics in the 1380s, by the early 1400s he had been dead for a decade and her own influence in national affairs was marginal at best. This explanation appears even more unconvincing in the face of Henry's equanimity in bringing the full deadly force of royal justice to bear against other high-status traitors. The answer to the conundrum can only lie in Maud's sex and in the consequent inability of the judicial authorities to find a place for her within late medieval cultural and legal frameworks that constructed the political crime of treason through the gendered binary of 'traitor' and 'true man'. Her case strengthens the argument that in a masculine body politic, treason was a crime that women were thought inherently incapable of committing.

By endorsing interpretations of treason that equated defiance of Henry with destroying the realm and people of England, the new king and his judicial officers bolstered his claims to embody sovereign political authority. This is not to argue that the precedents being established in King's Bench in the early 1400s were the product of any systematic attempt at constitutional reform or of the broad application of jurisprudential principles. Rather, they reflect the altogether more pragmatic aim of defending Henry's manly honour and asserting his legitimacy, while also anchoring his sons firmly within the patrilineal line of royal succession. Yet the unintended consequence of this short-term political agenda was that a more fundamental change in the constitutional relationship between the king, political subjects and the realm was taking place through case law in treason trials, even if this was not yet reflected in statute law.

The most immediate change, but one with enduring impact on the treatment of political dissent, was the crucial shift in English treason law from a moment in October 1399, when punishing mere words as treason was named as the unjust act of tyrant, to an environment wherein verbal criticism could get a man hanged, drawn and quartered as a traitor. This shift was predicated upon a deeper cultural understanding of the gendered nature of particular types of speech and in particular, the instrumental power that was attributed to men's words, spoken in public and avowed by them as true. As has been seen, the rhetoric of treason prosecutions not only gendered the crime of treason, it helped to gender the body politic against which traitors

106 Ross, 'Seditious Activities', p. 34; Given-Wilson, *Henry IV*, pp. 262, 448.

offended. By describing attacks on Henry and his sons as tantamount to attacks on the people and nation of England, treason indictments constructed a collective masculine political body that was conjoined to the corporeal body represented by the Lancastrian patrilineage. This strategic constitutional realignment would become more explicit in new legislation and in case law from 1406 onwards.

However, the Lancastrian regime did not have things all its own way. The cultural and legal relationship between men's speech and the performance of true manhood meant that their voices could survive as constituent yet resistant parts of the prosecution narratives of the state. Henry's judicial officials took great care to reinforce Latin indictment formulae and the evidence of coerced French-language confessions with the 'proof' of treason in traitors' own words but the authenticating power of the vernacular could also work in the reverse direction. When men's speech was presented as truth voluntarily revealed and given the status of legal proof, this unleashed the potential for that same speech to contest the prosecution narratives within which it was embedded. Resistance came in the form of verbal and textual performances of true manhood that reflected the traditional virtues of elite chivalric masculinity. Increasingly, opponents of the Lancastrian regime would also draw on the model of civic manhood, justifying their dissent through popular political discourses of the common law, common profit and the community of the realm.

5

CIVIC MANHOOD AND POLITICAL DISSENT

Chivalric manhood provided a cluster of shared values that men could invoke to defend themselves as true men and loyal political subjects, but masculine truth could equally be embodied through the performance of civic manhood. Civic manhood was inflected by the norms and values of the urban middling classes, including the literate professionals who staffed an expanding civil service and royal administration, and the members of urban craft and merchant guilds. The performance of civic manhood embraced universal masculine virtues of honour, homosocial loyalty, good lordship and service, but men of middling status were more likely to serve with the purse and the inkpot rather than the sword.[1] In the civic sphere, a man's worship and his reputation in the eyes of other men was paramount and this was gauged through his contributions to the common good and his upholding of right order, whether at the level of his household, guild, town government or the community of the realm. In a series of treason trials beginning in 1407, those accused drew on this model of civic manhood to justify their resistance to the Lancastrian regime as the actions of loyal subjects and true men. Although they were charged with trying to kill the king and his sons, careful reading of indictments and other evidence reveals they were not bent on murder; rather they sought to restore right order by removing an illegitimate usurper and reinstating the true king, Richard, to his throne. In public speeches and handbills posted in London and other urban centres, and in petitions sent to foreign courts, they drew on legitimate modes of political complaint to appeal to higher authorities to restore good governance to the realm.

The strategies of these political dissenters bore similarities to another group who were causing problems for the Lancastrian regime by the early 1400s: those identified as lollards. Lollardy was a form of religious heterodoxy chiefly concerned with church reform but it had an overtly political cast. Lollard doctrine asserted the superiority of secular over ecclesiastical authorities in temporal affairs, arguing that in certain circumstances and to benefit the common good, the government could disendow the church of its property and wealth.[2] Another core belief was that true Christians enjoyed a personal

1 As discussed in the Introduction, p. 11.

2 Peter McNiven, *Heresy and Politics in the Reign of Henry IV: The Burning of John Badby*

relationship with God that did not require the mediation of priests, and a central tenet of lollardy was that the scriptures should be translated into English and made available to all lay people so that they could have direct access to the divine Word.[3] Lollard reformers and the political dissenters charged with treason deployed similar methods and discourses to voice and justify their positions. They used the geopolitical potential of urban space to reach a wide audience with public petitions and bills that appealed to principles of law, justice and right order. They tapped into discourses of the common good and voiced their claims as representatives of a universal commons.[4] Both groups also drew on the power of English to authenticate the ethical truth of their words. The political dissenters who are the focus here would no doubt have concurred with the author of an early fifteenth-century lollard tract on vernacular translation, who argued that: 'Trouthe schuld be openly knowen to alle manere of folke, trowthe moveth mony men to speke sentencis in Yngelysche'.[5]

Lollard texts featured a distinctive rhetoric in which they described themselves as 'trewe Christian men' or 'trewe men' of the church, visualised not as the hierarchical institution of the earthly church but as a universal and eternal community of the pre-destined.[6] These individuals were not using the term 'man' in a gender-neutral sense to represent the category 'human'. As Schirmer convincingly argues, '[l]ollards represent themselves not only as

(Woodbridge, 1987), pp. 11–17. Anne Hudson's seminal book remains a valuable introduction to lollard beliefs: Anne Hudson, *The Premature Reformation: Wycliffite Texts and Lollard History* (New York, 1988). For the broader cultural and political background, see Fiona Somerset, Jill C. Havens and Derrick G. Pitard, eds, *Lollards and Their Influence in Late Medieval England* (Woodbridge, 2003).

3 Steven Justice, 'Lollardy', *The Cambridge History of Medieval English Literature*, ed. David Wallace (New York, 1999), pp. 662–89.

4 The best known example of this strategy as used by religious reformers was the vernacular petition known as the 'Twelve Conclusions of the Lollards', which was posted at Westminster Hall during the parliament of 1395: H. S. Cronin, 'The Twelve Conclusions of the Lollards', *The English Historical Review* 22 (1907), 292–304; Wendy Scase, 'The Audience and Framers of the Twelve Conclusions', *Text and Controversy from Wyclif to Bale. Essays in Honour of Anne Hudson*, ed. Helen Barr and Ann M. Hutchison (Turnhout, 2005), pp. 283–301. On discourses of the 'true commons' in lollard petitions: Wendy Scase, *Literature and Complaint in England, 1272–1553* (Oxford, 2007), pp. 87–112.

5 'Tractatus de Regibus', *Selections from English Wycliffite Writings*, ed. Anne Hudson (Cambridge, 1978), pp. 127–31 (p. 127, lines 3–5); Jill C. Havens, '"As Englishe Is Comoun Langage to Oure Puple": The Lollards and Their Imagined "English" Community', *Imagining a Medieval English Nation*, ed. Kathy Lavezzo (Minneapolis, 2004), pp. 96–128.

6 Elizabeth Schirmer, '"Trewe Men": Pastoral Masculinity in Lollard Polemic', *Masculinities and Femininities in the Middle Ages and Renaissance*, ed. Frederick Kiefer (Turnhout, 2009), pp. 117–29; Shannon McSheffrey, *Gender and Heresy: Women and Men in Lollard Communities, 1420–1530* (Philadelphia, 1995), pp. 145–56.

"*trewe* men" but as "trewe *men*", their fidelity to the Word bound up with an oppositional model of masculinity'.[7] We have already seen accused traitors using the gendered language of trueness, in concert with embodied performances of chivalric manhood, to defend themselves while turning the tables on their accusers. Treason trials in King's Bench from 1407 expose another facet of this defensive strategy. Drawing on the model of civic manhood, the accused positioned themselves as true men of the commons whose opposition to the Lancastrian usurpers was proof of their masculine loyalty to the rightful king, to the crown or to the national community. Lollards grounded their claims to be 'trewe men' in the eternal power of God's law, that is, the Word and scriptural truths unmediated by priests. In the political sphere, those charged with treason asserted their claims to be true men and loyal political subjects through the authorising language and practices of English common law. By performing gendered vernacular identity as 'trewe men' and invoking the authority of law – whether common law or God's law – both political and religious dissenters positioned themselves as legitimate representatives of a universal community. In doing so, they drew on a shared fund of discourses and practices that were deeply meaningful to the literate and politically informed men of the urban middling classes.

New legislation enacted in 1406 implicitly connected religious and political dissent through measures to penalise those who preached lollard theological doctrine as well as anyone who continued to circulate stories that Richard II was still alive. By 1414, statute law explicitly defined lollards as traitors by default, regardless of their political proclivities. Treason cases prosecuted in King's Bench between 1407 and 1417 reflected and progressively strengthened this association as the government's repression of political dissent became entangled with campaigns against the lollard heresy.[8] The Lancastrian regime portrayed those spreading lollard ideas and men challenging Henry IV's legitimacy as part of the same amorphous yet well-organised confederacy, although tangible social and political connections between individual offenders were often tenuous at best. Common themes surfaced in the legal rhetoric of treason prosecutions that reflected the government's fears about the intimate relationship between heresy and treason, particularly in relation to the production and circulation of subversive texts in English. New legal measures against these 'evils' that imperilled the unity of church and state gave secular authorities a mandate to root out and destroy such texts and their producers.

Some scholars consider any links between lollards and political dissenters to be entirely the product of Lancastrian fear mongering, asserting that the Lancastrian government deliberately manufactured connections between

7 Shirmer, '"Trewe Men"', p. 129, emphasis in original.

8 For the development of this trend over the fourteenth and fifteenth centuries: Ian Forrest, *The Detection of Heresy in Late Medieval England* (Oxford, 2005); M. E. Aston, 'Lollardy and Sedition 1381–1431', *Past & Present* 17 (1960), 1–44.

heresy and treason to expand its own power.[9] This explanation is too reductive for others, who argue that to approach popular dissent (whether religious or political) solely as the product of the prosecutorial imagination robs individuals of the potential to have an intellectual history of their own or to exercise independent political agency.[10] Treason proceedings were to a large degree shaped by the government's agenda and by the prescriptive language of new legislation, but prosecution narratives could inadvertently capture resistant performances of true manhood and loyal political subjecthood. In the process, they reveal cross-fertilisation between the gendered language, performative strategies and urban social networks of lollards and of accused traitors. One factor that helps to explain these convergences is the urban context in which both groups of dissenters were operating. Lollardy had its roots in theological debates taking place at Oxford in the 1370s but it quickly spread beyond the walls of the university. It attracted noble and knightly followers but also merchants, artisans and other men of middling status in urban centres like London, Norwich, Coventry and Bristol.[11] Maureen Jurkowski's detailed studies confirm that by the first decade of the 1400s, lollardy was finding supporters amongst practitioners of the common law and she has traced links between lawyers working at the central courts of Common Pleas and King's Bench and men known to be part of London lollard networks.[12] Lollardy also attracted men in the book trade and scribal profession because vernacular translation and publication were vital to the dissemination of heterodox ideas. Hence, anti-heresy campaigns targeted unauthorised translation of the scriptures and other religious texts.[13]

The struggle against heresy became more tightly bound up with secular politics from the time of Henry IV's accession thanks to the close relationship between the king and Thomas Arundel, the archbishop of Canterbury who also served four terms as England's Chancellor.[14] Arundel had returned from

9 For example, Strohm, *England's Empty Throne*, pp. 60–71; Richard Rex, *The Lollards* (New York, 2002), pp. 50–1, 82–3.

10 Ian Forrest, 'Lollardy and Late Medieval History', *Wycliffite Controversies*, ed. Mishtooni Bose and J. Patrick Hornbeck II (Turnhout, 2011), pp. 121–34; Arnold, 'The Historian as Inquisitor'.

11 K. B. McFarlane, *Lancastrian Kings and Lollard Knights* (Oxford, 1972); Margaret Aston and Colin Richmond, eds, *Lollardy and the Gentry in the Later Middle Ages* (New York, 1997); McSheffrey, *Gender and Heresy*, pp. 1–10, 37–45.

12 Maureen Jurkowski, 'Lawyers and Lollardy in the Early Fifteenth Century', *Lollardy and the Gentry*, ed. Aston and Richmond, pp. 155–82; Idem, 'Lollard Book Producers in London in 1414', *Text and Controversy from Wyclif to Bale*, ed. Barr and Hutchison, pp. 201–26; Idem, 'Lollard Networks', *Wycliffite Controversies*, ed. Bose and Hornbeck, pp. 261–78.

13 Hudson, *Premature Reformation*, pp. 200–8; Nicholas Watson, 'Censorship and Cultural Change in Late-Medieval England: Vernacular Theology, the Oxford Translation Debate, and Arundel's Constitutions of 1409', *Speculum* 70 (1995), 822–64.

14 Arundel held the office of Chancellor in 1386–9, 1391–6, 1407–9 and 1411–12. He

exile with Henry in 1399 and his endorsement had been crucial because it gave Henry's kingship sacral sanction. In turn, the archbishop was able to use his position at the centre of royal government to pursue his long-standing agenda of religious reform; most ominously, his support was repaid in 1401 with the enactment of England's first statute mandating the execution by burning of relapsed heretics.[15] With further measures such as the 1406 statute, Arundel used the influence he wielded through England's highest ecclesiastical and secular offices to bring the forces of royal justice to bear to unearth suspected heretics as well as critics of the Lancastrian regime. The connections the Lancastrian authorities drew in treason trials between lollards and alleged traitors were at times explicit. In other cases, the linkages were less overt or even absent in the surface narratives, but that both groups were targeted under the same legislation and enforcement measures implied guilt by association. When treasonous intent was linked, even implicitly, with heretical beliefs and practices, it helped to reinforce the image of the traitor as a personal enemy of the king but more so as an enemy of the national community and Christian people of England.

Between 1407 and 1410, the court of King's Bench heard a series of treason proceedings against men charged with circulating handbills in Westminster and London, as well as with sending anti-Lancastrian petitions to foreign courts. The prosecutions were triggered by new legislation enacted in the 1406 parliament that called for the arrest and imprisonment of lollard heretics and of men publicising the story of King Richard's survival. At the same time, parliament enacted an innovative succession statute that enshrined in law the shaky Lancastrian claim to the throne. These two pieces of legislation have not previously been considered in relation to each other. However, the evidence from treason prosecutions shows that the two statutes were intimately connected in their ideological content and in the types of activities – particularly 'false and evil' speech and publication – they sought to proscribe.

The Long Parliament of 1406, which sat in three sessions between March and December, proved highly contentious.[16] Henry IV was suffering the first of what would be repeated bouts of debilitating illness and he was unable to attend in person, so it was left to Arundel to manage an unruly parliament.[17] There were clashes between the temporal and ecclesiastical Lords, between

became archbishop of Canterbury in 1396.

15 A. K. McHardy, '*De Heretico Comburendo*, 1401', *Lollardy and the Gentry*, ed. Aston and Richmond, pp. 112–26.

16 For what follows on the 1406 parliament see A. J. Pollard, 'The Lancastrian Constitutional Experiment Revisited: Henry IV, Sir John Tiptoft and the Parliament of 1406', *Parliamentary History* 14 (1995), 103–19; Bennett, 'Henry IV, the Royal Succession and the Crisis of 1406'; Douglas Biggs, 'The Politics of Health: Henry IV and the Long Parliament of 1406', *Henry IV: The Establishment of the Regime*, ed. Dodd and Biggs, pp. 185–203.

17 This was the first episode of what would become an intermittent but debilitating illness

the Lords and Commons, and within the Commons itself over numerous issues, most of which had the government's perceived financial and military mismanagement at their core. The king asked for more taxes to fight the Welsh and Scots and to increase defences against the French, demands that the Commons were reluctant to accede to in light of their belief that subsidies agreed to in the 1402 and 1404 parliaments had been squandered by a profligate royal household. Disputes over finances provoked accusations that the church was failing to pay its fair share and the ecclesiastical Lords faced calls for reduced exemptions. More radically, some members advocated taking the church's worldly wealth into government hands, raising the spectre of the lollard doctrine of disendowment. Finally, in return for agreeing to subsidies, the Commons insisted on having greater oversight of the membership and activities of the royal council and as a result of the king's poor health, the session concluded with the appointment of a continual council headed by Arundel to govern on Henry's behalf.

The troubled parliament of 1406 came hard on the heels of sustained resistance from people who denied Henry's title to the throne. Between 1403 and 1406, in addition to the Essex conspiracy and other instances of treason discussed in the previous chapter, the king countered serious armed rebellions led by the Percys, the hereditary earls of Northumberland who had been Henry's most prominent noble supporters in 1399. One significant act of the 1406 parliament was to confirm the convictions of Henry Percy, the earl of Northumberland, and his ally Thomas Lord Bardolf as traitors.[18] When the Percys rose against Henry, they declared their support for Edmund Mortimer, the earl of March, whom they now claimed was the true heir by blood to Richard's throne. In the 1406 parliament, Henry responded to these challenges by enacting the first formal statute of succession in England's history. This enshrined in law the royal legitimacy of his own manly body and masculine patrilineage, setting out in detail the line of inheritance from Henry IV to Prince Henry and his sons, or in the event of the prince's death without issue, to his younger brothers.[19]

Henry reinforced this message about Lancastrian legitimacy when, in an elaborate public performance of homosocial fidelity, his greatest subjects were compelled to swear oaths of love and loyalty to him and his sons. The

that plagued Henry until his death in 1413: Peter McNiven, 'The Problem of Henry IV's Health, 1405–1413', *The English Historical Review* 100 (1985), 747–72.

18 *PROME*, 'Henry IV: March 1406', Part Two, Pleas, Items One–Fifteen. The Percy rebellions are examined in detail in the following chapter.

19 Ibid., Part One, Roll, Item Sixty (22 December). The final enactment of the statute added a reference to the possibility of descent in the female line, a tactical modification made in response to negotiations then taking place for a marriage between Prince Henry and one of the daughters of Charles VI: McNiven, 'Legitimacy and Consent', pp. 484–7 and n. 46.

succession statute included descriptions of four previous ceremonies of oath-taking between 1403 and 1405.[20] It went on to state that at the oath-swearing ceremony of Christmas 1405, 'the heralds of France had been present to remove all doubts, ambiguities and evil intention which might in any way be suspected'.[21] Immediately after this ritual, the parliament roll declared:

> Not withstanding all the said oaths … certain people with a wicked purpose and evil thoughts, imagining your destruction, most sovereign lord, and the disinheritance of your heirs, have swayed the hearts of your loyal lieges by their false allegations … and much wicked information has been reported to many parties overseas, to the great pleasure of your enemies.[22]

Coming as it did in the same parliament as the treason convictions of Northumberland and Bardolf, this passage is usually interpreted as a direct response to their rebellion.[23] However, while the Percys supported the Mortimer claim, the reference here to 'false allegations' being spread in England and sent overseas touched on a second group of political trouble-makers: those who continued to spread stories about Richard's survival. It was in the midst of these tensions surrounding the 1406 parliament that lingering unease about Henry's legitimacy and dissatisfaction with his rule collided with lollard calls for reform to create an atmosphere in which religious dissenters and those promoting the Ricardian rumour might be treated by the Lancastrian authorities as two facets of the same threat. The result was that immediately after the new succession statute was enacted on 22 December, another statute was enacted 'concerning the lollards and other spreaders and contrivers of news and falsities'.[24] According to the related Commons' petition:

> Some of these evil men and women say, and by false oaths and evidence, wickedly publish and cause it to be falsely proclaimed amongst the people of your realm, that Richard, formerly king of England … is still alive … causing widespread unrest amongst your faithful lieges and subjects … to the probable destruction of your aforesaid kingdom, and consequently of you, your sons, and all the aforesaid lords spiritual and temporal.[25]

The statute in response declared that if anyone:

> Should preach, publish or openly maintain or hold, use or run any schools of

[20] The other three ceremonies took place at Great Councils held in Worcester and Westminster in 1403, and in parliament in February 1404.

[21] *PROME*, 'Henry IV: March 1406', Part One, Roll, Item Sixty.

[22] Ibid.

[23] Bennett, 'Henry IV, the Royal Succession and the Crisis of 1406', p. 18; McNiven, 'Legitimacy and Consent', p. 484.

[24] *PROME*, 'Henry IV: March 1406', Part One, Roll, Item Sixty-two.

[25] Ibid.

> any sect or doctrine from now on contrary to the aforesaid Catholic faith ... or preaches, publishes or openly maintains, or writes or publishes any tract which incites people to remove or seize the temporal possessions of the aforesaid prelates and ministers of holy church ... or preaches, publishes or openly maintains that Richard, formerly king, who is dead, lives ... each and every one of them should be arrested, captured and thrown into prison.[26]

This legislation gave lay authorities a mandate to punish both religious and political offenders. A series of writs followed, commanding the officials of towns including London, Coventry, Shrewsbury and Norwich to arrest and imprison suspects in accordance with the statute.[27]

Anxieties about public speech and vernacular publication were central to the statute and to the petition that gave rise to it. This can be seen in the repetition of the phrase 'preaches, publishes or openly maintains' to describe the proscribed activities of lollards and those spreading Ricardian rumours, thus conflating the two groups as purveyors of the same types of false speech. The Commons' petition targeted the spreading of 'false news' in the textual form of handbills, public letters or petitions as well as oral preaching and verbal rumours.[28] While the petition named 'evil men and women' as offenders, treason prosecutions that followed the new legislation show it was only men who were indicted as traitors for engaging in these activities. This follows the gendered pattern established in previous treason proceedings, where women's words were dismissed as politically impotent gossip while men's public speech was constructed in law as a material act of treason.

The new statute included an unusual clause stating it was to remain in force only until the next parliament, with this qualifier being inserted as a result of the tense negotiations between Arundel, the Lords ecclesiastical and temporal, and the Commons. The king's relative weakness in 1406 had allowed the Commons (backed by certain supporters amongst the Lords temporal) to gain concessions on issues including management of the royal finances and the composition and powers of the king's council. As a *quid pro quo*, the Commons were pressured to support the new statute but they did so reluctantly.[29] Although the statute was only supposed to be in force until the next parliament, held in October 1407, there is no reference to it being revoked and other evidence shows that royal officials continued to enforce its terms. In 1408, Chancellor Arundel was sending writs to the civic officials of London and Coventry ordering them to arrest anyone preaching or teaching 'opinions

26 Ibid.

27 See for example, *CPR, 1405–1408*, pp. 352 (1407), 476 (1408).

28 *PROME*, 'Henry IV: March 1406', Part One, Roll, Item Sixty-two.

29 McNiven, *Heresy and Politics*, pp. 100–4; Maureen Jurkowski, 'The Arrest of William Thorpe in Shrewsbury and the Anti-Lollard Statute of 1406', *Historical Research* 75 (2002), 273–95 (pp. 281–5).

contrary to the Catholic faith'.[30] As shall be seen, treason indictments from the same period were also framed in terms of the 1406 statute, with the accused being charged with spreading false rumours and publishing bills saying that King Richard was still alive.

Neither the new statute of succession nor the statute against lollards and those spreading Ricardian rumours explicitly stated that people contravening these laws should be condemned as traitors. The legislation against lollards and rumourmongers said only that offenders should be arrested and 'brought in person into the next parliament to await, receive and answer such judgments as they have deserved'.[31] The succession statute did not stipulate how people should be treated if they challenged its terms but the inclusion of the paragraph regarding those who broke their oaths and rebelled, taken together with the conviction of Northumberland and Bardolf as traitors during this same parliament, certainly implied that anyone trying to undermine its terms should also be condemned as traitors. This legal position was soon to be consolidated through treason trials in King's Bench.

CRIMINALISING POLITICAL DISSENT: BILL CASTING AS TREASON IN KING'S BENCH 1407–10

Reports in the months following the 1406 parliament indicate that in defiance of the new statutes, the Lancastrian government was still being confronted by bold public expressions of political resistance. Typical of these was an outbreak of bill casting that coincided with a Great Council held at Westminster between 11 April and 11 June, 1407.[32] According to Thomas Walsingham, in early May, 'proclamations were displayed in many places in London as well as on the doors of St Paul's' stating that Richard was living in exile but would soon return in glory to reclaim his kingdom.[33] Walsingham hinted at a certain amount of popular support for this message because he said that when the offender was caught and punished, 'this moderated the joy which that fictitious story had inspired in many'. This episode is corroborated by an indictment from the Hilary term of 1408 naming Benedict Wolman, John Tange, 'Coleyn the fishmonger' and Walter Denyol, and alleging that in early May 1407, in the days prior to the Feast of the Ascension, they had been using the sanctuary of Westminster as cover from which to circulate bills telling of Richard's survival and imminent return. Through this 'false, felonious, and

30 *CPR, 1405–1408*, p. 476.

31 *PROME*, 'Henry IV: March 1406', Part One, Roll, Item Sixty-two.

32 On the Great Council: Edmund Wright, 'Henry IV, the Commons and the Recovery of Royal Finance in 1407', *Rulers and Ruled in Late Medieval England: Essays Presented to Gerald Harriss*, ed. Rowena E. Archer and Simon Walker (London, 1996), pp. 65–81 (p. 78).

33 *St Albans Chronicle II*, p. 499.

traitorous scheming', they had plotted to destroy the king, the prince of Wales, and the loyal peers and magnates of the realm.[34]

The timing indicates the target audience for these bills was the political community gathered in London for the Great Council. While Great Councils could not enact statutes or grant subsidies, they could wield considerable influence in determining diplomatic and military strategy or in resolving pressing issues of domestic governance. That of 1407 may have been seen as particularly significant in terms of its capacity to address subjects' grievances because of the new arrangements for the continual council that were one outcome of the 1406 parliament. In early 1407, Henry IV was in a position of physical and political weakness owing to his failing health and to a ban of excommunication he was under for his execution of Richard Scrope, the archbishop of York, in 1405. Henry's illness was seen by many, including possibly the king himself, as a divine punishment for his usurpation of the throne as well as for the archbishop's death.[35] Wolman and his fellows were likely emboldened by these circumstances to tell the people of London and Westminster that Henry was not their legitimate king. They also took the opportunity to express their masculine loyalty to Richard, to whom they swore to be 'true in their hearts and works'.[36]

The case against Wolman and Tange came to court in mid-1409. In addition to posting bills in London, they had sent letters to the 'emperor of the Germans' and to Isabelle, daughter of the king of France (Richard's former queen), declaring that Richard was alive and asking for help to restore him.[37] In their petitions, the writers tried to persuade these foreign courts that if Richard were indeed dead, then the earl of March was king by hereditary right. Either way, Henry IV should be evicted from the throne as an illegitimate usurper. This was exactly the type of 'wicked information' the government had been anxious to suppress in the 1406 statute of succession; the 1409 case shows that such verbal challenges to Henry's masculine honour and royal legitimacy were now being constructed in common law as treasonous deeds. Wolman and Tange's letters to France were likely seen as especially threatening because during 1406 and 1407, the dukes of Burgundy and Orléans had temporarily suspended their internecine struggles to unite in a campaign against English lands in Calais and Guyenne.[38] The statute of succession stressed that the French diplomatic representatives had recognised its terms

34 TNA KB 9/196/1 m. 13.

35 Davies, 'After the Execution of Archbishop Scrope'; McNiven, 'The Problem of Henry IV's Health'; Douglas Biggs, 'An Ill and Infirm King: Henry IV, Health, and the Gloucester Parliament of 1407', *The Reign of Henry IV: Rebellion and Survival*, ed. Dodd and Biggs, pp. 180–209 (pp. 184–6).

36 TNA KB 27/593 Rex m. 13d: 'eorum esset fidelis corde et opere'.

37 Ibid.

38 Given-Wilson, *Henry IV*, pp. 257–61.

and that, in the wake of the Percy rebellions, the men of England's political community had repeatedly sworn oaths of homosocial loyalty to Henry and his sons. In an atmosphere of renewed aggression by France, the judicial officers crafting the indictment against Wolman and his colleagues took the opportunity to portray their letters as a direct attack on Henry's person because they gave encouragement and moral justification to the king's foreign enemies. Augmenting this traditional interpretation of treason, charges that the accused men sought to disinherit the prince of Wales, now formally named as heir and fully incorporated at the heart of the masculine body politic alongside his father, directly invoked the new statute of succession and identified as traitors those who sought to deny Henry's patrilineage. This was a novel and more expansive construction of treason that royal judicial officers would make explicit over the following years.

The 1409 case against Wolman and Tange ended in an anti-climax for the prosecution because the two men were able to produce pardons and so were freed without trial. Wolman's pardon was dated 27 January 1409 at Westminster, taking advantage of a general pardon issued by Henry IV just days earlier.[39] This was offered 'in order that our subjects may bear more cheerful hearts towards us and our heirs, more truly to remain in faith and love', wording that echoed the oaths of loyalty and the statute of succession.[40] Pardon notwithstanding, in early 1410 Wolman was up before King's Bench again alongside a number of other men indicted for similar offences. John Honchton and John Hewet were charged with distributing 'certain false letters' in the parish of St Clement's 'outside the bar called the Temple of London'.[41] In a second case from the same term Wolman, Simon Warde and a goldsmith called John Whirewel were charged with making bills and letters in 'the parish of St. Margaret's in Westminster'.[42] Both cases originated from a set of Middlesex indictments dated to Michaelmas 1409.[43] Once again, the indictments charged Wolman and his fellows with circulating their texts in Westminster as well as sending them to the courts of France, Flanders, Wales and Scotland. In a third case, John Longe the shoemaker and John Longe the Younger – probably a father-and-son pair – were charged for publicly spreading the story of Richard's survival in Westminster and Holborn.[44] This last case exemplifies the conflation of men's oral and textual speech in the 1406

39 *CPR, 1408–1413*, p. 46.

40 Edward Powell, *Kingship, Law, and Society: Criminal Justice in the Reign of Henry V* (Oxford, 1989), p. 125 (quoting the terms of the pardon in TNA C67/34 m. 11).

41 TNA KB 27/595 Rex m. 1d.

42 Ibid., Rex m. 3d.

43 TNA JUST 1/554 m. 8 and 8d. Simon Walker resolved the confused dating of these records although he did not address the details of the charges or their implications: Walker, 'Rumour, Sedition and Popular Protest', pp. 61–2.

44 TNA KB 27/595 Rex m. 8.

statutes. While the Longes' indictment did not mention the making of bills or letters, it characterised their crime as speaking false and treasonous words in public ('dixerunt tam pupliore'), activities constructed in the statutes and prosecuted here as tantamount to publication.[45]

The Latin prosecution narratives in the 1410 cases presented a universalising schema in which the sequence of charges traced coherent and causal connections between men's false words and their treasonous deeds. Each indictment began with allegations that through their public political speech, the accused men had falsely, feloniously and traitorously plotted the destruction of Henry IV and the prince of Wales. This configured speech acts in the conventional pattern of the 1352 statute and its depiction of treason as 'compassing and imagining' the death of the king or his heir. The limits of treason were then stretched in charges that this public speech was intended to disinherit the king and his eldest son; to destroy the peers and magnates of England; and that it was circulated (either verbally or in the form of bills) with the intent of inciting subjects against the love and allegiance they owed to the realm. The charge of inciting subjects against their love and allegiance, which began to appear in prosecutions from 1402, had already expanded the scope of treason. Now, the boundaries were pushed further in indictment clauses that located men's treason in false words spoken or written against the magnates and peers of the realm, or that challenged the terms of the statute of succession through the charge of plotting to disinherit the king and his eldest son. This marked a subtle but significant shift in the definition of treason: here, the offence encompassed attempts to use vernacular public petitions to 'destroy' men other than the king and to undermine the authority of parliament to enact and enforce statutes that shaped constitutional arrangements and the governance of the realm. By moving the locus of treason beyond the body of the king and his male heirs to the men of England's governing elite, this formulation at once constructed treason as a crime against a national community and gendered that community as a masculine political body.

Given the combined weight of the 1406 statutes against speaking or publishing dissenting opinions, in conjunction with precedents already established in King's Bench to punish this type of political speech as a material act of treason, it may seem surprising that none of the men arraigned in 1410 were convicted. Like Wolman and Tange in 1409, the two John Longes were freed on the strength of pardons they produced.[46] Honchton and Hewet were able to find mainpernors, including two men from London and one from Coventry, to provide security for a future court appearance and were released but there is no record of them returning to stand trial.[47] Wolman, Whirewel

45 Ibid.

46 Ibid. The pardons were dated 26 December 1409, at the king's palace of Eltham: *CPR, 1408–1413*, p. 231. For the Longes' petition for pardon: TNA SC 8/310/15453.

47 TNA KB 27/595 Rex m. 1d and KB 29/50 m. 13.

and Warde elected a jury trial but thanks to an unusual intervention by the Commons in parliament, they were freed before this could take place. As the highest judicial tribunal in the kingdom, parliament could be appealed to on points of law in lower courts including King's Bench. On this occasion, parliament found that the indictments taken before the sheriff of Middlesex at Michaelmas 1409 were incorrectly prepared and lacked essential information. As a result, they were cancelled and the legal process annulled. The Commons further petitioned the king that 'the procurers, supporters, and abettors of the indictments recently wrongfully brought in your bench' should themselves 'be punished and chastised'.[48] It can plausibly be inferred that the annulment was achieved thanks to a private petition to the Commons on behalf of the indicted men.[49] Wolman had probably instigated this defensive move because the Commons had previously intervened on his behalf when he was imprisoned for suspicious activities in 1404.[50]

Wolman and his fellow bill casters drew on the shared values of civic manhood and on the geopolitical potential of urban space to enact their resistance to the Lancastrian regime while claiming to be loyal subjects defending law and right order. Several indictments stated the men had distributed their bills in and around the sanctuary precinct comprising Westminster Abbey and the parish of St Margaret's, which abutted the centre of royal administration and justice at Westminster Hall. Nearby in Holborn were the Inns of Court, which by the fifteenth century were the social and professional nerve centre for England's common lawyers. Westminster was the most highly privileged sanctuary in England and it offered permanent protection from prosecution at common law as well as exemptions from taxes and trading regulations. From the later 1300s, it boasted a growing residential lay community that included people evading criminal justice and private lawsuits, as well as merchants, artisans and tradesmen exploiting its commercial privileges.[51]

The jurisdictional, social and spatial characteristics of the sanctuary precinct

48 *PROME*, 'Henry IV: January 1410', Item Fifteen. The dorse of the original indictments is annotated with a memorandum that they had been cancelled by order of the king in parliament: TNA JUST 1/554 m. 8d.

49 There is no record of such a petition in the TNA SC 8 series of files but Dodd notes that in the late fourteenth and early fifteenth centuries, private petitions were only occasionally preserved in the records of parliament: Gwilym Dodd, *Justice and Grace: Private Petitioning and the English Parliament in the Late Middle Ages* (New York, 2007), pp. 6–7, 156–67.

50 Walker, 'Rumour, Sedition and Popular Protest', p. 61, n. 93.

51 Isobel Thornley, 'Sanctuary in Medieval London', *Journal of the British Archaeological Association* 38 (1932), 293–315; McSheffrey, *Seeking Sanctuary*, pp. 27–32; Gervase Rosser, *Medieval Westminster, 1200–1540* (Oxford, 1989), pp. 66–9, 122–44, 155–8, 217–21. On the sanctuary of Westminster Abbey in relation to common law jurisdiction: Lacey, *The Royal Pardon*, pp. 12–15.

made it a perfect base of operations for political bill casters. It gave access to a large, politically astute and educated audience while offering immunity from prosecution. Residents of the sanctuary and surrounding neighbourhood included lawyers and scribes, as well as skinners and parchment makers who were involved in the book trade.[52] This community of men, many of them familiar with the language and practices of the common law and of petitioning, could furnish the intellectual and material tools of the bill caster's trade. Their experience would have been particularly valuable to men seeking to craft texts capable of shaping political debate within the civic sphere of London and of persuading foreign dignitaries that their cause had merit. Benedict Wolman was just one of many bill casters who exploited the resources and geopolitical qualities of this urban space to voice his resistance to a usurping king.[53]

This can be seen in cases such as that of Honchton and Hewet, the two men who appeared in King's Bench for distributing their bills 'at the bar called the Temple'.[54] Bill casters traditionally posted their messages on the doors of St Paul's and Westminster Hall because both topographically and symbolically, these sites were central to national political culture as well as for the worshipful men of London's civic community. Temple Bar, too, was significant and the cancelled indictments from Michaelmas of 1409 show that this landmark attracted a number of men in addition to Honchton and Hewet.[55] The bar (probably at that time a simple chain barrier) was the main entry point by road into the city of London from Westminster and it marked a material and symbolic transition between these two urban zones.[56] For bill casters who sought to legitimise their resistance to the Lancastrian regime through a legal rhetoric of 'truth' and 'right', its proximity to the legal community of the Inns of Court was equally important. By 1410, the Temple Bar area was home to the societies of the Inner and Middle Temple, and to Lincoln's Inn a short distance away between Fleet Street and Holborn. The lawyers who lived and worked in these establishments were in the habit of offering legal services and consulting with clients in the surrounding public spaces.[57] Posting bills at Temple Bar can therefore be seen as a deliberate attempt to engage the political support and practical assistance of London's burgeoning community of professional men of law.

52 Rosser, *Medieval Westminster*, pp. 209–15; Sheila Lindenbaum, 'London Texts and Literate Practice', *The Cambridge History of Medieval English Literature*, ed. Wallace, pp. 284–309 (pp. 288–300).

53 For an expanded discussion of dissent through the lens of spatial theory: E. Amanda McVitty, 'Prosecuting Treason in Lancastrian London: The Language and Landscape of Political Dissent', *Medieval Urban Culture*, ed. Andrew Brown and Jan Dumolyn, Studies in European Urban History 43 (Turnhout, 2017), pp. 93–109.

54 TNA KB 27/595 Rex m. 1d.

55 TNA JUST 1/554 m. 7.

56 John Schofield, *Medieval London Houses* (New Haven, 1994), pp. 11–12.

57 J. H. Baker, 'The Third University of England', *The Common Law Tradition*, pp. 3–28.

Court records also point to social and professional connections between political bill casters and urban networks of religious dissenters. It was in the streets, taverns and marketplaces of London and Westminster that men of these communities crossed paths, and where their distinctive articulations of civic masculinity could cross-fertilise through public verbal and textual performances of true manhood. When treason proceedings were halted because the accused produced pardons, this shows that bill casters were able to draw on a certain level of local support for their activities, whether from fellow guild members or from a wider group of dissenters with links to lollard networks. Pardons did not come cheap – in the early fifteenth century, the fee for suing out a general pardon from Chancery was 16s 4d to the clerk of the hanaper plus 2s to the Chancellor – and common lawyers sympathetic to lollard views regularly assisted with their purchase.[58] When the 1409 proceedings against Wolman, Whirewel and Warde were annulled, it was probably because the three men enjoyed the assistance of a legal practitioner familiar with the technical requirements for criminal indictments and with the skills to petition the Commons to intervene. On that occasion, the nullified indictment against Wolman and his colleagues also named a John Wyghtlok among the offenders; in a 1417 treason indictment, Wyghtlok and Wolman were identified as confederates of a lollard common lawyer called Thomas Lucas.[59] Mainpernors were drawn from this same urban network of common lawyers working in and around Westminster, as well as from a wider pool that often included fellow guild members. In the case of Honchton and Hewet, two of their mainpernors were from London and one came from Coventry. Both cities were hotbeds of lollardy by 1407 and the target of repeated writs from Arundel commanding local officials to enforce the 1406 statute against lollards and those spreading Ricardian rumours.[60]

Historians of lollardy have noted that by the early 1400s, certain urban crafts were particularly associated with religious dissent. These included shoemakers and those in related leather-working trades; and men involved in the book trade including skinners, parchment-makers, book-binders and goldsmiths (who supplied gold leaf for illuminated manuscripts), as well as the scribes who copied lollard texts.[61] The treason cases pursued between 1407 and 1410 highlight several intersections between London's lollard networks and the bill casters operating in Westminster. Amongst the men accused were John Longe the shoemaker and John Whirewel the goldsmith, and their urban community included many other men with the means to produce

[58] John Bellamy, *Crime and Public Order in England in the Later Middle Ages* (London, 1973), pp. 193–4; Jurkowski, 'Lawyers and Lollardy'.

[59] TNA JUST 1/554 m. 8d. The 1417 case is discussed in further detail below.

[60] For example, *CPR, 1405–1408*, pp. 352 (28 April 1407), 476 (22 May 1408).

[61] Jurkowski, 'Lollard Networks', pp. 268–73; Idem, 'Lollard Book Producers'; McSheffrey, *Gender and Heresy*, pp. 1–10, 37–45; Justice, 'Lollardy', pp. 668–75.

lollard religious tracts as well as dissenting political bills. Men involved in the hospitality trade also lived in the sanctuary and the surrounding liberty of Westminster, where numerous inns and taverns catered to locals and visitors to the Abbey and royal courts.[62] Here, Wolman represented another intersection. When in 1417 he was named as an associate of the lollard lawyer Thomas Lucas, he was described as a 'hostiller' (innkeeper).[63] We must be cautious about accepting at face value the charge that Wolman was a lollard; the only direct evidence for this comes from the prosecution record and a comment in the *St Albans Chronicle* that he was as 'a citizen of London and a lollard'.[64] However, when Wolman was arrested in 1416, a psalter glossed in English was amongst the goods confiscated from his home.[65] Owning a religious work written in English was not definitive proof of lollardy but it was certainly far riskier after 1409, when Archbishop Arundel began systematically to enforce a ban on unlicensed English translations of religious works.[66] Based on the legal description, Wolman's psalter was probably an example of 'interpolation', whereby lay readers erased or edited passages in orthodox texts to align them with lollard teachings.[67] Such texts would have fallen afoul of Arundel's ban although they were more difficult for officials to detect.

THE LOLLARD LAWYER AND THE BILL CASTER

Ian Forrest contends that there is much to gain by moving away from viewing lollard communities in isolation and instead studying them in relation to wider social, occupational and geographical networks. As he puts it, 'the history of lollardy could benefit from assuming greater commonality between lollards and non-lollards'.[68] As the cases above demonstrate, the political bill casters operating from the Westminster sanctuary and lollard critics of religious orthodoxy formed overlapping communities characterised by vernacular publishing, knowledge of and contact with the common law and lawyers, and gendered self-authorisation as true men who were exercising the rights and duties of civic manhood by articulating legitimate grievances before the political community of the realm. Although tracing these connections is often difficult because of a lack of surviving sources, evidence for them can be found

62 Rosser, *Medieval Westminster*, pp. 122, 143.

63 *Calendar of Letter-Books of the City of London: I, 1400–1422*, ed. Reginald R. Sharpe (London, 1909), p. 165, <http://www.british-history.ac.uk/london-letter-books/voli> [accessed 16 January 2015]; TNA KB 27/624 Rex m. 9.

64 *St Albans Chronicle II*, p. 697.

65 TNA E 136/108/13; Maureen Jurkowski, 'New Light on John Purvey', *The English Historical Review* 110 (1995), 1180–90 (p. 1188 n. 1).

66 McSheffrey, *Gender and Heresy*, pp. 41–3.

67 Justice, 'Lollardy', p. 682.

68 Forrest, 'Lollardy and Late Medieval History', p. 126.

in the person of Benedict Wolman. As we have already seen, Wolman was a persistent offender who tangled with the legal system on multiple occasions between 1404 and 1417. The spatial and occupational details of his life locate him within this urban community of men characterised by their vernacular literacy, sometimes-heterodox religious beliefs, knowledge of the common law and tactical experience in using civic space to express political dissent. This was revealed most extensively in a case from 1416–17, when Wolman was prosecuted alongside the lollard lawyer Thomas Lucas.

Lucas and Wolman were indicted for treason for sending letters to Sigismund, the Holy Roman Emperor, as well as for spreading public bills in streets closer to home. The details of Lucas's professional career show how connections could be forged between political agitators like Wolman and lollard sympathisers.[69] Lucas was a fellow at Merton College in the 1390s and was a Master of Arts by 1403. In 1395, he was imprisoned along with three other Merton fellows for heretical religious views and was first explicitly named a lollard. Lucas's role at Merton had him travelling around the College's extensive estates on legal and administrative business. He was also a periodic visitor to the central law courts before and after his imprisonment, where he acted in lawsuits involving the College or individual fellows. He was still at Merton in 1408 but was expelled some time in 1409. By then, Lucas was establishing a new career in London as a common lawyer. From 1410, he was listed amongst the lawyers who acted as mainpernors for known lollards and in 1413, he began to represent clients in King's Bench. He was the advocate of record in at least three civil actions on behalf of men who were part of lollard networks, one of these being a suit involving the London goldsmith Robert Cringleford.[70]

We do not know how Thomas Lucas first crossed paths with the tavern-keeper Benedict Wolman but, given the spatial juxtaposition of the law courts and the Westminster sanctuary precinct, it is easy to imagine the two finding each other in the streets and hostelries of Westminster. Wolman's multiple court appearances from 1404 put him in touch with the local legal community, while Lucas's contacts with men like Cringleford, who was involved in the book trade, probably brought him into the same circles of parchment-makers and professional scribes whose skills were needed to make the bills and petitions Wolman and his associates were distributing. Certainly by 1416, if not earlier, Lucas and Wolman had joined forces.

After years of chronic illness, Henry IV had died in March 1413 and been succeeded by Henry V. The dynastic transfer of power from father to son was uncontested but it was not wholly unproblematic and questions

69 For what follows on Lucas's career, see Maureen Jurkowski, 'Heresy and Factionalism at Merton College in the Early Fifteenth Century', *The Journal of Ecclesiastical History* 48 (1997), 658–81.

70 Jurkowski, 'Lollard Book Producers', pp. 210, 213.

about Lancastrian legitimacy still festered. Henry V's anxiety to assert his title can be read in his first actions after his coronation, which included the ceremonial reburial of Richard in Westminster Abbey and the initiation of a comprehensive judicial reform programme intended to settle the political community.[71] This did not appease all the doubters: in 1416, Wolman and Lucas were jointly charged with treason for spreading vernacular handbills on the roads between Canterbury and London. These appealed to the higher authority of Sigismund, 'king of the Romans', to depose Henry V, disinherit him and his heirs, and restore Richard as the rightful king.[72]

Sigismund, king of Hungary and from 1411, Holy Roman Emperor, visited England in the summer of 1416 to negotiate a treaty with Henry V.[73] The emperor arrived at Dover on May Day and several chronicles reported an elaborate 'challenge' taking place there during which Sigismund demanded to know by what title Henry V held his lands. In at least one version of this story, the king replied that he held of no man except by his sword alone, invoking the potentially risky idea of rule by conquest rather than by dynastic right.[74] Other versions of the story incorporated a description of the king's brother Humphrey, duke of Gloucester, wading into the sea with his sword drawn and asserting that Sigismund would not be allowed to land until he disclaimed any right, as Holy Roman Emperor, to exercise sovereignty in England.[75] By implication, this statement acknowledged that a right to imperial overlordship existed in the first place. Both kings put on elaborate displays of chivalric manhood and these challenges, if they took place at all, should perhaps best be seen as part of the theatrics of a state visit. However, when Wolman and Lucas distributed their inflammatory bills to the crowds witnessing the emperor's arrival, they were engaging a public that might well have taken the challenges more literally than the royal and imperial entourages. For the ordinary man in the street, an appeal to the emperor to restore right order to the realm would have appeared a legitimate, if bold, move.

71 Paul Strohm, 'The Trouble with Richard: The Reburial of Richard II and Lancastrian Symbolic Strategy', *Speculum* 71 (1996), 87–111; Edward Powell, 'The Restoration of Law and Order', *Henry V: The Practice of Kingship*, ed. G. L. Harriss (New York, 1985), pp. 53–74.

72 TNA KB 27/625 Rex m. 9.

73 James Hamilton Wylie and W. T. Waugh, *The Reign of Henry V*, III (Cambridge, 1929), pp. 9–35; Norman Simms, 'The Visit of King Sigismund to England, 1416', *Hungarian Studies Review* 17 (1990), 21–9; C. T. Allmand, *Henry V*, new ed. (New Haven, 1997), pp. 233–56.

74 C. L. Kingsford, 'A Legend of Sigismund's Visit to England', *The English Historical Review* 26 (1911), 750–1.

75 Simms, 'Visit of King Sigismund', pp. 22–3. Wylie and Waugh (*Henry V*, III: pp. 9–11 and n. 10) argue that although a number of these accounts have been discredited as products of sixteenth-century imagination, there are earlier versions that can be corroborated from contemporary sources.

Wolman was first to face the consequences when in August 1416 he was interrogated before a tribunal headed by London's mayor and the justices of King's Bench. According to the trial record, in April 1416 in the London parish of St Dunstan West, Fleetstreet, Wolman and another man had 'falsely and traitorously' compassed and imagined the death of the king by 'confederat[ing] together' to depose Henry V and to disinherit him and his heirs. This construction of treason conflated a desire merely to displace Henry and remove his patrilineage from the royal succession with a plan to murder the king and his sons. To accomplish this, the accused 'falsely and traitorously did make and write a certain petition' to Sigismund stating that Richard II was still alive and asking 'the king of the Romans with a strong hand and powerful arm' to remove Henry and to restore Richard to his throne.[76] Wolman and his accomplice managed to persuade an imperial servant to present this petition to Sigismund, but Sigismund sent it straight on to Henry and the two men were arrested. Ordered to plead, they claimed innocence and were sent back to prison to await a jury trial, where Wolman's accomplice died. As for Wolman, his time had finally run out: he was found guilty and condemned to die. He was taken from prison at Newgate to the Tower and from there, 'drawn through the middle of the city, in the high streets of Cornhille and Westchepe, to the gallows at Tyburne', where he was hanged and beheaded, and his head was then posted on London Bridge.[77] Wolman's demeaning end marked the destruction of his civic manhood as he was expelled utterly from the urban body politic. His head, posted on London Bridge, sent a grim warning about the perils of public speech to the populace as a whole but especially to those men who were part of Wolman's dissenting networks in the liberty of Westminster.

Thomas Lucas faced trial the following year and the record named Wolman as well as John Wyghtlok (first indicted with Wolman in Michaelmas 1409) as his co-conspirators. The indictment described the direct petition to the emperor and added that the group had spread their bills on the roads between Canterbury and London. Lucas was also charged with asking the emperor to endorse disendowment of the clergy and with 'counselling, aiding and abetting the evil opinions and deeds' of the lollard rebel Sir John Oldcastle.[78] While there is no evidence that Lucas actively participated in Oldcastle's 1414 rising, in the months following those events he had acted as mainpernor for a number of men indicted in King's Bench or helped them to acquire pardons.[79]

[76] *Calendar of Letter-Books*, pp. 157–66; 'Memorials: 1416', *Memorials of London and London Life in the 13th, 14th and 15th Centuries*, ed. H. T. Riley (London, 1868), pp. 624–44, <http://www.british-history.ac.uk/no-series/memorials-london-life/pp624-644> [accessed 16 January 2015].

[77] 'Memorials: 1416'.

[78] TNA KB 27/624 Rex m. 9. The Oldcastle revolt is examined in the following chapter.

[79] Jurkowski, 'Lollard Networks', p. 271.

The Lucas indictment confirmed the bill casting coincided with Sigismund's formal progress from Dover to London via Canterbury. Henry V rode out to Blackheath to meet Sigismund and escort him to Westminster, where the emperor addressed the parliament that was then in session.[80] Sigismund's appearance before parliament underscored the importance of the imperial visit, not only for the king but also for England's political elite. It was an embarrassment to the Lancastrian government that on such a grand state occasion, the spectre of Richard's deposition and Henry's questionable title to the throne had once again been raised and had even reached the imperial ear itself. By spreading bills on the roads, Wolman and Lucas publicised their grievances to a large, civic-minded and politically aware urban populace. It seems that the emperor was sensitive to the political awkwardness this caused because at the conclusion of Sigismund's state visit, his imperial entourage conducted their own billing campaign, 'let[ting] fall along the streets and thoroughfares' broadsides with verses praising Henry V.[81]

Why would Wolman and Lucas think that in Sigismund, they would find a sympathetic ear? As Holy Roman Emperor, he styled himself as the supreme temporal power of Christendom. While rulers beyond the immediate orbit of imperial power in central Europe rejected his claim to overlordship, Sigismund's role in initiating the Council of Constance in 1414 enhanced his moral authority as an arbiter of disputes between western Europe's temporal and spiritual powers. The Council had been called primarily to resolve the Great Schism, which by 1414 saw the unity of the Catholic Church splintered by three rival popes. Sigismund also treated the Council as an opportunity to secure peace between England and France as a prerequisite to his ambitions for a new crusade, and this was why he visited England in 1416. Given Sigismund's imperial authority and his prominent role in resolving international disputes, Lucas and Wolman no doubt seized upon his visit to England as the perfect opportunity to petition for his intervention on behalf of Richard. By 1416, the Council of Constance engineered by Sigismund had already removed two rival popes. It does not stretch credulity to imagine Lucas and Wolman believing the emperor would be receptive to their petition asking him to remove a usurping king.

Lucas's additional request that clergy be stripped of their temporal wealth and offices is more puzzling. One of Sigismund's most prominent acts at the Council of Constance had been to secure the conviction and burning of the Bohemian heretic Jan Hus, who had exchanged supportive letters with various English lollards.[82] Almost certainly, then, Sigismund would have had no truck with Lucas's proposition. Moreover, the emperor's relationship with Henry V

[80] *St Albans Chronicle II*, pp. 688–91.

[81] *Gesta Henrici Quinti*, p. 157.

[82] The first extended study of connections between Bohemian Hussites and English lollards is Michael Van Dussen, *From England to Bohemia: Heresy and Communication*

was cordial; he was awarded the Order of the Garter during his English visit and Henry also gifted him a Lancastrian livery collar, an item Sigismund henceforth wore on public occasions. Wolman and Lucas's attempt to enlist the visiting emperor in their political cause can therefore be seen as doomed from the start. Nevertheless, their activities offered a more direct and sophisticated challenge to the Lancastrian regime than did the earlier episodes of bill casting, and it is telling that the government's attempts to punish such forthright public expressions of political dissent were not always endorsed by the political community. Although Wolman was found guilty of treason and executed, Lucas was acquitted by a jury and released to continue his legal career.[83]

Trial records leave only indirect traces of what Wolman and Lucas's bills actually said. However, the description of a petition to the emperor and of public handbills demonstrates continuity with the treasonous bills and letters Wolman and his associates had been circulating in London and sending to foreign courts since 1407. Although there is no way of proving Lucas's involvement in the drafting of those earlier texts, it is plausible that his regular presence in Westminster on legal business from the early 1400s had brought him into Wolman's social orbit. Lucas's legal knowledge and his training in the language and style of formal petitioning would have served the bill casters well in crafting persuasive appeals to foreign courts and to the national political community centred on London and Westminster. These skills would also have been needed to petition the Commons to annul the 1410 proceedings and to petition the king for pardons on other occasions.

CIVIC MANHOOD AND THE LANGUAGE OF THE COMMON LAW

How can the mediated narratives of legal records provide insight into the ways men like Wolman and Lucas articulated their political resistance? The original text of bills and letters was sometimes copied into the official records as evidence, and from this we can infer the grounds on which men constructed their claims to be true men and loyal political subjects. Rarely, an original copy of a bill survives, such as in the case of John Wyghtlok. Wyghtlok faced treason charges in July 1413 for nailing up pro-Ricardian bills in London and one of these offending documents was preserved in the records of King's Bench. It was written in first-person English so its contents would have circulated aurally with ease through the streets, markets and taverns of the city. The bill enacted a challenge using the pen rather than the sword, with Wyghtlok describing himself as a 'trewe man' speaking in defence of a crown and community of the realm that should rightfully be separated from the bodies

in the Later Middle Ages (Cambridge, 2012). Van Dussen discusses Lucas's petition on pp. 84–5, 105.

83 TNA KB 27/624 Rex m. 9.

of usurping Lancastrian kings.[84] Wyghtlok's textual performance of masculine truth appealed to shared notions of civic manhood and its ideals of homosocial loyalty, service and obedience. Counting out his years of steadfast fidelity as a 'trewe servant' to his lord, Wyghtlok identified himself as 'groom and aftir y[e] oman withe kyng Richard the tyme of [thirty] wynter'.[85] Petitioning from this deferential social position, he appealed to the lords, knights and burgesses in parliament to restore right order and good governance to the realm by placing Richard back upon his throne. Authorising his actions through the language of the common law, he then reached beyond this political elite to a wider civic body politic encompassing 'alle other that herith or seth this bill'.

Wyghtlok was not new to using the legalistic discourses and petitionary forms of civic culture, in conjunction with the geopolitical potential of urban public space, to express political dissent. The cancelled indictments of Michaelmas 1409 named him alongside Wolman as one of the bill casters operating from the Westminster sanctuary. He was named again alongside Lucas in 1417 but the authorities were unable to track him down to prosecute him; Wyghtlok had in fact been at large since escaping from the Tower during his 1413 trial. The records from the 1413 incident provide rich evidence for how the Lancastrian government was using treason law to bolster royal legitimacy in the period immediately following Henry V's accession.[86] An examination of the structure of the trial record and the interplay of languages within it reveals that Latin and vernacular speech interacted in ways that authorised but also contested the official account of Wyghtlok's guilt. The evidence also pointed to discursive and social intersections between Wyghtlok and London's lollard community.

Wyghtlok had timed his protests to reach the maximum audience at a moment when the Lancastrian regime was especially vulnerable. He started his bill casting campaign in February 1413, coinciding with Henry IV's summons to the Lords and Commons to attend a session of parliament but by this time, the king was gravely ill and he died on 20 March. The men summoned remained in London anticipating the first parliament of Henry V, which opened on 15 May. In the intervening period, Wyghtlok conducted a second round of bill posting, disrupting 'the parliaments of both the present king and of his said father … in contempt of the said kings and of their whole parliament'.[87] The illness that killed Henry IV had incapacitated him intermittently for years. Rumour had it that the old king was suffering from leprosy inflicted as divine punishment for sins that included his deposition of Richard, and there are indications that Henry came to believe this himself towards the

84 TNA KB 9/203, m. 1. For a discussion of Wyghtlok's bill as an example of popular petitioning: Scase, *Literature and Complaint*, pp. 105–8.

85 TNA KB 9/203, m. 1.

86 The plea roll record is TNA KB 27/609 Rex m. 14 and 14d. Cf. *Select Cases*, pp. 212–15.

87 TNA KB 27/609, Rex m. 14.

end of his life.[88] When Wyghtlok broadcast his story of Richard's survival to parliament and London's populace at the very moment of Henry IV's final decline and death, it created a public relations nightmare for the new king. The bills reminded the political community, including men who had been intimately involved in the transfer of power at Richard's deposition, of the conditional nature of Henry IV's claim to the throne. This had the potential to reawaken doubts about the dynastic legitimacy of the Lancastrian patrilineage and it threatened to tarnish the honour of the new king as well as that of his father. To appreciate Henry V's vulnerability at this juncture, we need to put to one side his post-Agincourt reputation as a paragon of chivalric manhood and exemplary kingship. He came to the throne confronting serious financial problems as well as a crisis of public order that was generating severe unrest among his subjects; he had been fortunate only in having no credible alternative heir emerge to challenge his claim.[89]

Faced with the need to manage this volatile political climate, Henry used Wyghtlok's treason trial to vigorously reinforce the validity of his royal title in the public legal arena of King's Bench; he even attended court in person for Wyghtlok's arraignment. Proceedings began with the reading of the formal indictment, which was introduced by an exhaustive retelling of Richard's resignation of the crown 'freely, willingly and absolutely … in full parliament' and of his death, which was attested 'by thousands upon thousands within the city of London and in other places' who had seen his corpse.[90] It then encapsulated and restated Henry V's dynastic claim, through his father, to the throne:

> The crown, the rule and the dominion of the realm of England with all that pertains to it having devolved and descended legitimately, of right and by inheritance to our present king Henry, fifth after the Conquest, as true king and our liege lord of England [*vero regi et domino nostro ligeo Anglie juste, jure et hereditarie devenerunt et descenderunt*] … to whom as our liege lord and sovereign everyone born within his territory is bound of right and by the law of nature to serve, honour and obey.[91]

Between 1399 and 1406 the men of England's political elite had been compelled on multiple occasions to swear oaths of loyalty to Henry IV and his sons that culminated in the 1406 statute of succession. These rituals of homosocial fidelity and obedience were intended to anchor the Lancastrian patrilineage as the secure centre of England's masculine body politic. Instead, the need for repeated performances of oath-swearing implicitly reinforced the fact that in 1399, Henry's elevation had only been possible because his fellow noblemen and the political community in parliament had assented to it. When

88 McNiven, 'The Problem of Henry IV's Health.'

89 Powell, 'The Restoration of Law and Order'; McNiven, 'Rebellion, Sedition', pp. 111–17.

90 TNA KB 27/609 Rex m. 14.

91 Ibid.

Henry IV died, no other claimant presented himself, but one still existed in the Mortimer heir. It is easy to forget that prior to the divine endorsement of Lancastrian rule provided by Henry V's victory at Agincourt in October 1415, his kingship was still fragile. These anxieties can be read in the indictment against Wyghtlok where it stressed the circumstances of Richard's deposition and death (at least as the Lancastrians would have it) and compounded the proofs for Henry's legitimacy: Richard's voluntary resignation, natural law, the patrilineal right of inheritance and the statutory sanction of common law. Although the 1406 statute of succession was not mentioned by name it was alluded to in the references to *juste* and *jure*, references that simultaneously reminded Henry's subjects of the oaths they had sworn to him.

This long opening passage prepared the ground for the charges against Wyghtlok that followed. With his fellow 'liars and speakers of false words', Wyghtlok had gone around 'announcing in public and asserting as true that the said late king Richard was still alive in Scotland and would soon return to the land of England'.[92] This 'murmuring and dissension' was causally connected to charges that Wyghtlok had plotted the death of the king and his father, that he was in league with the Scots and that his ultimate goal was 'the subversion of the realm'. As the offences moved from spreading verbal rumours about a king-in-exile, to planning to kill the current king and his father, to allying with England's enemies and subverting the realm, the prosecution narrative elevated public speech that was little more than rash talk by a rump of Ricardian loyalists into crimes of treason against the English state. The overall effect was to depict Wyghtlok as a traitor tearing apart the masculine body politic from within by destroying the constitutional whole represented by Henry's body and his Lancastrian patrilineage conjoined to the crown and realm of England.

Wyghtlok also faced charges of attacking Lancastrian kingship from another angle: he had rejected royal pardons issued by Henry IV and Henry V and thereby 'utterly repudiated the grace of God and the king'.[93] This charge doubtless referred to general pardons for treasons, felonies and rebellions issued by Henry IV in 1409 and by Henry V shortly after his accession in April 1413.[94] The royal pardon symbolised the monarch's semi-sacral status as God's earthly instrument of justice and mercy. By definition, anyone who sought a royal pardon recognised the man who conferred it as a legitimate sovereign governing by divine approbation. The 1413 indictment said that Wyghtlok knew he had been previously convicted of treason and sentenced to death; the charge that he had repudiated the royal grace conferred by a pardon stressed the heinous and now-unforgivable nature of his crimes. This version of events

92 Ibid.

93 Ibid.

94 Powell, *Kingship, Law, and Society*, pp. 82–5, 125, 134–5; Dunn, 'Henry IV and the Politics of Resistance', pp. 16–21.

deliberately obscured a critical fact: Wyghtlok had indeed been indicted for treason in Michaelmas 1409 but that indictment had been annulled thanks to the intervention of parliament. Until he was indicted in 1413, Wyghtlok had yet to be charged with, let alone convicted of, any crime requiring a pardon. Royal judicial officials had failed to secure any convictions against the bill casters they pursued between 1407 and 1410; now, they tried to pre-empt any possibility of annulment or acquittal in Wyghtlok's case. By collapsing together the 1409 and 1413 episodes of bill casting and rumour-mongering then saying that Wyghtlok had already been convicted of treason in 1409 for these activities, the prosecution laid a false trail to minimise the chances of a jury acquittal. The indictment's structure divulged this strategy at the point where it moved directly from the declaration of a past treason conviction to the present charges of bill casting.

It was only after this story of a repudiated pardon, which would condition a jury's reception of the charges to follow, that the indictment arrived at the crux of the case against Wyghtlok. He had:

> Falsely, treasonably and wrongfully affixed a certain document, in contempt of the said kings [Henry IV and Henry V] and of their whole parliament there, to the doors of the church of Westminster and elsewhere in various places in London and at Bermondsey and in various other places in the realm where people gathered together.[95]

Evidence of treason was then supplied in the form of Wyghtlok's bill, fully and precisely transcribed into the record from his original English document. Like other men's vernacular confessions and letters, this textual witness was meant to be treated by a jury as irrefutable proof of Wyghtlok's guilt, voiced in his own words. The bill's contents were read out in court; we know this because the transcription in the trial record was introduced by the phrase 'this bill is attached to these presents and follows in these words'.[96]

As was routine in common law felony and treason prosecutions, Wyghtlok was not allowed to call witnesses in his own defence, nor was he allowed legal counsel to represent him. Instead, his vernacular bill stood in for his oral testimony and the prosecution's intention was that this should be accepted as an undisputed confession of guilt. Yet despite this effort to control the narrative, the equivocal roles Latin and English played in authorising the prosecution record and in verifying the evidence of guilt created unpredictable tensions at the sites where the two languages interacted, both in the written trial record itself and when its contents were verbalised in the public space of the courtroom. At these sites, Wyghtlok can be found staging a resistant

95 TNA KB 27/609 Rex m. 14.

96 Ibid.

performance of civic manhood and loyal political subjecthood grounded in homosocial fidelity, service, obedience and masculine truth.

The indictment fashioned Wyghtlok as an enemy of the king but also of the body politic of the crown and national community of England by describing his pro-Ricardian bill as an attack equally aimed at Henry and at parliament and the realm. Wyghtlok, though, appropriated the legitimate model of petitioning and the authorising language of the common law to ask this same national community to restore right order and good governance to the realm by reinstating the real king. Wyghtlok opened his bill with a salutation that was reminiscent of petitions to parliament:

> To yow alle reverent and wurshepful Knyghtes of the Shires of Englond and burgeys of the burghs communes and all othir trowe liege men to the coroune of Englond, and to all other yat herith or seth this bille, in defaute of a bettir man I, John Wyghtlok ... do yow alle to wite [witness][97]

This correct *salutatio* showed the hand of skilled legal professional at work and as shall be seen, such a man was indeed indicted in the case. The first people the bill named were the knights and burgesses elected to parliament, who were addressed in the humble and deferential style that was typical of supplications from petitioners to those who had the power to address their grievances. Wyghtlok immediately expanded this appeal to 'all other true liege men to the crown' and, in a phrase that signalled his engagement in a civic sphere characterised by aurality, vernacularity and broad political participation, to 'all others that hear or see' his bill. The one person Wyghtlok did not name was Henry, a silence that implicitly excluded the king from the collective of worshipful and true men to which Wyghtlok voiced his complaint. By the early fifteenth century, the salutation clauses of petitions sometimes addressed the Lords and/or the Commons rather than directly addressing the king, and the text of Wyghtlok's petition showed familiarity with this convention.[98] However, the phrasing also drew a more deliberate contrast between the legitimate authority wielded by a universal political community of true men and the illegitimate power of the Lancastrian usurper.

Wyghtlok went on to claim that King Richard, 'youre liege lord and myn', was alive and would return to be 'amonge his trewe peple'.[99] He attempted to enlist the support of his urban audience of literate professional men by appealing to their expectations that their superiors in the political order would use their authority – potentially backed up by martial strength – to ensure justice and right order. He begged the 'trewe lords' to bring Richard into England and return to him the royal *dignitas* stripped at his deposition

97 TNA KB 9/203 m. 1.

98 Dodd, 'Kingship, Parliament and the Court'.

99 TNA KB 9/203 m. 1.

and 'ordeine for hym als swiche a lord shuld be ordeyned for to the plesance of God and salvacioun of the wurship of Englond'. While the prosecution condemned Wyghtlok for treasonously plotting the death of the king *and* the destruction of the realm, Wyghtlok's own words expressed a loyal and obedient servant's humble desire to see right order restored by re-joining the body natural of the real, surviving king to the body politic of his true people and realm of England.

When Wyghtlok used first-person English to voice his political grievances, this appropriated the state's judicial authority as it was exercised through the standard practices and language of the common law. By calling his text a *bille* and swearing to its truth, Wyghtlok modelled the submission of a written bill as a legitimate way to initiate a legal action. He then asked his audience to bear witness to the veracity of his testimony, endorsing his text as a form of legal proof:

> For as moche as ye be in doute of his lif, I, forseid John Wyghtlok, do yow alle to wite [witness] yat yat same persone kyng Richard yat ocupied the corone of Englonde ... is in warde and kepyng of the duk of Albanie in Scotland. To preve this sooth, I, forseid John Wyghtlok, wil swere before yow alle up on a book.[100]

Repetition of the phrase 'I, forseid John Wyghtlok' characterised his words as an authentic and unmediated oral plea, and it mimicked the legal formulae used by judicial officers to record confessions and witness testimony. Incorporating the sanctified legal ritual of swearing an oath 'upon a book' that his testimony was true, Wyghtlok augmented this form of proof with an appeal to the ethical truth value of men's words that was expressed through the customary notion of sooth.

Wyghtlok went on to pre-empt the state's processes of investigation and punishment. First he offered to entrust himself to the keeping of 'certeine trewe lordis espirituels and temporels, knyghtis, esquiers, burgeys' while his claim was investigated and verified, in effect offering himself up to voluntary captivity as a guarantor of his loyal and honourable manhood. In a telling reference to the use of *peine forte et dure* to extract legal pleas, he asked that he be 'with duresse of prisone en no wise empeired to the tyme it be knowyn whetthir my relacioun [account] be trewe or fals with the lordis espirituels and temporels and communes'. Finally, he demanded:

> If [his account] be foundyn trothe I axe fre issue oute of prisone and my name of a trewe man, and if it be beffoundyn fals then takis me out owte of prisone and lede me to the kyng Herry ... and the vilest deth that may be ordeined for me lete me have it.[101]

[100] Ibid.
[101] Ibid.

The sequence of his requests showed that Wyghtlok saw the political community represented by parliament as the institution most qualified to determine the veracity of his claims and judge his case. Such a request was not entirely in vain, for the annulment of the 1409 treason proceedings had demonstrated that the Commons in parliament could on occasion resist the royal prosecutorial apparatus.

What of Wyghtlok's lollard connections? The only place Wyghtlok was ever explicitly connected to lollardy was in the 1417 indictment of Thomas Lucas. Nevertheless, his bill contained signs of social and material convergence with London's lollard community. Following his offer to turn himself over to Henry and his sons, he imagined himself being:

> Take to the devil evir to lie in helle body and soule with outyn departyng and nevir to have mercy of god ne parte of no priere [prayer] in holichirche fro this day in to the day of doome [if his words should prove to be false].[102]

This image of hell without purgatory indicates some personal accord with lollard doctrine concerning death and judgment. Although Wyghtlok's willingness to 'swear upon a book' seems to contradict the general lollard reluctance to swear oaths, lollards accepted the use of oaths as a form of proof in judicial contexts as long as the oath reflected the true conscience of the man swearing it.[103] More significant was Wyghtlok's deployment of the distinctive vernacular appellation 'trewe man' and his claim to agency as part of a broadly representative commons. This mode of self-identity and the claim to political agency it supported had strong synergies with the language of lollard reform petitions and texts.

There was another intersection between Wyghtlok and London's lollard community, revealed in the way his protest was produced and circulated. The bill features the rhetorical structure and physical format of a formal petition and the hand is *anglicana*, widely used in the scribal profession and book trade of late medieval London.[104] As was typical for petitions from this period, while it was composed in the first person and purported to be an unmediated representation of Wyghtlok's own speech, Thomas Clerk was the man who physically wrote it. Clerk was tried for treason in the same term as Wyghtlok for posting the bills in Bermondsey and Southwark. A jury acquitted him on the treason charge but convicted him for having 'written and made' the bill.[105] In the early 1400s, the term 'clerk' was often used as a catchall for law students and others with legal training working below the senior ranks of the bar.[106]

102 Ibid.

103 Hudson, *Premature Reformation*, pp. 371–4.

104 Scase, *Literature and Complaint*, p. 106.

105 TNA KB 27/609 Rex m. 17.

106 Baker, *Introduction to English Legal History*, pp. 137–9.

Given the connections noted earlier between the lollard lawyer Thomas Lucas and the bill casters operating out of the Westminster sanctuary, as well as linguistic and rhetorical evidence that Wyghtlok's bill was drafted by someone with expert knowledge of the common law and of petitioning practices, could Thomas Clerk have been a legal associate of Thomas Lucas? A lack of records means this must remain speculation, but Lucas was working as a lawyer in Westminster in the early 1400s and taking cases in King's Bench by 1413. It is plausible that thanks to his relationship with Wolman, Wyghtlok had also entered Lucas's orbit. Another link in this chain was Sir Elias Lynet, who was indicted alongside Thomas Clerk in 1413 and who in 1409 had been indicted alongside Wyghtlok and Wolman.[107] Lynet had lollard connections and perhaps lollard sympathies, for in December 1413 the king commanded him to use his contacts to spy on people suspected of involvement in Oldcastle's rebellion.[108] The royal writ emphasised the need for secrecy, suggesting that Lynet was an insider who was trusted enough by the plotters to lure them into the open. Taken together, these factors trace networks of homosocial affinity between political bill casters and London's lollard lawyers and scribes.

Thomas Clerk's role in making the bill shows Wyghtlok was not simply a lone agitator. Rather, he was someone steeped in urban political culture with the knowledge to craft a sophisticated petition that conformed to legal conventions, while deploying a powerful vernacular discourse of true manhood that appealed to shared civic values of homosocial loyalty, worship, obedience and service to the common good. He also had the contacts to find an amanuensis with the skills to aid him in this task. Not only that, but Clerk's indictment as a traitor for writing and circulating the bill shows that, whoever he was, he was not only capable of producing Wyghtlok's text but was also willing to risk his own neck to publicise its contents.

When Wyghtlok's bill was read out in the public space of the courtroom, it gave voice to a series of volatile ideas about royal legitimacy and the nature and locus of political authority. At the conclusion of the bill's transcription in the King's Bench record, the prosecution attempted to regain control of the narrative. Changing back to Latin the record definitively stated:

> This bill and all the aforesaid things are and were falsely, treasonably and wickedly done and imagined by the aforesaid John Wyghtlok … with the purpose and intention of causing rebellion, murmuring and dissension in the realm and to stir up the people of the present king against their allegiance and to bring the Scots, Welsh and other enemies of the king and realm into the land of England to the perpetual subversion and destruction of the said realm.[109]

[107] TNA KB 27/609 Rex m. 17 (1413); TNA JUST 1/554 m. 8 (1409).

[108] W. T. Waugh, 'Sir John Oldcastle (Continued)', *The English Historical Review* 20 (1905), 637–58 (p. 639).

[109] TNA KB 27/609 Rex m. 14.

The following Wednesday, Wyghtlok was brought back into court in the presence of King Henry himself and ordered to plead. He vigorously denied plotting to kill Henry and all the other acts of treason imputed to him. However, when it came to his bill, 'as well as all the matters included therein, he openly avows it'.[110] Wyghtlok's bold answer suggests he saw his public campaigning as the honourable actions of a true man and loyal subject, not as the criminal deeds of a traitor. When he refused to disavow his sworn testimony about Richard's survival but instead authorised his actions by framing them as loyal service and obedience to the legitimate king, this confounded the state's construction of him as a wicked and false man. In the end, Wyghtlok did manage to evade punishment. After pleading not guilty, he was returned to the Tower to await a jury trial. A guard helped him to escape and as far as the records show, he was never recaptured. The unfortunate guard was, however, made to suffer a traitor's death in Wyghtlok's place; he was hanged, drawn and decapitated, and his head was spiked above the gate of the Tower.[111]

When Wyghtlok swore to the sooth and 'trothe' of his narrative, he was performing a model of civic manhood in which masculine worship was defended not with a sword, but with words sworn under oath and witnessed as an oral plea in a court of law. His bill used the legitimising form and language of petitioning, and its first-person composition erased Thomas Clerk's role in its production. This added weight to Wyghtlok's textual enactments of service, loyalty and obedience by exploiting the linguistic authority of English to verify his words as ethical and legal proof. When the bill was transcribed into the trial record and read out in the public arena of King's Bench, it introduced a dissident voice into the prosecution narrative. Even as the state tried to use this text as proof of treason, its status as sworn legal testimony bolstered the credibility of Wyghtlok's claim to be acting as a true man to the crown and people of England. In the process, it destabilised the union between the Lancastrian king and his patrilineage and the masculine body politic of the realm.

Literate, legally trained men like Thomas Clerk and Thomas Lucas provided points of contact between political and religious dissenters in the urban sphere, and Wyghtlok's case shows there were connections between these groups that were not simply the product of prosecutorial invention. But invention or not, the government's suspicions about dangerous links between heresy and treason were soon made concrete in new treason legislation. Within a year of Wyghtlok's appearance in King's Bench, parliament enacted a new statute that ordered secular authorities to hunt out and eradicate 'all kinds of heresies

110 Ibid.

111 Ibid., Rex m. 14d. This portion of the record is badly stained and barely legible, so my translation is supplemented by an eighteenth-century transcription in British Library, Additional MS 38525 fol. 20v.

and errors commonly called lollardy'.[112] It targeted 'those belonging to the heretical sect called lollardy as well as others of their confederacy, persuasion and leaning', and causally connected heresy with treasons aimed at 'destroying our most sovereign lord the king himself and all the various estates'. The statute went on to proscribe anyone who sheltered or aided offenders, specifically 'common scribes and their books'.

When the 1414 statute is not viewed as a tactical response to the rebellion of Sir John Oldcastle (considered in the following chapter), it is usually seen as one instance of a broader European trend that saw increasingly centralised nation-states enforcing sweeping laws against all forms of dissent. But the statute also betrayed a more specific Lancastrian concern with the types of vernacular publication common to lollards and to the political bill casters who challenged Henry's rule. These concerns converged in the 1417 indictment of Thomas Lucas, which was based upon the 1414 statute. Although this was the first of the prosecutions between 1407 and 1417 to refer directly to lollardy, it illustrated continuity with the 1406 statutes and reflected the drift towards more expansive common law precedents that defined men's public political speech as treason. The accused men faced familiar charges that they had plotted to kill the king and his sons, but also more innovative charges that they sought to depose Henry, to disinherit him and his heirs, and that they had spoken with the intent of persuading other men to break their oaths to the Lancastrian dynasty. In consequence, the law was reshaping the constitutional relationship between political subjects and the state by redefining what made a man traitor. From the opposite direction, though, the trial records reveal men renegotiating the terms of their own political subjecthood. Even through the mediation of prosecution narratives, we find accused traitors drawing on vernacular publication strategies and on the geopolitical potential of civic space to claim agency as true men, acting on behalf of a universal commons and of a body politic that could legitimately be separated from the body natural of an individual king.

[112] *PROME*, 'Henry V: April 1414,' Item Fourteen.

6

CHIVALRY, HOMOSOCIALITY AND THE ENGLISH NATION

I return now to where this study began, with treason amongst the men of England's political elite. The offenders were prosecuted in venues including parliament, the Court of Chivalry and King's Bench, and their cases trace significant changes in the treatment of treason across the first two decades of Lancastrian rule. Indictments and trial records drew on shared cultural expectations of true manhood to construct treason as a crime of personal betrayal, aimed at the king and the masculine social body of his patrilineage. In these cases, 'true manhood' took on a distinctly chivalric disposition as both prosecution and defence appealed to values of knighthood and 'good lordship', and to homosocial bonds secured by sworn oaths. Men named as traitors justified their resistance on the grounds that oath-keeping and 'trothe' were fundamental to legitimate kingship, so that a king who broke his sworn word fatally undermined his manly honour and his right to rule. From the prosecution perspective, the king and his judicial officials were guided by the conviction that close bonds between men were inherently corruptible, and that traitors were guilty of 'oaths of confederacy' and 'false covine' against the king.[1] Yet this traditional chivalric model of treason was being gradually subsumed by broader constructions of treason as an attack on the public authority of the English nation-state. This constitutional shift was signalled through the legal rhetoric of indictments and new statutes, and it was made incarnate in the spectacle of the traitor's execution.

THE PERCYS: FROM RESISTANCE TO REBELLION

Henry Percy, the earl of Northumberland, his son Sir Henry 'Hotspur' Percy, and the earl's brother Thomas Percy, earl of Worcester, had been Henry IV's most powerful allies when he invaded England in 1399, and their military and political

1 Anxieties about unstable masculine bonds were widely expressed in the late medieval period with the rise of so-called bastard feudalism. For general studies, see Michael A. Hicks, *Bastard Feudalism* (London, 1995); P. R. Coss, 'Bastard Feudalism Revised', *Past & Present* 125 (1989), 27–64. For representative discussions of this theme in literature: Tison Pugh, '"For to Be Sworne Bretheren Til They Deye": Satirizing Queer Brotherhood in the Chaucerian Corpus', *The Chaucer Review* 43 (2009), 282–310; Strohm, 'The Textual Environment of Chaucer's "Lak of Stedfastnesse"', *Hochon's Arrow*.

support played no small part in helping him secure the throne.[2] By the middle of 1403, the relationship had soured and a rising led by Hotspur and Worcester ended in their deaths at the battle of Shrewsbury on 21 July.[3] Northumberland was able to secure a pardon in early 1404, but he rebelled again in 1405 alongside Lord Bardolf. After they fled into exile, Northumberland and Bardolf were convicted as traitors during the 1406 parliament. They returned to England for a final battle in 1408, where they were killed.[4] Why did the Percys turn against the Lancastrian regime? Some historians have vouched for the accuracy of chroniclers who said that while the Percys supported Henry's ambitions to regain his ducal inheritance in 1399, they never sanctioned Richard's deposition and Northumberland had extracted a sacred oath from Henry that he would not try to seize the throne. Others contend that Henry's inability to meet the Percys' expectations for rewards in the early 1400s led them to challenge his royal legitimacy for their own ends.[5] Regardless of the Percys' real motivations, what is significant for the development of treason law is the way they drew on shared expectations about knighthood, masculine honour and service to the public good to justify abandoning the king. From the state's perspective, these chivalric discourses could challenge, but also complement and validate, more expansive definitions of treason as a crime against the people and nation of England.

When the author of *An English Chronicle* recounted the devastating collapse in relations between Henry IV and Hotspur, he deftly encapsulated the chivalric paradigm of treason. Accused by Henry of betraying him, Hotspur denied being disloyal and demanded the right to defend his honour in a personal combat with the king, declaring, 'Traytour am I non, but a true man and as a true mon I speke'.[6] The chronicle redaction post-dates events and it reflected the political biases of the writer's patrons, so it cannot be accepted as a verbatim report.[7] Nevertheless, the words put into Hotspur's mouth expressed enduring values

2 Sherborne, 'Perjury and the Lancastrian Revolution'; J. M. W. Bean, 'Henry IV and the Percies', *History* 44 (1959), 212–27; Michael Hicks, 'The Yorkshire Perjuries of Henry Bolingbroke in 1399 Revisited', *Northern History* 46 (2009), 31–41; Mark Arvanigian, 'Henry IV, the Northern Nobility and the Consolidation of the Regime', *Henry IV: The Establishment of the Regime*, ed. Dodd and Biggs, pp. 117–37.

3 Hotspur died from an arrow wound and Worcester was captured and executed.

4 For general accounts: Bean, 'Henry IV and the Percies'; Peter McNiven, 'The Scottish Policy of the Percies and the Strategy of the Rebellion of 1403', *Bulletin of the John Rylands Library* 62 (1980), 498–530; Andy King, '"They Have the Hertes of the People by North": Northumberland, the Percies and Henry IV, 1399–1408', *Henry IV: The Establishment of the Regime*, ed. Dodd and Biggs, pp. 139–59.

5 A useful summary of the historiography is provided in Hicks, 'Yorkshire Perjuries', pp. 32–4.

6 *An English Chronicle*, pp. 32–4 (p. 33). This chronicle portrayal is discussed in greater detail with reference to the construction of chivalric masculinity in McVitty, 'False Knights and True Men', pp. 474–5.

7 The manuscript dates to the mid-1400s but Stow argues that for the period 1399–1413, it relied on a mixture of Latin and English texts composed c.1400–20. On dating and

that structured political thought and action for the men of England's governing elite. The fundamental opposition between treason and true manhood was succinctly captured, as was the inextricable connection between masculine embodiment and publicly speaking truth.

Sources produced closer to events also described the Percys justifying their resistance to Henry IV by positioning themselves as loyal knights and true men. Most telling is a text now known as the 'Percy manifesto', which was circulating throughout England by mid-1403. Its purported content survived in the single chronicle account of John Hardyng, which must be read with some scepticism given his later career as a Yorkist propagandist.[8] However, his version is corroborated by royal letters, writs and legal records that show the Percys were circulating a text justifying their volte-face. The structure and rhetoric of this Latin document mirrored that of royal proclamations. Grounding its authority in the illustrious Percy patrilineage and in the high offices the family held, it opened with the salutation from 'We, Henry Percy, earl of Northumberland, Constable of England, and Warden of the West March … Henry Percy, his firstborn son and Warden of the East March … and Thomas Percy earl of Worcester', who declared themselves to be acting in their legal and ethical capacity as 'procuratores et protectores rei publice' against 'you Henry duke of Lancaster and your accomplices and favourites' ('complices tuos et fautores').[9] The text then itemised their grievances: that in 1399, Henry IV had broken a sacred oath sworn on the Host not to seize the throne but only to reclaim his inheritance as the duke of Lancaster; that he had broken further oaths to tax fairly and rule for the common good; that contrary to his word, he had stripped Richard of his royal prerogative and had then 'treasonously' imprisoned and murdered him; that he had usurped the kingdom of England, depriving the true heir Edmund Mortimer, the earl of March, of his right; and finally, that he had refused requests to ransom the young earl's uncle, Sir Edmund Mortimer, from Welsh captivity.[10] The

manuscript history: Stow, 'The Continuation of the *Eulogium Historiarum*'; Marx, 'Introduction', *An English Chronicle*, pp. xi–xiv.

8 *Chronicle of John Hardyng*, pp. 351–4. Hardyng produced two versions of his chronicle. The first, a pro-Lancastrian recension, in the 1450s, and a second pro-Yorkist recension dedicated to Edward IV in 1463; the text of the manifesto was added to the second version: C. L. Kingsford, 'The First Version of Hardyng's Chronicle', *The English Historical Review* 27 (1912), 462–82 (pp. 462–6); Simon Walker, 'The Yorkshire Risings of 1405: Texts and Contexts', *Henry IV: The Establishment of the Regime*, ed. Dodd and Biggs, pp. 161–84 (pp. 169–71).

9 *Chronicle of John Hardyng*, p. 352. For the Percys' offices and authority: Cynthia J. Neville, 'Scotland, the Percies and the Law in 1400', *Henry IV: The Establishment of the Regime*, ed. Dodd and Biggs, pp. 73–93.

10 *Chronicle of John Hardyng*, pp. 352–3. Given-Wilson (*Chronicles of the Revolution*, p. 192) points out that while Hardyng's account has been questioned, there are other independent sources indicating Henry swore some sort of oath regarding his intentions. Cf. Sherborne, 'Perjury and the Lancastrian Revolution'; Hicks, 'Yorkshire Perjuries'.

manifesto concluded by declaring that Henry and his 'complices … et fautores' were 'traitors and destroyers of the *res publica* of the realm' ('proditores et rei publice regni destructores').[11]

When the Percys identified themselves as procurators of the *res publica*, they drew on a potent late medieval corpus of constitutional and political theory to position themselves as defenders of the public good. Equally powerful, though, was their invocation of the traditional model of *diffidatio* to resist an illegitimate or ill-governed lord. This concept was present in their reference to *complices et fautores*, which recalled the Appeal of 1388 and the 1399 articles of deposition; the latter text had repeatedly accused Richard of putting the private interests of favourites above the common good of the realm. By deploying this charge against Henry, the Percys could claim to be exercising their customary noble right to counsel the king and reform royal government. The trope of 'wicked advisers' – frequently joined to allegations that kings were too intimate with particular men – often covered up specific division's over policy.[12] Nevertheless, it offered an instantly recognisable framework for explaining fractures in the masculine body politic. The Percys implied that Henry's illegitimate kingship was causally derived from his failures of chivalry, epitomised by his oath-breaking and by deceiving and murdering his king. These breaches of knightly fidelity and masculine honour rendered Henry a traitor. Finally, the complaint that Henry had not ransomed Sir Edmund Mortimer alluded to another violation of chivalry, as he refused to use his resources and influence – his knightly largesse – to aid his military retainers. A letter to the king from the earl of Northumberland, dated 26 June 1403, sheds light on how this failing was deployed as political critique. According to the earl, Henry had refused to honour promises to pay the Percys for military expenses incurred defending the Scottish marches, leaving the Percys in the shameful bind of being unable to pay their own men.[13] Northumberland asked that the promised payments be made urgently, warning that if the money was not forthcoming, 'the good name of the chivalry of your realm will no longer be preserved … and above all [cause] dishonour and distress' to the earl and his son, 'who are your loyal lieges'.[14]

The Percys produced at least one Latin version of their manifesto and it was also circulating in English, identifying it as part of the broader phenomenon of vernacular petitioning and bill casting in the popular political sphere. This was consistent with the publication strategy of Thomas Mowbray, the earl of Norfolk and Richard Scrope, archbishop of York, who in 1405 were

11 *Chronicle of John Hardyng*, p. 353.

12 Rosenthal, '"The King's 'Wicked Advisers'"'; Valente, *Theory and Practice of Revolt*, pp. 25–32; Fletcher, *Richard II*, pp. 75–6, 171–4.

13 For the background and a tally of payments owed: Bean, 'Henry IV and the Percies', pp. 221–4.

14 *PPC*, pp. 204–5 (p. 205).

circulating a document advocating political reforms.[15] Their vernacular text was 'published in the highways and byways of the city of York, and publicly fastened to the doors of monasteries, so that any person who wished could ascertain the nature' of their complaints.[16] As for the Percy manifesto, in a letter to the Privy Council of 17 July 1403, Henry IV complained that Henry Percy 'who has risen against us and our regality' had been referring to the king as 'nothing more than Henry of Lancaster', and that Percy had made and circulated proclamations claiming that Richard was still alive 'with the intent of inciting our people to rise with him in strengthening of his false purpose'.[17] The following day, writs were sent to the sheriffs of London and other urban centres ordering them to issue proclamations that no one should be 'afraid for report of any news' but stay obedient and loyal, 'resisting all them that presume to rise ... by reason of some evil information given them by colour of such news'.[18] The king's claim that the Percys were saying Richard was still alive was almost certainly false but it helped Henry deflect attention from the most damaging of the Percy accusations. These were that Henry had broken his sacred oath not to seize the throne and broken further promises to his subjects not to burden them with taxes; that he had murdered Richard; and that he had deviously deprived the earl of March of his dynastic right. McNiven argued that the most serious consequence of the Percy manifesto and their rising was to promote the cause of Edmund Mortimer as Richard's true heir.[19] However, Henry's failures of chivalric manhood, especially his oath-breaking, represented an equally damaging critique for a king who had relied on his reputation as an honourable knight and a 'man not a boy' to buttress his claim to the throne.[20]

When it came to contests of true manhood and treason, Sir Henry Percy proved a formidable opponent for the king. Percy's soubriquet 'Hotspur' blazoned his chivalric reputation and chronicle accounts of the battle of

15 The political protest of Mowbray and Scrope is often conflated with the second rebellion led by the earl of Northumberland in 1405. However, the political aims of the two groups differed and Walker has shown that their activities were only coincidentally related: Walker, 'The Yorkshire Risings of 1405: Texts and Contexts'.

16 *St Albans Chronicle II*, p. 443. The full text of the manifesto circulated by Mowbray and Scrope and preserved in the chronicle (pp. 442–5) shows they sought to reform Lancastrian government rather than replace it; they did not question Henry IV's legitimacy.

17 BL Cotton Cleopatra F III, fol. 145r. Cf. *PPC*, pp. 207–9 (where the text is identified under an older foliation as fol. 112).

18 *CCR, 1402–1405*, p. 181.

19 McNiven, 'Legitimacy and Consent', p. 483.

20 For the discourse of Richard's 'youth': Fletcher, 'Manhood and Politics in the Reign of Richard II'. For Henry IV's exploitation of chivalric ideals and institutions to validate his kingship: Tuck, 'Henry IV and Chivalry'; Hugh E. L. Collins, *The Order of the Garter, 1348–1461: Chivalry and Politics in Late Medieval England* (Oxford, 2000), pp. 76–8, 109–14.

Shrewsbury portrayed it as a trial by combat between two of England's most lionised knights. The Percy army was defeated and Hotspur was killed, but his untarnished chivalric reputation continued to torment Henry. People's refusal to believe that as the true man, Hotspur could have lost the combat materialised in stories circulating after Shrewsbury that he was not dead at all. These rumours were treated seriously by Henry IV, who was finally driven to have Hotspur exhumed and subjected to a traitor's shameful public execution by hanging his corpse between two millstones in Shrewsbury's marketplace.[21] Popular belief that Percy resistance was vindicated by Henry's betrayals persisted in more mundane places, too. In June 1409, the London tailor John Freston was finally pardoned in King's Bench in a treason case that had been initiated by general commissions of inquiry after the battle of Shrewsbury.[22] Witnesses testified that while Freston was residing in the sanctuary of St Martin le Grand in London, he had made treasonous allegations including that Henry IV had robbed his loyal liege people; by these words, Freston had shown himself to be a 'false traitor to our lord the king and to the crown'.[23] The Latin indictment expanded on these charges: Freston had helped to incite people to treasonous rebellion by saying that Sir Henry Percy had come to save them from the burden of taxes ('tallagia'); by claiming that Percy's goal was only to restore good governance; and by falsely stating that Percy was acting with true intentions for the benefit of the realm.[24] Henry IV's failures of chivalric lordship also featured in the case of John Kynggeslay, a Percy retainer who was imprisoned at Norwich in late 1405 after making treasonous comments to two esquires he met on the road.[25] Asked for news by the two men, Kynggeslay told them that following a battle, the earl of Northumberland had taken the earl of Westmorland (a leading supporter of the king against the Percys) prisoner.[26] Kynggeslay then urged the esquires to join up with Northumberland and Owain Glyn Dŵr in Wales, adding that Glyn Dŵr's forces were growing stronger by the day because he was able to

21 James Bothwell, *Falling from Grace: Reversal of Fortune and the English Nobility 1075–1455* (Manchester, 2008), p. 76.

22 See for example *CCR, Henry IV: 1402–1405*, p. 181 for the commission dated 23 July to the justices appointed for Hertfordshire and Buckinghamshire.

23 TNA KB 27/593 Rex m. 13 and 13d (m. 13). It was probably Freston's residence in the sanctuary that accounts for the time between his alleged offences and his appearance in court. On St Martin's sanctuary: Shannon McSheffrey, 'Sanctuary and the Legal Topography of Pre-Reformation London,' *Law and History Review* 27 (2009), 483–514 (pp. 484–5).

24 TNA KB 27/593 Rex m. 13.

25 TNA C 49/48/6. Kynggeslay was questioned by the royal council but later released. For his career: Walker, 'Rumour, Sedition and Popular Protest', pp. 31–2.

26 The battle referred to would have been that of mid-1405 involving Northumberland and Lord Bardolf. The Percy forces had in fact been defeated by Westmorland and Northumberland and Bardolf had fled to Scotland: Kirby, *Henry IV*, pp. 185–7.

pay his men. This echoed the Percys' complaints that the king had failed to keep his promises of money and arms, leaving them unable to honour their own knightly obligations.

The Lancastrian government characterised the Percys' treason in chivalric terms as personal betrayal but augmenting this customary definition, they faced charges of usurping the sovereign public authority of the state and perpetrating crimes against the nation of England. The prosecution narratives were shaped by the belief that the idealised homosocial affinities binding men together in a masculine polity centred on the king were being subverted by debased masculine attachments that seduced true men into treason. These suspicions were most vividly captured in Henry's conviction that the Percys had formed 'bonds of confederacy' against him, a notion that gained widespread credence from 1403. Hardyng made the most explicit reference to these bonds. After fighting alongside Hotspur at Shrewsbury, Hardyng changed sides to support the Lancastrians. In a later Yorkist redaction of his chronicle, he claimed that while serving as Henry IV's constable at Warkworth, formerly a Percy stronghold, he had uncovered there a collection of sealed agreements signed by every English nobleman apart from the earl of Stafford and swearing them to an alliance against Henry. Just prior to his account of the Percy manifesto, Hardyng mentioned 'dyvers other lordes' who had allied with the Percys 'and wer bounde to hym be theire lettres and sealles which I sawe and hade in kepynge'.[27] Whether or not there really was a cache of secret contracts, there was widespread belief in their existence. This can be inferred from writs like that of 7 September 1403 to the bailiffs of Worcester, ordering them to proclaim that:

> Whereas it is notorious, and by many reports has newly come to the king's ears, that a number of the children of iniquity, striving to sow discord between the king and the lords spiritual and temporal, and between the said lords, have wickedly published and do daily publish it, that great number of such lords consented in the evil designs and imaginings of [the Percys] and other traitors … the king has caused the said lords to be assembled at this council and to be examined, and has found that they consented not … but were true to him.[28]

The bonds were also alluded to in the January 1404 parliament. The earl of Northumberland had appeared before the assembly to plead for mercy for his part in the events of 1403 and Henry had pardoned him. Following their ceremonial reconciliation, the Commons petitioned the king:

> To make a declaration on behalf of the archbishop of Canterbury, the duke of

[27] *Chronicle of John Hardyng*, p. 351.

[28] *CCR, Henry IV: 1402–1405*, p. 187. The reference to the lords being examined at a royal council refers to the first of several occasions on which Henry's nobles were made to swear new oaths of loyalty to him and to the succession.

> York, and the other lords spiritual and temporal … slandered by certain malevolent persons to the effect that they were in collusion, agreement and conspiracy with Sir Henry Percy and Sir Thomas Percy … and that the same archbishop, duke and earl, and the lords and others mentioned above, should be declared and considered in full parliament to be loyal lieges to you.[29]

The idea that noblemen were binding themselves together against the king reflected the traditional view of treason as the violation of true knighthood. However, the political community was also coming to embrace definitions of treason as a crime against the nation. Both these models influenced Northumberland's plea for mercy. This was recorded in the parliament roll in the first-person English in which it was delivered, exactly preserving Northumberland's confession of guilt and his words of contrition. After reminding Henry that he had voluntarily submitted himself at York, Northumberland threw himself on the king's mercy 'as I that naghte have kept yowre lawys et statutys [statutes] … and specially of gederyng of power and gevyng of liverees'.[30] The earl's admission that he had given liveries to augment his military strength validated Henry's suspicions about men forming dangerous allegiances that violated their fundamental loyalty to him. At the same time, by breaking laws and statutes, Northumberland had infringed upon the collective public power represented by parliament, particularly in its enactment of new Statutes of Liveries in 1399 and 1401. The statute of 1399 was in fact one of the main concessions Henry had made to the Commons after he took the throne.[31]

Friction between the customary view of treason and more expansive constructions conditioned legal discourse during the 1406 parliament, too. Despite the pardon and reconciliation of 1404, Northumberland rebelled again in 1405 in company with Lord Bardolf. Their treasonous action was raised in parliament on 12 June 1406, when the Lords temporal asserted their right, as peers of the realm, to try the men before the Court of Chivalry.[32] The Record and Process of this deliberation and the judgment against the two noblemen were then confirmed in parliament on 19 June. Prominent among the charges was that Northumberland and Bardolf had 'traitorously usurped and accroached royal power'.[33] The term accroaching was drawn from the civil law rhetoric of *lèse-majesté*, which defined treason as an attack on the person of the king but also as a crime against the public authority of the state he embodied and represented. This notion of *lèse-majesté* was also

29 *PROME*, 'Henry IV: January 1404', Item Twenty-one.

30 Ibid., Item Eleven.

31 Given-Wilson, *The Royal Household and the King's Affinity*, p. 240; Given-Wilson, *Henry IV*, p. 393.

32 *PROME*, 'Henry IV: March 1406', Part Two, Pleas, Item One.

33 Ibid., Item Five.

implicit in charges that, acting on his own authority, Northumberland had treated with the king of Scotland and with ambassadors from France, 'to bring about the ruin of our lord the king ... in relation to his power and his kingdom of England'.[34] As proof of this, two warrants dated 11 June 1405 and endorsed with Northumberland's seal were presented. These said the earl had appointed attorneys on his behalf to 'accomplish and bring about any kind of agreements which may be made' with King Robert of Scotland and with the ambassadors of France as if they were 'doun and accorded by oure self in our owne propre persone'.[35] By negotiating on independent terms with foreign governments, Northumberland had usurped the sovereign diplomatic authority of the English state. He was also condemned for having turned on his own countrymen by attacking the town of Berwick and 'causing' the Scots to pillage and burn the town.[36] These crimes were described as 'treasons committed against the person of ... the king' but Northumberland was equally depicted as an enemy of the nation for treating with England's enemies and waging war against his fellow Englishmen.[37]

The Record and Process achieved two constitutional ends. When Northumberland urged the duke of Orléans to join him in a war against 'Henry of Lancaster, at present regent of England', it raised once again the issue of Henry's title. As discussed in the previous chapter, shortly before addressing the case against Northumberland and Bardolf, the parliament of 1406 had enacted England's first succession statute. While Henry used this statute and supporting oaths of loyalty to tackle the issue of his legitimacy from one direction, the Record and Process handled it from another. By defining Northumberland's activities as seeking 'to bring about the ruin of our lord the king ... with regard to his power and his kingdom of England,' the text reinforced the conceptual bond between Henry's body natural and the masculine body politic encompassing the regality and realm of England.[38] From a constitutional perspective, the Record also constructed treason as a crime against the state. Northumberland and his supporters had taken the field armed for war and with 'with pennons unfurled', arrayed men in battle and held the king's castles against him.[39] This rhetoric reflected the 1352 statute but in the context of the Court of Chivalry, it also drew on civil law doctrine that only the king, as the embodiment of sovereignty, had the authority to wage

34 Ibid., Item Seven.

35 Ibid., Items Eight and Nine. The quote is from Item Eight, being the warrant in English that confirmed the authority granted by the earl to his attorneys to treat with King Robert on his behalf.

36 Ibid., Item Ten.

37 Ibid., Item Fifteen.

38 Ibid., Item Thirteen.

39 For example, Items Four and Eleven.

war.[40] This drove home the distinction between the illegitimate private warfare of noblemen and just public warfare waged by the state.[41] The charges were amplified by statements that the noblemen had circulated proclamations that 'seditiously and treacherously' said they were trying to 'redress certain fictitious troubles and failings' in the kingdom and to 'remove … certain alleged malefactors surrounding … the king'.[42] This eliminated any possibility that Northumberland and Bardolf could justify their actions as knightly *diffidatio*, done with the intention of reforming royal government for the public good.

Accounts of Northumberland's death portrayed his treason equally as a personal betrayal and a crime against the nation. The *St Albans Chronicle* explained that Northumberland and Lord Bardolf had crossed back into England in February of 1408 and 'had a public proclamation made that they had come to bring about the consolation of the people of England … They therefore urged the people to follow them if they had any desire at all for liberty'.[43] At Bramham Moor, the noblemen were challenged by the sheriff of York 'displaying the standard of St George', a potent emblem of English national identity.[44] While on one level, Walsingham saw in this encounter a knightly trial by combat in which Northumberland intended to prove the truth of his cause with his body, the idea he had betrayed the nation of England was also represented in the sheriff with his St George banner. Northumberland was killed in the battle and the treatment of his corpse marked him as a traitor to knighthood but also as an enemy of the nation. He was 'stripped of his armour and beheaded' then his head was spiked and 'carried in public display through the city of London, and placed high upon the bridge'.[45] The stripping of armour was a ritual performed upon the bodies of high-status traitors to annihilate their honour and knightly manhood.[46] However, by the later fourteenth century English noblemen were generally spared the degrading public display of body parts, and hanging, drawing and quartering was frequently commuted to simple beheading.[47] When men's bodies were used in humiliating spectacles like the parading of Northumberland's head, this

40 Black, *Political Thought*, p. 90; and more generally, Frederick H. Russell, *The Just War in the Middle Ages* (Cambridge, 1975).

41 Keen, 'Treason Trials', pp. 95–6; Bellamy, *Law of Treason*, pp. 62–3, 95.

42 *PROME*, 'Henry IV: March 1406', Part Two, Pleas, Items Three and Five.

43 *St Albans Chronicle II*, pp. 530–5 (p. 531). The chronicle account of events is generally accepted as accurate, although the writer embellishes his narrative with various prophecies concerning the fall of the Percy family.

44 Bengtson, 'Saint George and the Formation of English Nationalism'.

45 *St Albans Chronicle II*, pp. 533, 535.

46 McVitty, 'False Knights and True Men', pp. 458–9. For general descriptions of these rituals: Keen, 'Treason Trials', pp. 88–91.

47 As seen for example in the case of the earl of Arundel, discussed in Chapter Two. See also Bothwell, *Falling from Grace*, pp. 64–6; Gillingham, 'Killing and Mutilating Political Enemies'.

stripped them of their masculine identity as knights but also of their political identity as English subjects.

THE TRAITOR AND HERETIC AS THREAT TO THE REALM

Like the Percys, Sir John Oldcastle began as a loyal supporter of the Lancastrian regime. He came from a relatively obscure knightly family but his martial abilities caught Henry IV's eye on campaign against the Scots in 1400, and from that time onwards he regularly served the king in military and judicial capacities.[48] In the early 1400s, he fought alongside the young Prince Henry against the Welsh rebels and as Lord Cobham, he attended parliament between 1410 and 1413.[49] These brief details present Oldcastle as an exemplary knight and royal servant. Just prior to his first attendance at parliament as Lord Cobham, Oldcastle even took on a French knight in a chivalric tournament at Lille.[50] Yet in January 1414, he was indicted for treason for leading a rising against Henry V that ended in the executions of thirty-eight men as traitors. The rising followed Oldcastle's conviction for heresy and subsequent alienation from the royal court. In September 1413, he had faced an ecclesiastical inquisition spearheaded by Archbishop Arundel, where he had been declared a heretic, excommunicated and handed over to the secular arm for burning. Because of Oldcastle's close friendship with Henry V, the king postponed his execution to try personally to convince him to recant. During this brief respite, Oldcastle escaped from prison in the Tower and set his plans in motion. While Oldcastle's compatriots died in 1414, he was on the run for three years but in 1417, he was finally recaptured and executed.[51] He was drawn and hanged as a traitor then 'burned hanging' to mark him as a heretic, a sentence that indelibly and causally connected one crime to the other.[52]

The persecution of Oldcastle and his adherents had immediate, fatal consequences for many of the accused men, but the legal narratives of prosecution and repression also had broader implications. The indictments, in combination with the new anti-lollard statute of April 1414, played on cultural dread about the heretic-as-traitor to extend the scope of treason as a crime against the state. Chroniclers portrayed Oldcastle's treason in customary terms as

[48] Oldcastle's judicial offices included those of justice of the peace and sheriff, and he also served as shire knight for Herefordshire in the January 1404 parliament. For his background and career: W. T. Waugh, 'Sir John Oldcastle', *The English Historical Review* 20 (1905), 434–56 (pp. 435–9); Maureen Jurkowski, 'Henry V's Suppression of the Oldcastle Revolt', *Henry V: New Interpretations*, ed. Gwilym Dodd (York, 2013), pp. 103–29 (pp. 104–5).

[49] Powell, *Kingship, Law, and Society*, p. 145.

[50] Waugh, 'Sir John Oldcastle', p. 439.

[51] On the heresy trial and subsequent rising: Powell, *Kingship, Law, and Society*, pp. 141–67; Strohm, *England's Empty Throne*, pp. 65–86.

[52] *PROME*, 'Henry V: November 1417', Item Eleven.

a fall from chivalric manhood but an alternative interpretation emerged in the official records. The authorising legal rhetoric of these sources exploited gendered conceptual linkages between heretics and traitors to portray them as a single group of 'enemies of the state', a masculine entity represented by but not coterminous with the manly body of the king. When heresy was described as the prototypical thought crime located in unnatural desires, and this was then connected directly or indirectly to material acts of treason, it reinforced recent common law precedents that a man's thoughts, intentions or words alone could be enough to render him a traitor. These 'imaginings' were constructed as treasonous deeds against the king but equally as attacks on the Christian people, 'estates' and nation of England.

In many ways, Oldcastle personified the traitor as a false knight, whose violations of honour and homosocial bonds undid his own manhood. It was through this lens of chivalry that contemporary observers interpreted his actions. In a 1415 poem, the Lancastrian court poet Thomas Hoccleve excoriated Oldcastle as someone who had once been 'a manly knyght' but who had 'lost the style of cristenly [Christian] prowesse', and admonished him to 'ryse up a manly knyght out of the slow [slough] of heresie'.[53] For Hoccleve, Oldcastle's heresy and his resulting betrayal of 'our feithful cristen Prince and King' were the inevitable outcome of his fall from chivalry. Hoccleve even implied that Oldcastle could still redeem himself if he were to 'clymbe no more in holy writ' and instead return to reading the chivalric literature appropriate to a man of his status, like 'Lancelot de lake, or Vegece of the art of Chivalrie' (that is, Flavius Vegetius Renatus, author of the popular military manual *De re militari*).[54]

The *Gesta Henrici Quinti* and the *St Albans Chronicle* featured similar interpretations. The *Gesta* described Oldcastle as 'one of the most beloved and greatest men of [Henry's] household', who was 'strong of body but weak in virtue' ('fortis viribus set virtute debilis').[55] *Viribus* conveyed the idea of a body that was sexed male but that lacked the inner virtues of true manhood.[56] Walsingham expressed anxieties about the erosion of homosocial bonds of knighthood in his assertion that while some of Oldcastle's followers were motivated by their lollard beliefs others were driven by avarice. He went on to describe 'crowds of men hastening along together' after Oldcastle, having been 'enticed by promises of large rewards'.[57] Oldcastle's fall from chivalric virtue was made explicit in Walsingham's claim that one participant, a wealthy

53 Thomas Hoccleve, 'To Sir John Oldcastle', *Hoccleve's Works: I. The Minor Poems*, ed. Frederick J. Furnivall, Early English Text Society E. S. 61 (London, 1892), pp. 8, 11–12 (stanzas 2 and 14).

54 Ibid., p. 14, stanza 25. Cf. Lewis, *Kingship and Masculinity*, pp. 18, 94–6.

55 *Gesta Henrici Quinti*, pp. 2–3.

56 Lewis, *Kingship and Masculinity*, p. 95.

57 *St Albans Chronicle II*, p. 637.

brewer, had made a deal that in return for his support, 'he should receive from the hands of John Oldcastle the order of knighthood'.[58] To this end, the brewer brought with him 'two war-horses ... harnessed with gold' and a pair of gilt spurs. This story may well have been invented.[59] Nevertheless, the evocative description of Oldcastle degrading the order of knighthood by selling it the highest bidder vividly encapsulated the traditional perception of treason as the corrupt inversion of chivalric true manhood.

We do not know how Oldcastle explained his decision to turn against Henry. Chroniclers reported that he had circulated vernacular bills in London defending himself but the only evidence for his reasoning has been filtered through later accounts, with the most prominent of these being by Tudor writers whose interpretations were heavily influenced by Reformation politics.[60] However, Powell argued that Oldcastle's rebellion can be viewed as knightly *diffidatio* in response to Henry's failure to protect him from Archbishop Arundel and therefore, 'as the rising of an injured vassal against the lord who had forsworn him'.[61] If there is any veracity in John Bale's account, then the discourse of knighthood also shaped Oldcastle's confession of faith, which he purportedly wrote and delivered to the king after he was excommunicated in September 1413. According to Bale, Oldcastle told the king that one hundred knights and esquires would stand as his purgators, and offered to submit himself to trial by combat.[62] By portraying Oldcastle as willing to prove the truth of his faith upon his body, Bale was engaging the sensibilities of his Reformation readership. However, Waugh points to elements of Bale's text that suggest he was working from an older source, now lost, in which the chivalric right to trial by combat to contest a charge of treason would not have been out of place.[63]

The legal records of Oldcastle's trial drew on the chivalric model of treason but to a large extent this was subsumed by judicial constructions of treason as a crime against the people and nation of England. As with the Percys, the understanding of treason as a personal betrayal was represented by fears that corrupt homosocial affinities had subverted natural masculine bonds between political subjects and the king. In the indictment arising from a commission of oyer and terminer of 10 January 1414, Oldcastle, the lollard

58 Ibid., p. 641.

59 Walsingham names the brewer as William Murley of Dunstable, but there is no evidence of this person being indicted or executed after the rising: *St Albans Chronicle II*, p. 640, n. 912.

60 Details of his noble defiance featured in John Bale's *A Brefe Chronycle* (1544) and John Foxe's *Acts and Monuments*. For these sources and the manuscript history: Waugh, 'Sir John Oldcastle', pp. 434–5, 451–6; Strohm, *England's Empty Throne*, pp. 66–7, 70, 230 n. 10.

61 Powell, *Kingship, Law, and Society*, pp. 148–9, 156 (p. 149).

62 Waugh, 'Sir John Oldcastle', p. 450.

63 Ibid., p. 451 n. 85.

chaplain Walter Blake and Sir John Acton were charged with planning a *privatim insurgerent* to advance their *nephando propositio*.[64] The term 'private insurgency' distinguished this as unsanctioned aggression and pre-empted any defence that Oldcastle's actions were a legitimate performance of *diffidatio*. The term *privatim*, when linked to the term *nephando*, suggested that Oldcastle and his followers had formed a secret confederacy against the king. As discussed earlier, *nephando* invoked the most extreme form of perverse male attachment, the sin of sodomy, which was characteristically referred to in late medieval theological tracts and legal texts as *nephandum peccatum* or 'unspeakable sin'. Canon and civil law connected sodomy to *lèse-majesté* and heresy in a triumvirate of hidden crimes that were rooted in unnatural deviance.[65] Invoking a universally understood legal and intellectual framework in which gender inversion signalled wilful rebellion against divinely-ordained natural order, the traitor, the heretic and the sodomite all stood as existential threats to the integrity of the masculine body politic. Echoing the gendered rhetoric of *nephandum* in the Oldcastle indictment, the idea of unnatural bonds also surfaced in the April 1414 statute, which targeted 'those belonging to the heretical sect called lollardy as well as others of their confederacy'.[66] The discursive link between lollardy as a sect and the forming of dangerous confederacies deliberately seeded the idea that the problem was not lone malcontents but a well-organised cabal.[67] For the Lancastrian regime, it must have seemed that in Oldcastle's betrayal and rebellion, their deepest forebodings about perverse homosocial affinities had been fully realised.

Although the prosecution records were inflected by themes of treason as personal betrayal, this chivalric interpretation was outweighed by rhetorical constructions that framed the activities of Oldcastle and his followers as crimes against the state. The oyer and terminer commission authorised the king's officers to inquire into 'all treasons and insurrections committed by lollards and all treasons, insurrections, rebellions and felonies', wording that implied two different groups and two sets of crimes. This distinction was almost immediately erased in writs for the investigation of 'treasons, insurrections, rebellions and felonies' committed by 'the king's subjects, commonly called lollards, and others'.[68] By tacking on 'and others' to this group, and

64 TNA KB/27/611 Rex m. 7; *Select Cases*, pp. 217–20.

65 McVitty, 'False Knights and True Men', pp. 465–6; Forrest, *Detection of Heresy*, pp. 150–1.

66 *PROME*, 'Henry V: April 1414', Item Twenty-four.

67 Anne Hudson, 'A Lollard Sect Vocabulary?', *Lollards and Their Books* (London, 1985), pp. 164–80.

68 *CPR, 1413–1417*, p. 175. Powell (*Kingship, Law, and Society*, pp. 152–3) notes that the formulaic language of sixteen additional provincial commissions issued on 11 January, and of their resulting indictments, follows that of the London and Middlesex commission and indictments.

associating acts of treason with identity as a lollard, this rhetorical move implied that every man involved in the rising had betrayed his king but also the Christian community of England.

The resulting indictments featured explicit constructions of treason as a crime against the nation as well as against the masculine political body that encompassed the king and his patrilineage. First in the sequence of charges was having 'falsely and treasonably proposed and imagined' to kill the king and his brothers, and to 'deprive the … king and his heirs of the inheritance of his aforesaid realm'.[69] 'Proposing and imagining' the murder of the king aligned with the 1352 statute and this could plausibly stretch to include the murder of the king's brothers, who had been recognised as his heirs should he die childless. However, by augmenting this charge with the allegation that the plotters intended to disinherit the king and his heirs, the indictments established legal precedent to treat challenges to the 1406 succession statute as acts of treason. This meant that any questioning of Lancastrian dynastic legitimacy, even using the title 'Henry of Lancaster', was an act of treason. The accused were further charged with having 'falsely and treasonably plotted' against the estate of the realm ('falso et proditorie machinando tam statum regium') as well as the church and faith 'within the said realm of England'.[70] The term *statum regium*, twinned with accusations that the plotters intended to destroy the community of Christian believers, constructed traitors as enemies of the entire English nation. This was made explicit when the offenders were said to:

> Have falsely and treasonably plotted … to constitute John Oldcastle as regent of the said realm [of England], and to establish many more governments [*quamplura regimina*] according to their wishes within the aforesaid realm like a people without a head, to the ultimate destruction of the catholic faith and clergy as well as of the estate and majesty of the royal dignity [*status et majestatis dignitatis*] within the said realm.[71]

Building on charges of plotting to kill and disinherit Henry and his male heirs, this passage shifted the focus of treason from acts directly against the king's person and patrilineage to acts against the Christian faith, through which temporal polities were rightly ordered within a universal Christian community. When the plotters were described as intent on destroying the 'estate and majesty of the royal dignity of the realm', this advanced a constitutional framework in which royal power was abstracted from the person of the king and reified in the notion of *majestatis*, the public authority of the state. Finally, the record graphically depicted Oldcastle as a traitor who would

69 TNA KB 27/611 Rex m. 7.

70 Ibid.

71 Ibid.

dismember the English nation from within by reducing it to a monstrous body politic without a head.

There is no evidence that Oldcastle thought to make himself regent but regardless of the veracity of this allegation, it was incorporated into the indictment to do political and ideological work. By representing Oldcastle's resistance as an attempt to sunder the social and political unity of the nation of England, it foreclosed any possibility that his actions might be perceived either as honourable knightly *diffidatio* or as a just challenge to an illegitimate ruler. When the prosecution narrative asserted that Oldcastle planned to make himself regent of England, it drew into its associative net other troublemakers who had not participated in the rising but who were nevertheless viewed as subverting Lancastrian rule. These included bill casters promoting the story of Richard II's survival and men who persisted in championing the Mortimer cause while defiantly addressing the king as 'Henry of Lancaster'. This broader strategy produced indictments such as one naming that persistent Ricardian bill caster Benedict Wolman amongst a group charged with 'treasons and felonies' in support of Oldcastle.[72] The belief that Oldcastle was promoting the cause of the deposed king also surfaced in Walsingham's account of Oldcastle's final appearance before parliament in 1417. According to the chronicler, when Oldcastle was ordered to reply to the charges, he responded 'that he had no judge amongst them while his liege lord, King Richard, was still living'.[73]

The legal position that lollards 'as well as others of their confederacy' were traitors to the nation as well as enemies of the king was cemented in the April 1414 statute.[74] This drew on the language of the January indictments and on the precedents established by the conviction and execution of thirty-eight men as traitors.[75] Its opening clause stated that the law was enacted because of 'great uprisings … and insurrections', immediately framing all the activities it went on to describe as treason through the accusation that those involved had 'arrayed … in warlike fashion in form of rebellion'.[76] Like the January indictments, the legislation targeted 'those belonging to the heretical sect called lollardy as well as others of their confederacy, instigation, and urging'.[77] By making repeated rhetorical connections between 'heretics and lollards' and 'lollards *and others*', as well as criminalising beliefs in 'heresies *and*

72 TNA KB 27/611 Rex m. 13. Once again, Wolman was able to produce a pardon.

73 *St Albans Chronicle II*, p. 729.

74 *PROME*, 'Henry V: April 1414', Item Twenty-four; *Statutes*, II, pp. 181–4 (c. vii).

75 These thirty-eight men were executed at St Giles' Fields, on the outskirts of London, on 12 January; seven of them were burned as heretics as well as hanged as traitors: Powell, *Kingship, Law, and Society*, p. 151.

76 TNA KB 27/611 Rex m. 7.

77 *PROME*, 'Henry V: April 1414', Item Twenty-four.

other errors', the overall effect of the statute was to mark anyone with suspect religious *or* political beliefs as both heretics *and* traitors.[78]

The terms 'treason' or 'traitor' were not directly used in the 1414 statute, although *prodicionibus* and *proditorie* appear throughout the related trial records. Instead, the statute condemned 'all kinds of heresies and errors'. That the men guilty of these 'errors' were traitors by definition was proved by their deeds, itemised in a sequence beginning with 'abolishing and subverting the Christian faith and the law of God'; moving on to destroying the king and 'various estates of the same kingdom' as well as 'all manner of governance'; and culminating in intentions to 'utterly [destroy] the laws of the land'.[79] This charted a direct path from heresy, to the customary idea of treason as an act against the king's person, to the most expansive conception of treason as a crime against the estates of the realm and the laws of England. Each element in the sequence built cumulatively upon the previous one, creating a searing image of transgressors as traitors to God, the king, divine and common law, and the English nation. Underpinning this legal discourse was the gendered binary of natural/unnatural that connected treason and heresy. This produced the traitor as the quintessential 'false man' and simultaneously masculinised the abstract constitutional entities of nation, state and political community against which he offended.

The new statute empowered royal authorities 'to make enquiries concerning all those who uphold any errors or heresies *such as* lollardy, or who are their aiders, shelterers, supporters, or sustainers' ('et queux sont lour maintenours, recettours, fautours, susteignours').[80] The terms *recettor*, *fautour* and *susteignour* were typically found in the ecclesiastical records of heresy inquisitions.[81] However, the statute implied there were 'errors' besides lollardy to be exposed, along with their 'supporters or sustainers'. This was reinforced in a statement that all previous statutes 'for the correction and punishment of heretics and lollards, made in the past and not repealed, are to remain in force', confirming that the government expected the 1406 statute against 'lollards and other spreaders and contrivers of news and falsities' to continue in use alongside the new legislation.[82] While the 1414 statute made no explicit reference to the repression of political speech, the earlier statute left much scope for such speech to be prosecuted as treason.

78 Ibid., emphasis added.

79 Ibid.

80 Ibid., emphasis added. Forrest (*Detection of Heresy*, pp. 43–6) discusses the implications of the new statute for expanding secular jurisdiction.

81 Arnold, 'Lollard Trials and Inquisitorial Discourse', pp. 84–5; Anne Hudson, 'The Examination of Lollards', *Historical Research* 46 (1973), 145–59.

82 *PROME*, 'Henry V: April 1414', Item Twenty-four; *PROME*, 'Henry IV: March 1406', Part One, Roll, Item Sixty-two. There is no evidence the 1406 statute was ever revoked; prosecutions from 1407 onwards indicate it was still in force.

By linking treason and heresy in the indictments relating to the Oldcastle rising and then reinforcing this connection in the 1414 statute, the Lancastrian regime effected both legal and constitutional changes. The statute systematised the state's direct involvement in the investigation and suppression of heresy, and by prioritising the interests of secular rather than ecclesiastical justice it helped to extend royal jurisdiction. By 'eliding the distinction between heresy and treason', the statute redefined heresy as armed rebellion and therefore enabled its pursuit through the secular courts.[83] The response to Oldcastle's rebellion also heralded judicial and constitutional change when it came to treason. When the legal discourse categorised offenders as enemies of God as well as of the king and extended the threat they posed to encompass the English church and Christian body politic, this expanded the scope of treason well beyond attacks on or rebellion against the king. The conceptual and rhetorical links created between heresy and treason in the secular judicial sphere opened up an associative network of more indirect crimes that could be punished as treason. By implication, these included holding or expressing opinions that were considered 'heresies' in religious terms but also those that were viewed as 'errors' from a political perspective. This was consistent with civil law jurisprudence according to which treason included not only direct acts against the king but also attacks on or insults to the public authority vested in the government and its officers, as well as in the instruments and symbols of sovereign state power.

BETRAYAL OF THE NATION

Henry V's problems with men close to him turning traitor did not stop with Sir John Oldcastle. On 5 August 1415, Henry Lord Lescrope of Masham, who served as one of the king's trusted judicial officers on the 1414 Oldcastle commission, was himself tried and executed for treason. Lescrope's conviction provides an emphatic articulation of treason as a crime against the nation. In the Record and Process of his trial, he was condemned for betraying the king but also 'the tongue in which he was born' ('linguam in qua natus est').[84] However, the government's attempts to equate attacks on the king with a betrayal of the nation as it was represented in the idea of 'mother tongue' were complicated by Lescrope's use of English to defend himself. In vernacular first-person letters written directly to the king, Lescrope and two co-conspirators drew on the customary idea of treason as a violation of knighthood, coupled with the ethical and legal proof value of men's words in English, to mitigate their actions and solicit the king's mercy as his true, if misguided, liege men.

83 Forrest, *Detection of Heresy*, pp. 43–6 (p. 45).

84 *PROME*, 'Henry V: November 1415', Item Six.

The Southampton plot involved Lescrope, the king's cousin Richard earl of Cambridge, the Northumbrian knight Sir Thomas Grey of Heton and Edmund Mortimer, the earl of March in an alleged conspiracy to kill Henry V and restore Richard II or, if he should prove to be dead, to place Mortimer on the throne as his rightful heir.[85] Pugh detailed the possible familial, political and financial motivations of the participants in his 1988 study, which remains the generally accepted version of events.[86] Although opinions differ about the extent of the conspirators' belief in Richard's survival or exactly what they hoped to achieve, most scholars agree that some sort of rising was being discussed. The exception was Strohm, whose examination of the trial records led him to conclude the plot was a Lancastrian '"mock-up", invented so that its supposed principals would have *something* to which they might confess'.[87] Regardless of the real extent of the threat, the Southampton incident emerges as a significant episode in the development of English treason law and related constitutional thinking. The Lancastrian regime punished the offenders as enemies of the English nation and its collective interests as well as personal enemies of Henry V. Through judicial processes of confession, trial and execution, customary conceptions of treason as the inverse of knighthood came into conflict with definitions of treason as a crime against the state, but the latter finally outweighed the former and neutralised the offenders' defensive claims.

Contemporary observers saw the Southampton plot through the lens of chivalry and portrayed the conspirators' treachery as the product of corrupted homosocial bonds. The *Gesta Henrici Quinti* opened with a portrait of the king at Portchester Castle making final preparations to sail for France to reclaim his 'right' that 'the French, by their blameworthy and unjust violence, have for so long … striven to usurp and withhold'.[88] This characterisation of Henry V's military invasion as a just war to recover his rightful inheritance echoed the chivalric narratives used to justify his father's armed invasion of England in 1399. It was at this portentous moment that Henry discovered he had been betrayed by 'Richard, earl of Cambridge, his cousin by blood [*consanguineum suum germanum*], Henry, lord Scrope, an intimate member of his own household and one who was almost second to none … among those in the king's confidence', and by Sir Thomas Grey, 'a renowned and noble knight if only he had not been dishonoured by the stain of treason'.[89] Walsingham described how these 'three powerful men in whom [the king] had the greatest

85 The affair has come to be known as the Southampton plot because it was exposed while Henry V was at Portchester Castle preparing to depart for France.

86 Pugh, *Southampton Plot*. See also McNiven, 'Rebellion, Sedition', pp. 112–14; Keen, *England in the Later Middle Ages*, pp. 258–9.

87 *England's Empty Throne*, pp. 86–99 (p. 89, emphasis in original).

88 *Gesta Henrici Quinti*, p. 15.

89 Ibid., p. 19, Latin on p. 18; my translation.

confidence conspired to assassinate him' and termed them 'parricides', framing the conspirators' actions in the most intimate terms of familial betrayal.[90] He went on to accuse the men of using flattery and deception to embroil the earl of March, with March 'swearing a bodily oath' ('corporali prestito juramento, firmaret') to join their secret scheme.[91] The story of a corporeal ritual being performed to seal men together in an unnatural cabal against their king evoked in negative terms the bodily performances involved in the ceremony of knighting, exemplifying the cultural angst that homosocial bonds were inherently frangible and liable to corruption.

Arguably, Cambridge and Grey were the ringleaders and Cambridge at least had good reason to be resentful of the king, who had given him scant reward for years of military service to both Henry and his father.[92] Lescrope, by contrast, had long been a loyal retainer in Lancastrian service in military, administrative and judicial capacities. It was his close personal relationship with Henry V that influenced his elevation to the office of Treasurer in 1410–11 (when Prince Henry had been in control of the royal council), and Lescrope's admission to the elite chivalric Order of the Garter in 1410 was likewise a mark of Henry's esteem.[93] After serving on the January 1414 commission into Oldcastle's activities, in February 1414 Lescrope was one of three royal envoys sent to France to negotiate Henry's marriage.[94] As late as June 1414, he was being entrusted with sensitive diplomatic missions on behalf of the king.[95] The chroniclers emphasised the magnitude of Lescrope's violation of this trust while underplaying the involvement of Cambridge, Grey and March. The *Gesta* condemned Lescrope as 'the more culpable an enemy because the more intimate a friend' while Walsingham dwelt on Lescrope's feigned loyalty and deception.[96] Asserting that Henry trusted Lescrope's advice above that of any other man 'if ever private or public plans were negotiated', he said the king's policy was that if official embassies were sent to France, they should always have the benefit of Lescrope's superior intelligence and character.[97] Walsingham reinforced the strength of the king's masculine

90 *St Albans Chronicle II*, p. 659.

91 Ibid., p. 661, Latin on p. 660, my translation. Whatever the actual scheme was, it was undone when March lost his nerve and told the king of the conspiracy against him.

92 Cambridge's ennoblement in 1415 was not accompanied by any grant of lands and he was kept short of money by the king; Grey also had persistent money problems: *Southampton Plot*, pp. 61, 91–2, 98, 104.

93 Collins, *Order of the Garter*, pp. 43, 114–16.

94 Pugh, *Southampton Plot*, p. 25; Jurkowski, 'Henry V's Suppression of the Oldcastle Revolt', pp. 110–11.

95 TNA E 101/132/4 for his expense account for a journey to Calais; TNA E 30/1531 (25 June 1414) is the report of a meeting of English and Burgundian commissioners at Leicester, and instructions to Lescrope to treat further with the duke of Burgundy.

96 *Gesta Henrici Quinti*, p. 19.

97 *St Albans Chronicle II*, pp. 659, 661.

bond with Lescrope in his declaration that 'among the English race there was hardly a man so dear to the king as Henry Scrope, apart from his own brothers'.[98] While the chronicler went on to explain the plot partly as the product of French scheming and bribery, it was Lescrope's intimate betrayal to which he repeatedly returned.

This interpretation was echoed in the Record and Process as it was copied into the parliament roll. This alleged the men had 'falsely and treasonably conspired together and bound themselves to one another to the effect that, having gathered to themselves many others both of the retinue of the lord king and of his other lieges', they would carry out their plan to install March as king if Richard should prove to be dead.[99] Cambridge, Lescrope and Grey had not only forged themselves into a secret confederacy, they had also subverted the allegiance of other men. This legal rhetoric was reminiscent of charges in earlier cases that traitors intended to incite others against their love and allegiance, but the reference to 'retinues' anchored this transgression firmly within the homosocial world of chivalric loyalties forged through martial service. The trial record went on to make much of Lescrope's membership of the Garter, 'instituted for the strengthening of the faith, the king, the realm, and justice', a description that evoked the core virtues of knightly manhood while simultaneously stressing the extent to which Lescrope had betrayed these values.[100] This message was reinforced in a final warning that no one should use Lescrope's violation as a reason to malign other men who continued to bear the Order with honour.

At Southampton on 2 August, a jury of local men indicted Cambridge, Grey and Lescrope in a hastily assembled judicial tribunal headed by the king's brother Thomas, duke of Clarence. Cambridge and Grey denied any acts of treason, but they admitted to engaging in some suspect conversations and threw themselves on the mercy of the king. Lescrope admitted talking to the other men but denied they had ever discussed harming the king. He added that he had become involved with the sole aim of confounding any plot from within, but he nevertheless put himself in the king's grace for concealing things from him. Lescrope then demanded to be 'tried and judged by his peers of the realm', wording that suggests he expected to defend his honour in the Court of Chivalry.[101]

Soliciting the king's mercy required an admission of guilt and a demonstration of abject submission to the king's will. To initiate this process, all three men had to provide some explanation for what they had been up to, resulting in letters of confession.[102] The letters were extracted once the men had been

98 Ibid., p. 661.

99 *PROME*, 'Henry V: November 1415', Item Six.

100 Ibid.

101 Ibid.

102 The originals are TNA E 163/7/7 ms. 1–8. These are badly stained and damaged in parts,

imprisoned so they cannot be viewed as voluntary disclosures free of coercion but they were not wholly supplicatory rhetorical performances, either. They were composed in first-person English and their level of evidentiary detail placed them within the rhetorical and linguistic framework of testimony given under oath in a court of law. According to the *Gesta*, the offenders were executed 'after they had made public confession' and the Record and Process confirms that the letters were read out before the tribunal at Southampton.[103] These public performances were intended to prove the crime of treason in the offenders' own words and to validate its expeditious punishment. Yet the stories the letters told and the admissions they made were far from straightforward. Invoking the idea of treason as the antithesis of knighthood, the writers veered between humble admissions of wrongdoing, veiled justifications and attempts to deflect blame onto others.

Grey's confession began with his abject self-representation as a man who knew he had destroyed his knightly honour. He described bringing 'the utter most shame to me and all my kin' and imagined that 'I were buried alive … and my name never to be rehearsed'.[104] This foretold the obliteration of manly identity, not only for the condemned traitor but also for the masculine social body represented by his lineage.[105] Grey conceived of treason as an intimate betrayal as he admitted to Henry that he was drawn into 'speaking and working and counselling against your person'.[106] He located the moment of his fall precisely in relation to his performance of knighthood, saying that it was when he was returning home from London, where he had contracted with the king to provide a retinue for the French campaign, that he had a fateful meeting with Cambridge. Grey blamed Cambridge for seizing this opportunity to lead him into error, bewailing 'Alas! the time of that retinue making, for it has brought me to this shame and undoing'.[107] His despairing admission served to remind the king of Grey's history of loyal knightly service while simultaneously deflecting responsibility onto the earl as the main offender.

Citing poverty and covetousness as reasons for his transgressions, Grey also hinted at the idea of *diffidatio* by making a veiled allusion to Henry keeping him short of money and thus failing in his lordly obligations. The

so have been consulted alongside translations into modern English: Pugh, 'Appendix II', *Southampton Plot*, pp. 160–77. Pugh reconstructed these with the aid of copies made in 1882 by James Gairdner, then Deputy Keeper of the Public Records Office. For the manuscript history, including confirmation these are genuine 'autograph letters of confession', see Pugh, *Southampton Plot*, pp. xiii, 160–1.

103 *Gesta Henrici Quinti*, p. 19.

104 TNA E 163/7/7 m. 1; 'Appendix II', p. 161.

105 This social death was legal and financial, as well as cultural, because forfeiture stripped the offender's heirs of titles, lands and offices: Danielle Westerhof, *Death and the Noble Body in Medieval England* (Woodbridge, 2008), Chapters Five and Six.

106 TNA E 163/7/7 m. 1; 'Appendix II', p. 161.

107 Ibid.

notion of *diffidatio* became more prominent when Grey explained why the earl of March had agreed to the scheme. He first recounted how Henry V had extracted a ruinous fine of 10,000 marks from March for the latter's marriage, adding that Lescrope had had to loan March the money to pay it. In a second parchment fragment, probably a continuation of the same letter, Grey said that he had been shown a letter from March, 'written with his own hand, how he had been [to] your gracious lord. And how foul you had fared with him in the payment for his marriage. And so he saw no way but you would undo him'.[108] Elsewhere, Grey claimed that it was Lescrope who, by speaking 'the highest and the haughtiest' to March, had pressured him into asserting 'his right of the crown'.[109] Grey's letter was a mélange: admissions of wrong-doing were followed by attempts to deflect blame from himself by depicting Cambridge and Lescrope as the ringleaders, and these were accompanied by attempts at justification through suggestions it was the king's mistreatment of his faithful liege men that had driven them to desperate ends. Grey returned finally to contemplating the destruction of his own knightly honour and lineage, but concluded by claiming that this was the result of Cambridge's greater betrayal, and 'I have slain all my kin through his false counsel'.[110]

The earl of Cambridge wrote at least two letters to the king between 31 July and his execution on 5 August.[111] In the earlier text, he provided the most coherent and detailed account of the plot and if any of the confessions bears the marks of deliberate manufacture by the prosecution, it is this one. Cambridge implicated his fellows on several points of treason itemised in the 1352 statute, including planning to ally with the Scots to ride in arms against the king and to seize royal castles in Wales.[112] He made no mention of a plot to kill the king, an admission that would leave no ambiguity that Cambridge was a traitor. He did, however, admit to offences amounting to treasonous speech, something that might or might not be considered within the legal scope of treason depending on the nature of the tribunal and the opinion of a jury. He said the conspirators had planned to circulate:

> A proclamacyoun, which schulde hadde bene cryde in the erle name, as the heyre to the coroune of Ynglond, ageyns yow, my lege lord, calde, by an untreu

108 TNA E 163/7/7 m. 2; 'Appendix II', p. 165.

109 TNA E 163/7/7 m. 1; 'Appendix II', pp. 163–4.

110 TNA E 163/7/7 m. 2; 'Appendix II', p. 165.

111 One text survives as TNA E 163/7/7 ms. 4 and 5, which appear to be two fragments from the same letter. Two letters, one from between 31 July and 2 August, and the second written between 2 and 5 August, were also preserved separately in BL Cotton Vespasian C XIV, fol. 39 and Cotton Vespasian F III, fol. 7, transcribed in *Foedera*, IX, pp. 300–1. There are similarities between the letter in the Exchequer file and the first of the two Cotton Vespasian texts. This, along with the fact that E 163/7/7 m. 4 includes several lines of erasure suggests the former may have been a first draft of the latter.

112 *Foedera*, IX, p. 300; BL Cotton Vespasian C XIV, fol. 39.

> name, Harry of Lancastre usurpur of Yngland, to the entent to hadde made the more poeple to hade draune to hym, and fro yow.[113]

Addressing the king as 'Henry of Lancaster' had already been adjudged an act of treason in earlier cases such as that of Northumberland and Bardolf. Cambridge also referred to that other hazardous speech act, spreading rumours of Richard's survival but he was careful to deny any part in this element of the plot. He first said that the Mortimer claim was to be advanced only if Richard proved to be dead but immediately added, 'as y wot wel that he wys not alyve'. He then blamed two Northumbrian knights for hatching the plan 'for the bryngyng yn of that persone, wych they name Kyng Richard … oute of Scotland'.[114] He continued by beseeching the king for mercy and to 'have yee coupassyoun on me yowre lege man' in remembrance of Christ's Passion. However, in the final passage of his letter, Cambridge tempered his submission with a more defiant performance of knighthood that implied his readiness to prove the truth of his words through trial by combat:

> And yf heny of thes persones, whos names arne contenyd in thys bylle, holdyn contrary the substaunce of that I have wretyn at thys tyme, y schalle be redy, wyth the myth of God, to make hyt good as yee, my lege lord, wylle awarde me.[115]

When Cambridge wrote this first letter, he probably hoped that by detailing the plot and naming the other conspirators, while simultaneously showing ready to prove the truth of his words with his body, he could win the king's pardon. His second letter reveals this hope was ebbing away. Instead, there was abject contrition as Cambridge presented himself to Henry as 'yowre humble subgyt and very lege man', although he still tried to stress the greater culpability of others by claiming his transgressions were the result of 'steryng of odyr folke eggyng me thereto'.[116] Cambridge's use of the term 'very' (*veri*) was an orthographic variant of the French *verai*, meaning 'true'. Thus in his final plea for mercy he clung to chivalric identity, echoing Hotspur's apocryphal words that he was 'no traitor but a true man'.

In his confession, Lescrope also tried to perform knightly manhood to resist the allegations of treason.[117] Unlike Cambridge and Grey, Lescrope never admitted to betraying Henry, either wilfully or through other men

113 Ibid.

114 Ibid. This might have referred to a doppelgänger – described in some accounts as an 'idiot' or simpleton – harboured for some years at the Scottish court of the duke of Albany: McNiven, 'Rebellion, Sedition', pp. 108, 110.

115 Ibid.

116 *Foedera*, p. 301; BL Cotton Vespasian F III, fol. 7.

117 Lescrope's letter of confession is TNA E 163/7/7 ms. 6 and 7. The final membrane in the file, E 163/7/7 m. 8, is in the same hand and appears to be instructions regarding Lescrope's will.

'egging him on'. At most, he confessed to having 'with great uncunning' concealed things from the king and he staunchly maintained he had infiltrated the conspiracy only to foil it.[118] Given Lescrope's history of service to the king, this is plausible and is a stance made more credible by Lescrope's prominent role in thwarting Oldcastle's rising. Lescrope's letter is the only source to mention any connection to lollardy or to Oldcastle. Quite possibly, he thought this conspiracy was connected to the earlier plot, which the king had empowered him to punish. Oldcastle was still on the run in mid-1415; perhaps Lescrope suspected the conspirators knew where he was and thought that if he earned their trust, he might discover Oldcastle's hiding place. Throughout his confession, Lescrope stressed to Henry his unswerving performance of loyal knighthood, asking him to remember 'when I stood with you … in France and Flanders' and farther back in time, 'service that have continued with him that was our liege lord [of us all] your fathe[r]'.[119] He then described trying to frighten the plotters out of doing anything by warning them of the perils that would fall if they persisted, and showing them that regardless of how they tried to oppose the king, they would inevitably fail. Finally, he attested that March and the others, being suitably cowed, had 'vowed me they should not come there but fully leave all such works after this'.[120]

Confessing that he 'did great folly' by not telling the king immediately about the conspiracy, Lescrope defended himself by saying that 'yif I had herde a grounded purpose taken, the whych I … to have told it you bot yif I might have siesid [ceased] it my self I would have'.[121] In other words, if things had progressed beyond mere talk, Lescrope would have involved the king but he evidently believed he could prevent it coming to this. His confidence on this score must have been reinforced when March, Cambridge and the others had given him their sworn word that they would desist. When Lescrope had secured these promises in late July, Henry was making final plans for the invasion of Normandy; it would be unsurprising if he sought to avoid distracting the king with a matter he considered resolved.[122] He went on to assert that after the men had made their vows to him, 'this I never heard no more nor thought on', emphasising the veracity of his words by stating that 'truly our sovereign lord this is true as far as I … communed in such matters'.[123] His defence, grounded in his own masculine reputation and knightly honour, continued to the end of the letter. He beseeched the king's

118 TNA E 163/7/7 m. 6; 'Appendix II', p. 167. The original is badly damaged.

119 TNA E 163/7/7 m. 6; 'Appendix II', p. 168.

120 Ibid., p. 169.

121 TNA E 163/7/7 m. 7. This membrane is a continuation of m. 6, although better preserved. Cf. 'Appendix II', pp. 170–1.

122 According to the first part of Lescrope's confession, the promises were extracted during a meeting at March's lodgings on 25 July: 'Appendix II', p. 169.

123 'Appendix II', p. 170.

grace, 'synce this is the first tre[s]pas that evr I fel' and then agonised that if Henry did not pardon him, his 'worshyp be utterly destruyd'.[124]

Discussing the power of chivalric ideals in fifteenth-century political culture, Watts stressed that the ruling elite placed supreme value on worship and manhood.[125] A man attained and preserved masculine worship by embodying knightly prowess, courage and largesse but equally through his speech and demeanour, and most importantly by keeping his word. Lescrope's confession accentuated the tensions between speaking and not speaking that underpinned this relationship between men's words and their worship. By failing to speak, to tell Henry of the plot against him as soon as he knew about it, Lescrope had imperilled his own manhood. Through the rhetorical and linguistic performance of confession, he tried to authenticate his claim that despite his failure of speech, he remained a true man. He admitted that by staying silent, he had been 'uncunning' and 'did great folly'.[126] Yet he had only done this out of misguided loyalty, to deter the king's cousin and other close associates from enacting their doomed plan. By finally voicing everything to Henry in his vernacular first-person testimony, he sought to prove the truth of his words that 'I also never erst offended in no wise nor never will more'.[127]

The confessional letters and pleas for mercy were to no avail. Grey was condemned to death by the jury empanelled at Southampton while Lescrope and Cambridge were convicted by their fellow noblemen. The evidence in all three cases was revisited and the validity of the executions confirmed in the November parliament. The Record and Process preserved on the roll incorporated the traditional view of treason as a personal betrayal but more prominent, and of greater long-term significance, was its construction of treason as a crime against the English nation. It is important to remember that the conspiracy had been exposed mere days before Henry V sailed for France, in an atmosphere in which patriotic fervour might well influence how the king's judicial officers framed the offenders' crimes. Lescrope and Cambridge were judged at Southampton by 'lords and magnates of the realm of England, and peers of the said Richard earl of Cambridge and Henry Lord Lescrope, who were present there in preparation for the lord king's expedition overseas'.[128] This identified the offenders as part of England's political and military elite while simultaneously highlighting their purported desire to destroy the national martial enterprise that their king had called them to lead.

The chronicle accounts were also inflected by perceptions of treason as a betrayal of the English nation. According to the *Gesta*, it was 'the stench of French promises or bribes' that motivated Lescrope and his fellows

124 TNA E 163/7/7 m. 7.

125 Watts, *Henry VI*, pp. 31–9.

126 'Appendix II', pp. 167, 170.

127 Ibid., p. 168.

128 *PROME*, 'Henry V: November 1415', Item Six.

to bring disaster upon the English expedition.[129] Walsingham went even further. Having said that there was no man of the 'English race' closer to the king than Lescrope, he went on to portray him as English in external appearance and behaviour, but French in his inner identity and intentions: 'He was deceitfully contriving ill-fortune for the realm by supporting the French' and was 'supporting his own side with his looks, but the French with his mind'.[130] Notably, while the confessional letters made some allusions to Scots involvement, the chronicles eschewed this angle altogether and instead focused on the conspirators' alliance with the French, now clearly identified in the national imagination as England's arch enemy.

The Record and Process was heard in parliament on 8 November, in the heady atmosphere of victory after God himself had endorsed Lancastrian kingship through the English triumph at Agincourt. News of this had reached London on 29 October and on 23 November, Henry made his ceremonial entry to the city.[131] The *Gesta* described a crowd of thousands of London citizens riding to Blackheath to congratulate the king and thank him 'for his work on behalf of the public good [*laboribus publicis*]'.[132] Henry was escorted through the city, where pageants featured larger-than-life representations of English identity. These included the statue of a giant bearing the royal arms on the southern entrance to London Bridge and, on a tower spanning the bridge, a statue of St George. On a wooden castle constructed in Cheapside, St George was depicted again alongside 'the arms of members of the royal house and of the great nobles of the realm'.[133]

When the Southampton trials are considered against this patriotic backdrop, their implications for treason law become clear. By planning to wreck the king's French expedition, the plotters had proved themselves traitors to the English nation as it was now most vividly embodied in the divinely favoured Henry V. Although the conspirators had confessed to a convoluted scheme in support of either March or a Ricardian pretender, none of them said anything about wanting to kill the king and his brothers. On the face of it, their plan was implausible at best and according to Lescrope, it never progressed beyond wishful thinking and private conversations. As royal officials had learned in past trials, it was not easy to convince juries such talk amounted to treason, so the charge of regicide was likely added to the indictment to guarantee

129 *Gesta Henrici Quinti*, p. 19.

130 *St Albans Chronicle II*, p. 661.

131 Pugh, *Southampton Plot*, p. 178.

132 *Gesta Henrici Quinti*, p. 103, Latin on p. 102.

133 *Gesta Henrici Quinti*, pp. 101–13 (p. 109); Nicola Coldstream, '"Pavilion'd in Splendour": Henry V's Agincourt Pageants', *Journal of the British Archaeological Association* 165 (2012), 153–71. The giant was probably Gogmagog, prominent in the legendary history of Britain: Jeffrey Jerome Cohen, *Of Giants: Sex, Monsters, and the Middle Ages* (Minneapolis, 1999), pp. 29–31, 35–6.

convictions. But this charge served a political function, too. By depicting the conspirators' disgruntled talk as a physical attack on Henry's person and on his knightly honour as this was epitomised by his martial ambitions, the legal discourse bound his manly body more tightly to the masculine body politic of the nation. The message that treason was a betrayal of England and of the *publicis* for which Henry had laboured so valiantly was made explicit when the record affirmed that the three men had been justly 'convicted of high treason committed by them against the lord king and his majestic realm [*regiam majestatem*]'.[134] It is notable that 'majesty' was attached here to the realm rather than to the royal person. By extending majesty beyond the king's individual political body and vesting it in the realm, it recalled the charge in the Oldcastle case that the traitors sought to destroy the 'estate and majesty of the royal dignity'.[135] However, it took this idea to the next level of abstraction by identifying two distinct but intertwined acts of treason: one against the person of the king, and the other against the *majestas* or sovereign public authority of the state.

It was in the judgment against Lescrope that treason was defined most emphatically as a crime against the nation. Lescrope was excoriated as a disgraced ex-Knight of the Garter whose chivalric honour had been utterly undone by his crimes. The extent of his violation was stressed in the death he was to suffer. He was to be drawn through the streets of Southampton, publicly beheaded and his head sent north to be displayed on Micklegate Bar in York, the place with which his noble family was most closely associated. The degradation of public drawing, bodily division and display sent the clear message that, as Lescrope feared, his manly worship had indeed been utterly destroyed. The execution ritual expressed the traditional understanding of treason as a betrayal of chivalric manhood. However, this cultural and legal construction was in the end subsumed into a broader notion of treason when the record concluded that the display of Lescrope's head was to serve as a warning 'lest anyone henceforth so wickedly and audaciously should assume such audacity to transgress and rebel against his liege lord and the nation in which he was born [*lingua in qua natus est*]'.[136] This passage captured the understanding of nationhood as originating in shared language, strengthening precedents set in earlier trials that described traitors as destroyers of English language and law. This legal rhetoric gained additional power in Lescrope's case by incorporating birth, an equally potent signifier of national identity. The judgment heralded a crucial shift in the way political subjecthood was being constructed through treason law, as Lescrope's legal identity as a traitor stripped him of ethnic identity as an English man and the political privileges this entailed.

134 *PROME*, 'Henry V: November 1415', Item Six.
135 TNA KB 27/611 Rex m. 7.
136 *PROME*, 'Henry V: November 1415', Item Six.

His sentence serves as a waypoint for a wider renegotiation of the relationship between political subjects and the state, from being a 'subject of the English king' to being an 'English subject'.[137] The transition was also marked on the traitor's body. Lescrope's severed head, hanging from the gates of York, was visible to a large urban polity of all social backgrounds; it announced that treason was a violation of the entire English community, and not simply a betrayal of the personal loyalties and chivalric values of its political elite.

PRESERVING THE MASCULINE BODY POLITIC

The judgment against Lescrope had extended the scope of treason to incorporate betrayal of the nation, but such extensions were not always accepted by the political community. Royal judicial officials faced difficulties getting juries to accept more expansive constructions of treason, especially when men were indicted for acts of political speech absent of any real proof of physical deeds. These factors were at work in the case of Sir John Mortimer, who was arrested in 1418 and kept imprisoned until 1420 when he was indicted for saying treasonable things against the king. This indictment was not taken to trial, but Mortimer was still in prison in 1422 when he was indicted again. A jury acquitted him on that occasion and he was then re-indicted on the earlier charges. Once more, the case did not go to trial. Apart from two brief escapes, the unfortunate Mortimer remained in prison until 1424 when he was executed as a traitor for his second escape. His conviction was finally secured thanks to a new statute that extended the definition of treason to include breaking prison while held there on suspicion of treason.

Mortimer was a knight who had little influence in national affairs and despite his surname, was not known to be related to the Mortimer earls of March. Apart from an article by Powell, to whom we owe our knowledge of Mortimer's background and the legal machinations that ended in his execution, the case has attracted little notice.[138] Powell focused on what he saw as the anomalous extension of the 1352 statute to convict Mortimer, although he concluded that the reasons behind his 'strange death' remain unexplained. However, when Mortimer's case is placed alongside the ad hoc extensions and precedents established in previous trials it can be seen as part of a continuum along which the scope of treason was being stretched beyond traditional constitutional limits. The proceedings against Mortimer featured elements that had appeared previously, including men's speech punished as material acts and the idea that words or deeds against the king were also attacks on the nation. There were also some significant differences. One of these was the new statutory offence of escaping from prison, which was to be treated

[137] For a wide-ranging analysis of this shift, see Ruddick, *English Identity and Political Culture in the Fourteenth Century*.

[138] Powell, 'The Strange Death of Sir John Mortimer'.

as tantamount to a confession of treason. This law inverted the more familiar progression from men's thoughts to words to deeds, for now a physical act was equated to a verbal utterance – that of judicial confession. Moreover, Mortimer was indicted for speech that differed both in kind and degree from the overt rejections of Lancastrian rule discussed previously and when a trial jury refused to condemn it, the state was forced to other expedients to get its man. Nevertheless, the expansive conception of treasonous speech in the Mortimer indictments foreshadowed statutory sanctions on seditious or merely insulting speech seen in Tudor treason laws.[139]

Mortimer enjoyed a conventional military career, appearing first as an esquire in Guyenne in 1401 and going on to serve in various capacities under Henry IV and Henry V. He fought at Agincourt and was knighted before 1417, when he was given a senior naval command to patrol the Channel and protect English shipping.[140] Something drastic changed, though, between then and February 1418, when Mortimer was forced to take out an enormous surety for 1000*l* and swear to 'bear himself toward the king as his true liege'.[141] In December 1418, he was imprisoned. There is no record of the reasons for his arrest but he was still in the Tower when he was formally indicted in 1420. This indictment stated that in the summer of 1418, in the town of St Albans, Mortimer had treasonously said that he wished Henry were a pauper like he was, and that if he was with the king of France and had enough men, he would destroy Henry and push him out of Normandy.[142]

This indictment departed from earlier prosecutions involving deviant political speech. First, there were no details of where or in what context Mortimer's words were uttered, and there were no bills being posted or petitions being circulated. The indictment said only that Mortimer's remarks were made 'in the town', implying that he may simply have been overheard. More importantly, Mortimer did not say anything that challenged Henry V's legitimacy or his kingship. He did not raise the ghost of Richard II or refer to any alternative claim in the name of a purported Mortimer relative; nor did he call the king 'Henry of Lancaster'. He did not criticise excessive taxation or wicked counsellors. His comments about wishing the king were as poor as he was – perhaps a complaint related to the surety – and driving Henry out of Normandy were typical of the commonplace griping voiced in streets, taverns and marketplaces. They echoed, albeit in cruder terms, criticisms being voiced in parliament by 1419 about the mounting costs of Henry's increasingly unpopular French campaign and the consequent diversion of English tax

139 Bellamy, *Tudor Law of Treason*, pp. 30–6, 51–9; Roger B. Manning, 'The Origins of the Doctrine of Sedition', *Albion* 12 (1980), 99–121.

140 Powell, 'The Strange Death of Sir John Mortimer', pp. 85–6.

141 *CCR, 1413–1419*, pp. 456–7.

142 TNA KB 9/218/2 m. 45.

revenues to Normandy.[143] Even for the authorities, it seems it was a step too far to treat such vague grumblings as treason because Mortimer was not tried. The indictment bore witness to its own uncertainty on this point, for there was no trace of the standard legal rhetoric of treason in the form of charges that the offender had 'compassed and imagined' the death of the king.

Although this first attempt to prosecute Mortimer was not tested in court, he remained a prisoner in the Tower until April 1422, when he managed to escape along with Thomas Payn, formerly secretary to Sir John Oldcastle, and two foreign prisoners of war. Mortimer was soon recaptured and on 15 May he was again indicted for treason. This time, the charges were more targeted. First, he had 'falsely and treasonously conspired and imagined the death of our lord the king and many other evil and wicked things against the king and his realm of England', and along with his accomplices, he had conspired 'to bring about the destruction of the person of … the king and of the realm'.[144] This rhetoric had become typical of treason indictments and it identified the traitor as posing a material threat to the person of the king but also to the realm and people of England. The next charge was more unusual: Mortimer had treasonably conspired to escape the Tower and to help the king's prisoners to escape.[145] One of these men was Johan de Brakemonde, a knight in service to the dauphin of France, and the other was Martalinus de Flisca of Genoa; both were described as 'mortal enemies of the king and realm'.[146] By accusing Mortimer of aiding foreign 'enemies of the realm', the indictment portrayed him as a traitor to his nation as well as his king. Mortimer's identity as a false knight was emphasised in additional charges that he planned to go into Wales and raise a rebellion to make war on England, and that he intended to become a retainer of the dauphin of France and prey on English shipping in the Channel. Disguising his chivalric betrayals, Mortimer would then infiltrate 'English castles and towns in France with many soldiers, by acting as if they were true and loyal English men' ('tanquam essent veri Anglia et fideles').[147] The indictment concluded that Mortimer had planned and done these things contrary to his allegiance to the king and to the realm of England. In other words, he was to be viewed as a threat to the English nation and Englishmen at home and abroad, as well as to the king.

When Mortimer appeared before King's Bench, he pleaded not guilty and asked for a jury trial. Given the evidence of his escape with two prisoners

143 Given-Wilson, 'Introduction' to *PROME*, 'Henry V: October 1419'; G. L. Harriss, 'The Management of Parliament', *Henry V: The Practice of Kingship*, pp. 137–58 (pp. 148–51).

144 TNA KB 27/644 Rex m. 11.

145 While prison escapes had been mentioned as part of previous treason trials, such as that of Sir John Oldcastle, conviction had on those occasions been secured on other grounds. On the novelty of this charge: Bellamy, *Law of Treason*, pp. 130, 172–3.

146 TNA KB 27/644 Rex m. 11.

147 Ibid.

of war, and the harm he allegedly intended to wreak on English military and merchant interests, a jury of London men could have been expected to have no hesitation in convicting Mortimer. This was clearly the verdict Henry and his justices were anticipating, for they would not have brought the case to trial otherwise; they had already shown willing to keep Mortimer imprisoned without trial indefinitely.[148] Moreover, the jury had been selected and sworn in under the king's serjeants, a procedural formality that flagged Henry's personal interest in the trial. Despite this careful groundwork, the jury acquitted Mortimer. The verdict was an unwelcome surprise to the judges. They taxed the jurors as to whether or not they had understood their duty in rendering the verdict, to which the jury replied in the affirmative and restated their verdict of 'not guilty'.[149]

Even though the jurymen unequivocally vouched that Mortimer was not guilty of treason, he was sent back to the Tower. Five days later, the 1420 indictment for treasonous words was revived and delivered into King's Bench but once more, it was not taken to trial. Reluctance to put Mortimer in front of another jury indicates royal judicial officials doubted their ability to have their definition of treason accepted by the political community. Instead on 27 May, Mortimer was removed for a time to the Lancastrian stronghold of Pevensey Castle, but by the end of 1423 he was back in the Tower.[150] After Henry V's death in August 1422, he had become the problem of the conciliar regime of the infant Henry VI.[151]

In the parliament that ran from October 1423 to February 1424, steps were taken to get rid of Mortimer once and for all. First, a new statute of treasons was enacted.[152] The Commons' petition that heralded its introduction into parliament requested that if any man was arrested on an indictment, appeal or even the mere suspicion of treason, 'and is committed and detained in the king's prison for any reason, and escapes voluntarily from the said prison, that such an escape shall be adjudged and declared treason'.[153] The petition acknowledged that breaking prison was outside the scope of the 1352 statute; nevertheless, it was now to be treated as a voluntary admission of guilt and the offender was to be convicted without trial. In law, this transformed the physical act of breaking prison into the speech act of confession. The phrase 'detained … for any reason' left a further loophole. It meant that even men

148 This was in spite of three petitions from Mortimer to the Commons and Lords in parliament, pleading for their intercession with the king: SC 8/125/6236 (May 1421); SC 8/24/1171 (December 1421); SC 8/336/15882 (October 1423).

149 TNA KB 27/644 Rex m. 11. See also Powell, 'The Strange Death of Sir John Mortimer', p. 88 n. 32.

150 *CCR, 1419–1422*, p. 242.

151 Henry V's brother Humphrey, duke of Gloucester, was the Protector.

152 *Statutes*, II, pp. 226–7 (c. xxi).

153 *PROME*, 'Henry VI: October 1423', Item Sixty.

who had not been subject to any formal accusation or legal procedure could still be executed as confessed traitors if they broke prison. Here was a law that was ripe for abuse, a concern that led the Commons to conclude their petition by requesting that it should stay in effect only until the next parliament. This was just long enough for it to be used against Mortimer. After the statute was enacted, the jailer William Kyng, a servant of Robert Scot the lieutenant of the Tower, conveniently helped Mortimer to escape. He was promptly recaptured, indicted and on 26 February, brought before parliament to be adjudged a traitor.[154]

Despite the reach of the new statute, other steps had also been taken to ensure Mortimer's conviction. On 14 February William Kyng told parliament that while Mortimer was in prison, he had spoken against the king and had offered the jailer bribes to help him escape to carry out his treasonous plans. Kyng's testimony, which does not appear in the parliament roll but which was recorded by a London chronicler, disclosed that the jailer was acting on orders as an *agent provocateur*.[155] Kyng described winning over Mortimer's trust by telling him 'he loved hym and wold love hym kyndely and truely' though he would not offend Henry VI's regent, Humphrey duke of Gloucester, nor any 'true liege man of the kyng', a qualifier the jailer probably hoped would protect him from repercussions.[156] Kyng recounted telling his master, Scot, 'that Mortymer was false and wolde be false prisoner, if he myght', to which Scot replied that if Mortimer made any intimations of escape, Kyng should go along with him and 'favour him as his frende'. Kyng then provided the only evidence that Mortimer had voiced any criticisms about Lancastrian legitimacy or the Mortimer claim, stating that when he asked Mortimer what he planned to do after escaping, Mortimer said he would go to Wales and raise an army:

> And seid he wolde fere the Duke of Gloucestre and smyte of his hedde and al the Lordes heddes … And he seid also that therle of the March was but a dawe, save that he was the grettist, noblist, and worthiest blood of this land … And this Mortymer seid, that therle of the March shulde be kyng, if he had right and trouth And he shulde be his here [heir]. And if therle of the March wolde not take the Rule of the Realme and the Crowne, this Mortymer seid that he wolde take upon hym the Rule and the Crowne for he was next heir thereto.[157]

To these damning accusations, Kyng added that Mortimer had told him that

154 Ibid., Item Eighteen.

155 BL Cotton Julius B I, fols. 67v–68v. See also *Chronicles of London (1189–1509)*, ed. Charles Lethbridge Kingsford (Oxford, 1905), pp. 282–3. In other respects, the chronicle account closely follows the parliament roll so there is no reason to doubt that this part of the narrative is unreliable.

156 BL Cotton Julius B I, fol. 67v.

157 Ibid., fols. 68–68v.

if his plans in Wales did not work out, he would join the dauphin in France. The account ended with Kyng offering to prove the truth of his testimony 'upon the same Mortimer with his body'.[158] That Kyng's appearance before parliament was an elaborate set-up was made clear when, immediately after his challenge to combat, the chronicler reported that the new statute had been enacted and Mortimer had subsequently escaped, been recaptured, and was by the authority of parliament 'dampned to be drawen and hanged as for a treitour'.[159]

Kyng's allegations fit the model of previous treason convictions involving rash talk that threatened to reignite the question of Lancastrian legitimacy. The reference to March as a 'dawe' or halfwit who should assert his title to the throne but lacked the strength to do so was reminiscent of Sir Thomas Grey's confession that the Southampton plotters had thought March 'but a hog', and that Lescrope had to speak 'the highest and the haughtiest' to him to prompt him to 'challenge his right'.[160] Other elements, such as the reference to Mortimer joining forces with the dauphin, were drawn from the unsuccessful indictment of 1422. However, the Mortimer prosecution went further because it was not the king who was named as the traitor's main target, but the duke of Gloucester and other lords. While threats against Henry V's sons, brothers and other magnates had featured in treason indictments since the early 1400s, these crimes were always twinned with plotting the death of the king. To consider threats to the duke or to other lords as treason even in the absence of any explicit threat to the king was a novel construction that extended the scope of treason law to encompass attacks on the broader ruling elite, including men beyond the immediate royal patrilineage.

The record of Mortimer's conviction reinforced the message that he was a threat to the English political community as a whole, not only to the king or his royal uncles. After the charges against Mortimer were read out to him as he stood before parliament, the Commons 'affirmed the indictment in all respects as a true and faithful indictment' and 'beseeched' the Lords to do the same.[161] Several times, the record says the indictment was found true by the *tota communitas*, terminology that encompassed the Commons in parliament but also the community of the realm. The active part played by the Commons in finding the verdict true, rather than simply confirming an existing judgment, was a telling contrast to the parliamentary convictions of Northumberland in 1406, Oldcastle in 1417, and Lescrope, Grey and Cambridge in 1415. In 1406, the Commons had simply asked to be told what action would be taken against the rebel earl; in Oldcastle's case they petitioned that the 1414 judgment of King's Bench be enforced. Similar wording was used about Lescrope and his

158 Ibid., fol. 68v.

159 Ibid.

160 'Appendix II', pp. 162–3. 'Dawe' meaning 'a stupid fellow': *MED*.

161 *PROME*, 'Henry VI: October 1423', Item Eighteen.

fellows, with the Commons requesting that the record of the Southampton tribunal be affirmed in parliament. Bellamy argued that in Mortimer's case the Commons viewed themselves as a grand jury sitting on an inquest.[162] This likely overstates their control of parliamentary judicial processes but nevertheless, by presenting the Commons as active participants in finding the verdict, the royal council was able to portray the dubious conviction of Mortimer as a lawful judgment endorsed by the national political community.

Mortimer's status as an enemy of the realm was further reinforced in his sentence. He was to be:

> Led to the aforesaid Tower and then drawn through the centre of the aforesaid city up to the gallows at Tyburn, and be hung on the gallows ... and stretched out on the ground, and his head cut off, and his intestines burnt, and his body divided into four parts, and his head placed on the gate of London bridge, and the said four parts of his body be put separately on the other four gates of London.[163]

This unusually harsh punishment and the prominent display of Mortimer's mutilated corpse before the London public marked him out as a traitor to the king but also, given the charges against him, to the nation of England. Degraded and deprived of his manly identity as a knight and an English political subject, his male body was torn asunder to preserve the integrity of the masculine body politic of the realm.

The reasons for Mortimer's long persecution and his violent death remain a mystery. Powell surmised that he can only have been targeted because of his name, accepting as unproblematic the jailer William Kyng's testimony that Mortimer had boasted of being heir to the earl of March and that he intended to claim the throne himself. While agreeing that no connection can be traced between Mortimer and the earls of March, Powell argued 'such a relationship must surely have existed, however, for without it the Lancastrian regime's vendetta against [him] is incomprehensible'.[164] It is however possible that it was not Mortimer himself who was the source of the government's anxieties but that, in the wake of the Southampton plot, Henry V worried that another group of nobles might be using him as a front for their own ends. Although he was a knight of modest means and obscure parentage, Mortimer had some powerful associates. He had no problems finding guarantors for the 1000*l* in 1418; in February 1420, a mainprise made in Chancery named James earl of Ormond as one of five guarantors for Mortimer's good behaviour, pledging £40 that he would be 'a true prisoner to the king'.[165] As a member of the Irish nobility, Ormond might have had connections to the earl of March, who had

162 Bellamy, *Law of Treason*, p. 172.

163 *PROME*, 'Henry VI: October 1423', Item Eighteen.

164 Powell, 'The Strange Death of Sir John Mortimer', pp. 88, 91.

165 *CCR, 1419–1422*, p. 63.

extensive estates in Ireland and was to be appointed the king's lieutenant there in March 1423.[166]

There is another angle from which this case starts to make more sense. The Lancastrian regime's persecution of Mortimer indicates continuing anxieties about dynastic security, even after the military success of Agincourt and the diplomatic coup of 1420's Treaty of Troyes, which made Henry heir to the French throne. This might seem puzzling but it is important to note that despite the initial patriotic zeal for Henry's French wars, by 1420 support was waning and the Commons were increasingly reluctant to grant additional subsidies. The English political community also had reservations about the Treaty of Troyes, reflected in Commons' petitions asking that English taxes not be diverted to government in France and urging that the two realms the Lancastrians now claimed should be kept quite separate.[167] Powell assumed that when the regime went after Mortimer, it was reacting to a genuine threat (however impotent). Yet given the general climate of increasing political criticism, it is perhaps more plausible that in the absence of any obvious connection to the earls of March, Mortimer's discontented ramblings in combination with his emblematic name presented the Lancastrians with a prime opportunity to enact some powerful political theatre at a time when an infant king, a regency council, and an expensive and increasingly unpopular war created significant potential for instability and unrest.

There are clues to this rationale in the 1420 and 1422 indictments, neither of which mentioned the Mortimer claim or Lancastrian legitimacy. These elements did not appear at all until the case came before the 1423 parliament and even then only in the suspect testimony of Mortimer's jailer. The elaborate scheme used to finally dispatch Mortimer allowed the royal council to raise the Mortimer claim, and therefore the issue of Lancastrian legitimacy, in the public political sphere explicitly in order to quash it. There was precedent for this strategy. Discussing earlier treason cases involving the Ricardian rumour, McNiven argued that it was in the Lancastrian regime's interests to allow stories of the former king's survival to circulate and to associate them with proclamations supporting the Mortimer claim or with more pragmatic complaints about judicial corruption and excessive taxation. The government could then 'charge people with taking a treasonable stance which also had the merit of being based on nonsense, and use this claim to discredit more rational challenges to Lancastrian authority'.[168] After the Southampton plotters had been exposed and destroyed, the Mortimer claim could be seen

166 For the Mortimer family's land-holdings: Alistair Dunn, 'Richard II and the Mortimer Inheritance', *Fourteenth Century England II*, ed. Chris Given-Wilson (Woodbridge, 2002), pp. 159–70.

167 Allmand, *Henry V*, pp. 366–7, 376–7; Harriss, 'The Management of Parliament', pp. 150–1.

168 McNiven, 'Rebellion, Sedition', p. 117.

in the same light. The Southampton affair revealed that even amongst the conspirators, the earl of March was not considered a serious contender for the throne.[169] Once March had divulged the plot to Henry V and helped to convict his former allies as traitors, the teeth had been drawn on any credible threat from that quarter. In 1424, Mortimer was not only hanged and beheaded, but he also suffered the most brutal and degrading punishments for treason, those of disembowelling and quartering. By making such a graphic public example of him, Henry VI's council made a pre-emptive strike against anyone else who would grasp the opportunities created by regime change and a royal minority to raise questions about the legitimacy or effectiveness of Lancastrian government.

The conviction of Mortimer by the *tota communitas* represented in parliament, followed by the gruesome spectacle of his punishment, was a political message about cause-and-effect that would have lingered in the public imagination through the post-mortem display of his body parts in prominent sites around the city. As such, it had both immediate and longer-term consequences. The execution ritual showed that Mortimer had paid the ultimate penalty for his past acts of treason, but it was also intended to foreclose on future acts of critical political speech. This was a chilling response to men like the jurors of 1422, who had decided that despite Mortimer's words and intentions against the king and the English nation, he was not guilty of treason. Mortimer's conviction was finally achieved only through a series of dubious legal machinations. Regardless of irregular procedures, this outcome created a precedent for the punishment of less specific, more equivocal expressions of political dissent as acts of treason. We can therefore trace connections between Mortimer's case and the more expansive terms in which, from the later fifteenth century onwards, critical, insulting or even 'annoying' political speech against the king or the public authority vested in the officers and symbols of the state was defined and punished as treason.[170]

Between the Percy rebellions in the early 1400s and Mortimer's death in 1424, treason prosecutions reflected and helped to foster a transformation in the constitutional relationship between the king, the English state and its political subjects. The traditional perception of treason as the inversion of knighthood was still a powerful cultural influence on the way traitors were perceived, and chivalric discourses were deployed by the accused to defend themselves as loyal subjects and true men. However, in the legal sphere

[169] The conspirators had viewed him as an inferior alternative to either Richard, if he were alive, or to a more general northern rebellion.

[170] For examples of this expansion: Wicker, 'The Politics of Vernacular Speech'; Harris, 'Censoring Disobedient Subjects'. Bellamy (*Tudor Law of Treason*, p. 25) discusses a 1531 statute which defined as treasonous any activities that were contrived to 'annoy the king, his ambassadors, messengers or servants when they were executing the king's business', along with provisions against slandering 'the royal jurisdiction'.

the idea of treason as a personal betrayal of homosocial bonds was being displaced by more expansive definitions of offenders as men who had betrayed their nation, the Christian community and the collective interests of the realm. This in turn helped to underpin a broader transition in the way men envisaged and performed political subjecthood, marked by a gradual shift away from viewing allegiance in terms of their individual manly loyalty to the king, to viewing loyalty as being constituted in relation to the more abstract entities of the nation, the English people and the public authority of the state.

CONCLUSION

Conflicts over treason are at their root conflicts over how constitutional structures and relationships are conceptualised and made manifest. By describing the traitor's offences and identifying the entities against which they offend, treason laws inscribe the limits of legitimate authority in the polity and delineate the nature and sources of that authority. As a corollary, when the law strips traitors of their subjecthood – a punishment that in medieval England usually meant the loss of life itself – processes of trial and punishment determine how political subjects are constituted in relation to sovereign authority and the individuals and entities that embody it. Any history of treason is therefore also inherently an inquiry into political thought and practice, and the limits of the politically possible at any particular historical juncture. To date, legal scholars and constitutional historians have developed interpretations of treason law in medieval England largely without regard to gender. This has rendered invisible the pivotal role of masculine performance in negotiating constitutional conflicts over where sovereign power lay and how it could be wielded. That the medieval body politic was envisaged by default as a male body, functioning primarily through relationships between men, has perhaps seemed so obvious as to require no critical analysis. Outside a handful of pioneering studies on kingship and masculinity, the gendered nature of the polity and its implications for the ways power was claimed, performed and resisted are still too often overlooked in political and legal histories of medieval England.[1]

Viewing treason through the lens of gender, this study has laid bare the male body as the discursive, conceptual and material nexus of conflicts over royal legitimacy, sovereign authority and loyal political subjecthood. This has profound implications for the ways we understand treason as a legal construct, a political weapon, a tool for constitutional thinking and as a cultural category that helped to construct and mediate masculine identity in medieval England. As I have shown, while the technical parameters of treason in any particular case were uncertain and subject to debate, shifting legal definitions were nevertheless constructed upon and negotiated through a shared political

1 Separately, scholars of medieval queenship have effectively incorporated gender into accounts of political history, although with the focus on women rather than men.

imaginary in which the traitor stood as the opposite of the true man. Treason had its origin in the breaking of bonds between men, bonds most powerfully embodied in the oaths that sealed homosocial loyalties and stood as public guarantors of honourable true manhood. The crime of treason was proved upon men's bodies in trials by combat, where men's words were made flesh and their truth was tested before God. It was expiated though public rituals of execution, when the bodies of individual men were divided and destroyed to preserve the conceptual unity of the masculine body politic.

The history of treason in medieval England is incomplete without gender because it was anxieties about masculine honour, homosocial fidelity, kingship and royal legitimacy that fuelled the treason proceedings discussed in this book. At the heart of the political traumas of Richard II's reign were contests over the king's manly honour and his attempts to embody and exercise sovereign authority as an adult male monarch. His allies and his opponents saw each other and were seen in terms of corrupted homosocial affinities and of false knighthood that undermined the idealised chivalric bonds between the king and the nobles who saw themselves as his natural advisers. According to some commentators, the unnatural bonds between Richard and the men surrounding him had even crossed the line into that most pernicious inversion of natural gender order, as accusations of treason were coupled to hints of sodomy. In 1388 and 1397, the legal rhetoric of treason proceedings was heavily inflected by discourses of true and false manhood. However, as cases like that of Robert de Vere and the duke of Gloucester showed, the true man and the traitor were mutually constitutive identities that could not always be easily separated in practice. De Vere's actions in support of Richard at Radcot Bridge saw him branded a traitor but he could equally be seen as a true man and ideal knight, performing loyal military service in defence of his lord. Gloucester's last words affirmed that his resort to honourable knightly *diffidatio* had been forced upon him by the king's deceptions and oath-breaking. His vernacular first-person confession authenticated his avowal that he had acted in good faith to preserve Richard's honour as well as the common good of the realm. In a deadly verbal combat, Arundel, too, wagered his own chivalric honour and the backing of the 'true commons' against the liars and false men surrounding the king, and won for himself a brief political martyrdom.

For Henry IV, treason trials provided ideal opportunities to perform legitimacy by binding his own usurping manly body and the masculine social body of his Lancastrian patrilineage more tightly to the political body of the crown. In proceedings against the Counter-Appellants and the Epiphany rebels, and in the dispute between Morley and Salisbury, the shifting ground of statutory enactments and the flexible definitions of treason deployed in parliament and the Court of Chivalry incorporated interpretations of treason as an attack on the *chose publique*, the *communalté* and the English language, which stood as a metonym for English nationhood. When Henry defined acts against his person as treason against the public authority of the state, the community of the realm and the nation of England, this strengthened his own claim to embody sovereign authority. He then reinforced his hold on the throne by exercising royal justice against his most powerful subjects. Long after the constitutional rupture of 1399, the act of separating the crown from Richard's defective male body and of attaching it to the Lancastrian king and his patrilineage continued to be re-enacted through the rhetoric of treason proceedings. The 1413 trial of John Wyghtlok showed that even many years after his father's accession, Henry V still saw the need to retell the story of Richard's removal and to assert his own legitimacy on the grounds of dynastic bloodright and the law of patrilineal succession.

For the men who took the decision to depose Richard and replace him with Henry, one compelling reason for pursuing such a risky path had been that Henry was 'a man not a boy'. Henry exploited his early chivalric reputation, presenting himself to the political community as a honourable and true man who embodied all the masculine virtues the English expected in their kings. However, Henry IV's failures of chivalric honour – most emblematically represented in accusations of oath-breaking and murder – soon emerged as formidable grounds for criticism and resistance to his rule, alongside the more fundamental question of his legitimacy. His need to extract repeated oaths of loyalty to himself and his sons, backed up by the novel 1406 succession statute, reflected abiding Lancastrian insecurities about the inherent fragility of political ties between men upon which monarchical rule depended. These insecurities found expression in generalised charges that traitors intended to destroy the bonds of love and allegiance between the king and his subjects, as well as in more specific fears about false covine and secret contracts of confederacy. Masculine fidelity secured by oaths was valorised in theory but became problematic in practice, because the questions always lurked of 'fidelity to whom?' and 'for what ends?' These were constitutional questions, worrying at the problem of where sovereign power lay and how a tyrannical or illegitimate king could be challenged. Men could credibly justify their resistance to Henry on the grounds he was an oath-breaker and a usurper, perhaps even a murderer, and they countered treason charges by avowing themselves as true men to the crown, the *res publica* or the wrongfully deposed king.

Under Richard II and the Lancastrian kings, changes in the way treason was defined and prosecuted were the result of opportunist responses to urgent political problems rather than the product of considered jurisprudential thinking. Nevertheless, they had far-reaching constitutional impacts. As has been seen, it was not only elite men close to the king who faced charges of treason. As critiques of Lancastrian kingship multiplied and circulated in taverns, streets and market squares, and through the popular medium of handbills and public petitions, men from all walks of life were accused of treason for denigrating the king or denying his right to rule. To shore up Lancastrian legitimacy, new and progressively more expansive definitions of treason were being endorsed in common law through treason trials in King's Bench. Indictments and sentencing clauses expressed the traditional understanding of treason as an attack on the person of the king or his sons, but this was augmented by rhetorical constructions that defined traitors as enemies of the law and language of England; as threats to the *populum*, estates, and the national community; or, in the case of the Oldcastle rebellion, as threats to the *majestas* of the realm, now fully abstracted from the body of the king. Reading trial records, legislation and other evidence through the framework of gender analysis reveals the masculine body politic being imagined and produced through discourses of treason that turned on questions of male honour and homosocial loyalties. As the scope of treason expanded, the constitutional entities of the crown and community of the realm were also implicitly masculinised as they were bound to (or divided from) the male body of the king and the masculine social body of his patrilineage. Even such abstract constructions as the *chose publique*, the *majestas* of the realm or the English nation were masculinised through their utter entanglement in battles fought over true and false manhood – whether that of the king or of those who defied him and denied his legitimacy.

While traditional legal and political approaches to the history of treason in medieval England are necessary, this study has shown they are not sufficient to tell the full story. Incorporating gender into the analysis has exposed deeper cultural dynamics that shaped the actions of individuals and therefore influenced the way events unfolded. Gender also explains important gaps in our current understanding of how treason was defined and prosecuted, and provides wider insights into how political subjecthood was negotiated and performed. As has been seen, very few women were ever implicated in treason proceedings and those who were quickly retreated to the sidelines. Some women came into and disappeared from the records in anonymity, such as the tailor's wife who voiced a scathing denunciation of Henry IV and his son, or the women who testified to seeing Richard alive and well in Westminster two years after his death. Higher profile women like Maud de Vere and Constance Despenser became embroiled in and even instigated treasonous plots but they were awarded more private and far less severe punishments than their male accomplices. This reflected the belief that women lacked political agency by definition and therefore could not be culpable of the political crime of treason. Excluding women altogether from the category of people who could commit treason spared women the brutal punishments inflicted on men but at the same time, treason laws were one more factor that implicitly denied women the privileges of political subjecthood. It is tempting to speculate that women's perceived lack of agency might paradoxically have given them greater freedom to operate below the radar of masculine authorities. This is a question beyond the scope of the current study but it certainly warrants further investigation.

Significantly, it is gender that explains the establishment of critical legal precedents concerning treasonous speech that went on to underpin repressive early modern treason laws. Scholars have traditionally examined this development from the standpoint of conventional legal history, with debates centring on whether the prosecution of speech – whether verbal or textual – in the absence of overt acts was covered by the 1352 statute and therefore constitutionally valid. Approaching treason as a cultural category and not merely a legal one, I have demonstrated that this crucial legal shift is better understood as the product of a sociocultural context in which men's speech was a tangible element of manly embodiment. When men spoke their words in public and avowed them as true, it transmuted masculine speech acts into material deeds that could do corporeal harm. This was a legal interpretation that reflected anxieties about 'sins of the tongue' such as defamation and blasphemy, and the gendered distinction that had by the later fourteenth century developed between words as mere words and words as injurious deeds. It was this cultural transformation that fostered a judicial environment in which a man's deviant political speech could justifiably and logically be punished under the common law as a physical act of treason.

In Pollock and Maitland's classic study of English legal history, treason was evocatively described as 'a crime which has a vague circumference and more than one centre'.[2] Legal scholars have agreed on its constitutional and political significance in medieval England while struggling to pin down its exact meaning and scope, differing over how it was defined in statutes and comparing this to prosecutorial practice. I have worked from an alternative perspective that fully incorporates cultural perceptions of treason into the analysis and that considers not only how the authorities defined treason in statutes and prosecution narratives, but also the varied defensive strategies of the men accused. This approach confirms that the meanings of treason were always too fluid and contested to be contained by any one definition. As has been seen, despite legal precedents that constructed treason as a crime against the state, treason continued to exist along a continuum, with customary notions of treason as an intimate betrayal or a violation of homosocial loyalties sometimes reinforcing and sometimes contesting emerging perceptions of treason as a crime against the *res publica* or as the betrayal of the English nation. Treason could never be a matter of black-and-white determination because its meanings rested upon the equally unstable foundations of true and false manhood. True manhood was embodied and proved through the performance of shared masculine virtues of honour, worship, loyalty and service, but asserting identity as a true man was never a straightforward matter of 'ticking the boxes'. A man's true (or false) manhood depended entirely upon recognition and acceptance of his masculine status by other men, so that trueness had to be repeatedly enacted and defended. As legal categories, the

2 F. Pollock and F. W. Maitland, *The History of English Law before the Time of Edward I*, II (Cambridge, 1895), p. 503.

traitor and the true man were therefore unfixed identities, always subject to contest because they relied upon perception and on the consistency and authenticity of a man's embodiment of trueness in the eyes of other men. By fully integrating questions of gender and masculine performance, my exploration of treason helps to explain the endemic instability that characterised late medieval English political culture. The political system depended on personal relationships between individual men to function – relationships of trust, good lordship, obedience and service that were secured by verbal oaths and bodily performance. However, treason trials exposed just how fragile those relationships were and how difficult it could be to distinguish the true man from the traitor.

The legal and constitutional uncertainties of treason derived from the provisional and mutable nature of manhood itself, and this investigation proffers broader insights into masculine identity and political subjecthood in medieval England. In their public speech, petitions, political manifestos and letters, political dissenters and accused traitors deployed the language of true manhood to appeal to a constellation of shared masculine values and expectations. However, these values were internalised and performed in different ways to justify political resistance or to enact loyal political subjecthood. For men like Sir Simon Burley and Lord Morley, true manhood meant true knighthood. They drew on the traditional chivalric understanding of treason as a man's intimate betrayal of his lord and sought to defend their knightly honour by resort to the chivalric procedure of trial by combat. In their manifesto, the Percys invoked chivalric values when they condemned Henry IV for his unknightly oath-breaking, a fundamental violation of honour that rendered his kingship illegitimate. Yet while they argued for the rights of the earl of March as the alternative candidate, they positioned themselves more overtly as manly defenders of the common good and the *res publica*. For men of more ordinary status, trueness was also a core value, but it was enacted through the model of civic manhood. Civic manhood encompassed universal virtues of honour, loyalty and service but these were adapted to the literate civic sphere and the practical possibilities of urban men of more middling status. For these men, service was far more likely to be intellectual, administrative or financial than martial, and their political resistance took the form of bill casting and public petitioning rather than armed rebellion. The political ideals of obedience to right order and service to the common good were of paramount importance in civic culture. This was exemplified in Wyghtlok's petition, where he identified himself as a long-serving yeoman to King Richard but ultimately justified his actions as a true man to the crown, commons and 'true people' of the realm. Through these varying expressions of political agency and political resistance, we can see that although chivalric manhood might have been a hegemonic ideal in medieval England, it was matched by different but equally powerful performances of civic manhood.

While the main intervention of this study has been to place gender at the centre of conflicts over treason, close reading of trial records and other sources has also generated new knowledge about vernacularity and linguistic politics in late medieval England. As this study has demonstrated, prosecution narratives often incorporated first-person English directly into the official legal record, sandwiched between the third-person French of coerced confessions or witness testimony and the formalised Latin of indictments and sentencing clauses. This usage was unusual because while English was the aural language of the common law, French and Latin were still used almost exclusively in formal written records. The English-language material incorporated into trial records was either endorsed as 'written by my own hand' or it appeared in the form of copies of bills or letters being circulated by accused traitors. From the care taken to provide accurate transcriptions, and the way the English content was situated in relation to French and Latin components, it becomes clear that this was intended to serve as material proof of treason in the traitor's own words, the textual equivalent of his oral confession before the court. This would be consistent with the growing status of English as a language of record in other government contexts, and with the power attributed to the vernacular to endorse a written text as an authentic and accurate proxy for an oral/aural proceeding.

However, as an authenticating device, English could subvert as well as authorise and the interaction of Latin, French and vernacular discourses could open fractures in prosecution narratives. In the confessions of men like the earl of Cambridge and Abbot Thomas, first-person English verified their supplications as sincere, but it also enabled evasion, as they deflected the fault onto others while at the same time avowing they remained the king's loyal liege men. The power of the vernacular to authenticate the veracity of resistant performances of true manhood and loyal subjecthood was nowhere more apparent than in the post-mortem conviction of the duke of Gloucester. His first-person confessional text had to be heavily edited before it could be presented publicly before the 1397 parliament, and the care taken to falsify the record in this way highlights the incendiary potential of a man's sworn word to undermine the official prosecution narrative against him. From the perspective of linguistic politics, as well as legal culture and scribal practices, this study adds to the growing body of research that considers the use of English in government contexts. Importantly, by focusing in detail on records relating to the prosecution of treason, it sheds new light on operations of power and on the way language itself functioned in judicial contexts to negotiate the relationship between the state and political subjects.

The *longue durée* history of treason shows that many of the themes I have explored here continued to resonate, not only throughout the early modern period but also down to the present day. In a tense political climate where modern democracies are struggling to balance principles of freedom of speech with curbs on public 'hate speech', the contested status of dissenting political speech in late medieval England may seem eerily familiar. Now as much as in the fifteenth century, the boundaries between politically offensive but legally allowable speech and words that have crossed a line to become criminal actions remain ill-defined and open to dispute. Over the years I was working on this book, discourses of treason once again became prominent in the public political sphere. Brexit campaigners were terming their opponents 'enemies of the people' and accusing them of betraying the nation; Chinese state media were condemning Hong Kong's pro-democracy protestors as traitors; and in the United States, debate raged over whether government whistle-blowers were 'traitors' or 'patriots'.[3] Elsewhere, the parallels were more direct, as some politicians contemplated reviving the 1352 treason statute to prosecute citizens fighting for Islamic State.[4] These discourses of treason carry inherent assumptions about who does and does not belong. When we talk about loyalty and betrayal, we are by implication debating what it is that defines the political subject or citizen, and therefore what makes any individual someone who merits the protections and privileges that status entails. This necessarily forces us to engage with enduring questions of where sovereign power lies; how individuals are constituted in relation to that power; and what the limits of legitimate political authority are, especially as it is expressed in the coercive power to execute justice. Contextualising our current legal and constitutional debates within the longer history of treason may help us to better grasp the principles at stake and perhaps, develop more nuanced judicial and political responses to contemporary challenges.

3 James Blitz, 'Brexit Briefing: Enemies of the People', *Financial Times*, 5 November 2016, <https://www.ft.com/content/010325da-a28a-11e6-82c3-4351ce86813f> [accessed 1 October 2019]; 'More Americans see man who leaked NSA secrets as 'patriot' than traitor: Poll', *Reuters*, 13 June 2013, <https://www.reuters.com/article/us-usa-security-poll/more-americans-see-man-who-leaked-nsa-secrets-as-patriot-than-traitor-poll-idUSBRE95B1AF20130612> [accessed 25 September 2015].

4 'The Guardian view on fighting Isis: medieval treason laws are the wrong weapon', *The Guardian*, 19 October 2014, <https://www.theguardian.com/commentisfree/2014/oct/19/guardian-view-on-fighting-isis-trason-laws-wrong-weapon> [accessed 6 November, 2016].

BIBLIOGRAPHY

MANUSCRIPT SOURCES

London, The National Archives

C 49	Chancery and Exchequer: King's Remembrancer, Parliamentary and Council Proceedings
E 30	Exchequer: Treasury of Receipt, Diplomatic Documents
E 101/132	Exchequer: King's Remembrancer, Various Accounts
E 136/108	Exchequer: King's Remembrancer, Escheators' Particulars of Account
E 163	Exchequer: King's Remembrancer, Miscellanea
JUST 1	Justices in Eyre, of Assize, of Oyer and Terminer, and of the Peace: Rolls and Files
KB 9	Court of King's Bench, Crown Side: Indictment Files, Oyer and Terminer Files and Information Files
KB 27	Court of King's Bench, Plea and Crown Sides: Coram Rege Rolls
KB 29	Court of King's Bench, Crown Side: Controlment Rolls and other Memoranda Rolls of the Clerk of the Crown
SC 8	Special Collections: Ancient Petitions

London, British Library

Additional MS 38525
Cotton Cleopatra F III
Cotton Julius B I
Cotton Vespasian C XIV
Cotton Vespasian F III

PRINTED PRIMARY SOURCES

The Anonimalle Chronicle, 1333 to 1381: From a MS Written at St Mary's, ed. V. H. Galbraith (Manchester, 1970).

'Appendix II: The Confessions of Sir Thomas Gray of Heton, Richard, Earl of Cambridge and Henry, Lord Scrope of Masham', trans. T. B. Pugh, *Henry V and the Southampton Plot of 1415* (Gloucester, 1988), pp. 160–77.

A Book of London English 1384–1425, ed. R. W. Chambers and Marjorie Daunt (Oxford, 1931).

Calendar of the Close Rolls, 47 vols. (London, 1900–63).

Calendar of Letter-Books of the City of London: I, 1400–1422, ed. Reginald R. Sharpe (London, 1909).

Calendar of the Patent Rolls, 53 vols. (London, 1891–1916).

A Chronicle of London from 1089 to 1483; Written in the Fifteenth Century and for the First Time Printed from Mss. In the British Museum, ed. N. H. Nicolas and E. Tyrell (Felinfach, 1995).

Chronicles of London (1189–1509), ed. Charles Lethbridge Kingsford (Oxford, 1905).

Chronicles of the Revolution, 1397–1400: The Reign of Richard II, ed. and trans. Chris Given-Wilson (Manchester, 1993).

Chronique de Jean Le Bel, ed. Jules Marie Édouard Viard and Eugène Déprez (Paris, 1977).

Chronicque de la Traïson et Mort de Richart Deux Roy Dengleterre, ed. Benjamin Williams (London, 1846).

An English Chronicle, 1377–1461: Edited from Aberystwyth, National Library of Wales MS 21068 and Oxford, Bodleian Library MS Lyell 34, ed. William Marx (Woodbridge, 2003).

Eulogium Historiarum sive Temporis, 3 vols., ed. F. S. Haydon (London, 1858–63).

Fabyan, Robert, *The Great Chronicle of London*, ed. A. H. Thomas and I. D. Thornley (London, 1938).

Favent, Thomas, *History or Narration Concerning the Manner and Form of the Miraculous Parliament at Westminster in the Year 1386, the Tenth Year of the Reign of King Richard the Second after the Conquest, Declared by Thomas Favent, Clerk*, trans. Andrew Galloway, in *The Letter of the Law: Legal Practice and Literary Production in Medieval England*, ed. Emily Steiner and Candace Barrington (Ithaca, 2002), pp. 231–52.

Gesta Henrici Quinti. The Deeds of Henry the Fifth, trans. Frank Taylor and John S. Roskell (Oxford, 1975).

Hardyng, John, *The Chronicle of John Hardyng*, ed. Henry Ellis (London, 1812).

Historia Vitae et Regni Ricardi Secundi, ed. George B. Stow (Philadelphia, 1977).

Hoccleve, Thomas, *Hoccleve's Works: I. The Minor Poems*, ed. Frederick J. Furnivall, Early English Text Society E. S. 61 (London, 1892).

Holmes, G. A., 'Judgement on the Younger Despenser, 1326', *The English Historical Review* 70 (1955), 261–7.

Knighton, Henry, *Knighton's Chronicle 1337–1396*, ed. and trans. G. H. Martin (New York, 1995).

Memorials of London and London Life in the 13th, 14th and 15th Centuries, ed. H. T. Riley (London, 1868).

The Parliament Rolls of Medieval England 1275–1504, ed. C. Given-Wilson, P. Brand, A. Curry, R. E. Horrox, G. Martin, W. M. Ormrod and J. R. S. Phillips, CD-ROM (Leicester, 2005).

Proceedings and Ordinances of the Privy Council of England: Volume 1, 10 Richard II MCCCLXXXVI to 11 Henry IV MCCCCX, ed. N. H. Nicolas (London, 1834).

Rymer's Foedera, 10 vols., ed. Thomas Rymer (London, 1739–45).

Select Cases in the Court of King's Bench, VII, ed. G. O. Sayles, Selden Society 88 (London, 1971).

Selections from English Wycliffite Writings, ed. Anne Hudson (Cambridge, 1978).

The Statutes of the Realm, 9 vols. (London, 1810–25).

The St Albans Chronicle: The Chronica Maiora of Thomas Walsingham. Volume I 1376–1394, ed. and trans. John Taylor, Wendy R. Childs and Leslie Watkiss (Oxford, 2003).

The St Albans Chronicle: The Chronica Maiora of Thomas Walsingham. Volume II 1394–1422, ed. and trans. John Taylor, Wendy R. Childs and Leslie Watkiss (Oxford, 2011).

'A True Copy of the Roll of Proceeding in an Appeale of Treason before the Conestable and Marshall between Thomas Lord Morley, Appellant, and John De Montague, Earle of Salisbury, Defendant, Anno Primi Henrici Quarti', ed. M. H. Keen and M. Warner, in *Chronology, Conquest and Conflict in Medieval England. Camden Miscellany XXXIV* (London, 1997), pp. 169–95.

Two Wycliffite Texts, ed. Anne Hudson, Early English Text Society O. S. 301 (Oxford, 1993).

Usk, Adam, *The Chronicle of Adam Usk 1377–1421*, ed. and trans. C. Given-Wilson. (Oxford, 1997).

The Westminster Chronicle, 1381–1394, ed. and trans. L. C. Hector and Barbara F. Harvey (New York, 1982).

SECONDARY WORKS

Ailes, M. J., 'The Medieval Male Couple and the Language of Homosociality', in *Masculinity in Medieval Europe*, ed. D. M. Hadley (London, 1999), pp. 214–37.

Allmand, C. T., *Henry V*. New ed. (New Haven, 1997).

Anderson, Benedict, *Imagined Communities: Reflections on the Origin and Spread of Nationalism*, Revised ed. (London, 1983).

Archer, Rowena E., and Simon Walker, eds, *Rulers and Ruled in Late Medieval England: Essays Presented to Gerald Harriss* (London, 1996).

Arnold, John, 'The Historian as Inquisitor: The Ethics of Interrogating Subaltern Voices', *Rethinking History* 2 (1998), 379–86.

——, *Inquisition and Power: Catharism and the Confessing Subject in Medieval Languedoc* (Philadelphia, 2001).

——, 'Lollard Trials and Inquisitorial Discourse', in *Fourteenth Century England II*, ed. Chris Given-Wilson (Woodbridge, 2004), pp. 81–94.

Arvanigian, Mark, 'Henry IV, the Northern Nobility and the Consolidation of the Regime', in *Henry IV: The Establishment of the Regime, 1399–1406*, ed. Gwilym Dodd and Douglas Biggs (York, 2003) pp. 117–37.

Aston, Margaret E., 'Lollardy and Sedition 1381–1431', *Past & Present* 17 (1960), 1–44.

Aston, Margaret, and Colin Richmond, eds, *Lollardy and the Gentry in the Later Middle Ages* (New York, 1997).

Bagerius, Henric, and Christine Ekholst, 'Kings and Favourites: Politics and Sexuality in Late Medieval Europe', *Journal of Medieval History* 43 (2017), 298–319.

Baker, John H., *An Introduction to English Legal History*, 2nd ed. (London, 1979).

——, *The Common Law Tradition: Lawyers, Books, and the Law* (London, 2000).

Bardsley, Sandy, 'Sin, Speech, and Scolding in Late Medieval England', in *Fama: The Politics of Talk and Reputation*, ed. Thelma Fenster and Daniel Lord Smail (Ithaca, 2003), pp. 145–64.

——, *Venomous Tongues: Speech and Gender in Late Medieval England* (Philadelphia, 2006).

Barr, Helen, and Ann M. Hutchison, eds, *Text and Controversy from Wyclif to Bale. Essays in Honour of Anne Hudson* (Turnhout, 2005).

Barron, C. M., 'The Tyranny of Richard II', *Bulletin of the Institute for Historical Research* 41 (1968), 1–18.

Barron, Caroline, 'The Deposition of Richard II', in *Politics and Crisis in Fourteenth-Century England*, ed. John Taylor and Wendy R. Childs (Gloucester, 1990), pp. 132–49.

Bartlett, Robert, *Trial by Fire and Water: The Medieval Judicial Ordeal* (Oxford, 1986).

——, 'Medieval and Modern Concepts of Race and Ethnicity', *Journal of Medieval and Early Modern Studies* 31 (2001), 39–56.

Bean, J. M. W., 'Henry IV and the Percies', *History* 44 (1959), 212–27.

Bellamy, John G., *The Law of Treason in England in the Later Middle Ages* (Cambridge, 1970).

——, *Crime and Public Order in England in the Later Middle Ages* (London, 1973).

——, *The Tudor Law of Treason: An Introduction* (London, 1979).

Bengtson, Jonathan, 'Saint George and the Formation of English Nationalism', *Journal of Medieval & Early Modern Studies* 27 (1997), 317–40.

Bennett, Michael, 'Edward III's Entail and the Succession to the Crown, 1376–1471', *The English Historical Review* 113 (1998), 580–609.

——, *Richard II and the Revolution of 1399* (Stroud, 1999).

——, 'Henry of Bolingbroke and the Revolution of 1399', in *Henry IV: The Establishment of the Regime*, ed. Dodd and Biggs, pp. 9–33.

——, 'Henry IV, the Royal Succession and the Crisis of 1406', in *The Reign of Henry IV: Rebellion and Survival, 1403–1413*, ed. Dodd and Biggs, pp. 9–27.

Biggs, Douglas, 'The Politics of Health: Henry IV and the Long Parliament of 1406', in *Henry IV: The Establishment of the Regime*, ed. Dodd and Biggs, pp. 185–203.

——, 'An Ill and Infirm King: Henry IV, Health, and the Gloucester Parliament of 1407', in *The Reign of Henry IV: Rebellion and Survival*, ed. Dodd and Biggs, pp. 180–209.

Billoré, Maïté, and Myriam Soria, eds, *La trahison au Moyen Âge: De la monstruosité au crime politique (Ve–XVe siècle)* (Rennes, 2009).

Black, Antony, *Political Thought in Europe, 1250–1450* (Cambridge, 1992).

Bose, Mishtooni, and J. Patrick Hornbeck II, eds, *Wycliffite Controversies* (Turnhout, 2011).

Bothwell, James, *Falling from Grace: Reversal of Fortune and the English Nobility 1075–1455* (Manchester, 2008).

Brand, Paul, 'The Languages of the Law in Later Medieval England', in *Multilingualism in Later Medieval Britain*, ed. D. A. Trotter (Cambridge, 2000), pp. 63–76.

Britnell, R. H., and A. J. Pollard, eds, *The McFarlane Legacy: Studies in Late Medieval Politics and Society* (New York, 1995).

Broad, Jacqueline and Karen Green, *A History of Women's Political Thought in Europe: 1400–1700* (Cambridge, 2014).

Broomhall, Susan and Jacqueline Van Gent, eds, *Governing Masculinities in the Early Modern Period: Regulating Selves and Others* (Farnham, 2011).

Burgtorf, Jochen, '"With My Life, His Joyes Began and Ended": Piers Gaveston and King Edward II of England Revisited', in *Fourteenth Century England V*, ed. Nigel Saul (Woodbridge, 2008), pp. 31–51.

Burgwinkle, William E., *Sodomy, Masculinity, and Law in Medieval Literature: France and England, 1050–1230* (New York, 2004).

Butterfield, Ardis, *The Familiar Enemy: Chaucer, Language, and Nation in the Hundred Years War* (Oxford, 2009).

Cadden, Joan, *Meanings of Sex Difference in the Middle Ages: Medicine, Science, and Culture* (Cambridge, 1993).

Canning, Joseph, *Ideas of Power in the Late Middle Ages, 1296–1417* (New York, 2011).

Carpenter, Christine, 'Political History and Constitutional History: Before and After McFarlane', in *The McFarlane Legacy*, ed. Britnell and Pollard, pp. 175–206.

——, *The Wars of the Roses: Politics and the Constitution in England, c. 1437–1509* (Cambridge, 1997).

Cassidy-Welch, Megan, 'Testimonies from a Fourteenth-Century Prison: Rumour, Evidence and Truth in the Midi', *French History* 16 (2002), 3–27.

Castor, Helen, *The King, the Crown, and the Duchy of Lancaster: Public Authority and Private Power, 1399–1461* (New York, 2000).

Cheney, C. R., ed., *A Handbook of Dates for Students of British History*. Revised by Michael Jones. New ed. (Cambridge, 2000).

Chiffoleau, Jacques, 'Dire l'indicible. Remarques sur la catégorie du nefandum du XIIe au XVe siècle', *Annales. Histoire, Sciences Sociales* 45 (1990), 289–324.

Chrimes, S. B., 'Richard II's Questions to the Judges, 1387', *Law Quarterly Review* 72 (1956), 365–90.

Clanchy, Michael T., *From Memory to Written Record: England 1066–1307* (London, 1979).

Clark, James G., 'Thomas Walsingham Reconsidered: Books and Learning at Late-Medieval St. Albans', *Speculum* 77 (2002), 832–60.

Clark, Linda, ed., *The Fifteenth Century III: Authority and Subversion* (Woodbridge, 2003).

——, *The Fifteenth Century VI: Identity and Insurgency in the Late Middle Ages* (Woodbridge, 2006).

Clark, Linda, and Christine Carpenter, eds, *The Fifteenth Century IV: Political Culture in Late Medieval Britain* (Woodbridge, 2004).

Clarke, M. V., 'Forfeitures and Treason in 1388', *Transactions of the Royal Historical Society* 14 (1931), 65–94.

Clementi, D., 'Richard II's Ninth Question to the Judges', *The English Historical Review* 86 (1971), 96–113.

Cohen, Esther, 'Symbols of Culpability and the Universal Language of Justice: The Ritual of Public Executions in Late Medieval Europe', *History of European Ideas* 11 (1989), 407–16.

——, *The Crossroads of Justice: Law and Culture in Late Medieval France* (Leiden, 1993).

Cohen, Jeffrey Jerome, *Of Giants: Sex, Monsters, and the Middle Ages* (Minneapolis, 1999).

Cohen, Jeffrey Jerome, and Bonnie Wheeler, eds, *Becoming Male in the Middle Ages* (New York, 1997).

Coldstream, Nicola, '"Pavilion'd in Splendour": Henry V's Agincourt Pageants', *Journal of the British Archaeological Association* 165 (2012), 153–71.

Coleman, Joyce, *Public Reading and the Reading Public in Late Medieval England and France* (New York, 1996).

——, 'Aurality', *Middle English*, 199 (2007), 68–85.

Collette, Carolyn P., *Performing Polity: Women and Agency in the Anglo-French Tradition, 1385–1620* (Turnhout, 2006).

Collins, Hugh E. L., *The Order of the Garter, 1348–1461: Chivalry and Politics in Late Medieval England* (Oxford, 2000).

Connell, R. W., *Masculinities*, 2nd ed. (Berkeley, 2005).

Connell, R. W., and James W. Messerschmidt, 'Hegemonic Masculinity Rethinking the Concept', *Gender & Society* 19 (2005), 829–59.

Coss, P. R., 'Bastard Feudalism Revised', *Past & Present* 125 (1989), 27–64.

Craun, Edwin D., *Lies, Slander, and Obscenity in Medieval English Literature: Pastoral Rhetoric and the Deviant Speaker* (Cambridge, 1997).

Cressy, David, *Dangerous Talk: Scandalous, Seditious, and Treasonable Speech in Pre-Modern England* (New York, 2010).

Cronin, H. S., 'The Twelve Conclusions of the Lollards', *The English Historical Review* 22 (1907), 292–304

Cullum, P. H., and Katherine J. Lewis, eds, *Religious Men and Masculine Identity in the Middle Ages* (Woodbridge, 2013).

Cunningham, Karen, *Imaginary Betrayals: Subjectivity and the Discourses of Treason in Early Modern England* (Philadelphia, 2002).

Cuttler, S. H., *The Law of Treason and Treason Trials in Later Medieval France* (Cambridge, 2003).

Davies, R. G., 'After the Execution of Archbishop Scrope: Henry IV, the Papacy and the English Episcopate, 1405–8', *Bulletin of the John Rylands University Library of Manchester* 59 (1976), 40–74.

Davies, Rees R., 'The Peoples of Britain and Ireland 1100–1400. III. Laws and Customs', *Transactions of the Royal Historical Society*, Sixth Series, 6 (1996), 1–23.

——, 'The Peoples of Britain and Ireland, 1100–1400. IV. Language and Historical Mythology', *Transactions of the Royal Historical Society*, Sixth Series, 7 (1997), 1–24.

——, *The Revolt of Owain Glyn Dŵr* (New York, 1997).

Davis, Isabel, *Writing Masculinity in the Later Middle Ages* (Cambridge, 2010).

Davis, Natalie Zemon, *Fiction in the Archives: Pardon Tales and Their Tellers in Sixteenth-Century France* (Stanford, 1987).

Dodd, Gwilym, 'A Parliament Full of Rats? *Piers Plowman* and the Good Parliament of 1376', *Historical Research* 79 (2006), 21–49.

——, *Justice and Grace: Private Petitioning and the English Parliament in the Late Middle Ages* (New York, 2007).

——, 'The Spread of English in the Records of Central Government, 1400–1430', in *Vernacularity in England and Wales, c.1300–1550*, ed. Salter and Wicker, pp. 225–66.

——, 'Thomas Paunfield, the "Heye Court of Rightwisnesse" and the Language of Petitioning in the Fifteenth Century', in *Medieval Petitions: Grace and Grievance*, ed. W. M. Ormrod, Gwilym Dodd and Anthony Musson (York, 2009), pp. 222–41.

——, ed., *Henry V: New Interpretations* (York, 2013).

——, 'Kingship, Parliament and the Court: The Emergence of "High Style" in Petitions to the English Crown, c.1350–1405', *The English Historical Review* 129 (2014), 515–48.

——, 'Languages and Law in Late Medieval England: English, French and Latin', in *The Cambridge Companion to Medieval Law and Literature*, ed. Candace Barrington and Sebastian Sobecki (Cambridge, 2019), pp. 17–29.

Dodd, Gwilym, and Douglas Biggs, eds, *Henry IV: The Establishment of the Regime, 1399–1406* (York, 2003).

——, eds, *The Reign of Henry IV: Rebellion and Survival, 1403–1413* (York, 2008).

Dodd, Gwilym, and Anthony Musson, eds, *The Reign of Edward II: New Perspectives* (York, 2006).

Doig, James A., 'Political Propaganda and Royal Proclamations in Late Medieval England', *Historical Research* 71 (1998), 253–80.

Dudink, Stefan, 'The Trouble with Men: Problems in the History of "Masculinity"', *European Journal of Cultural Studies* 1 (1998), 419–31.

Dumolyn, Jan, and Jelle Haemers, '"A Bad Chicken Was Brooding": Subversive Speech in Late Medieval Flanders', *Past & Present* 214 (2012), 45–86.

——, 'Political Poems and Subversive Songs. The Circulation of "Public Poetry" in the Later Medieval Low Countries', *Journal of Dutch Literature* 5 (2015), 1–22.

Dumolyn, Jan, Jelle Haemers, Hipólito Rafael Oliva Herrer and Vincent Challet, eds, *The Voices of the People in Late Medieval Europe: Communication and Popular Politics* (Turnhout, 2014).

Dunham, William Huse, Jr., and Charles T. Wood, 'The Right to Rule in England: Depositions and the Kingdom's Authority, 1327–1485', *The American Historical Review* 81 (1976), 738–61.

Dunn, A. H., 'Henry IV and the Politics of Resistance in Early Lancastrian England, 1399–1413', in *The Fifteenth Century III*, ed. Clark, pp. 5–23.

Dunn, Alistair, 'Richard II and the Mortimer Inheritance', in *Fourteenth Century England II*, ed. Chris Given-Wilson (Woodbridge, 2002), pp. 159–70.

Dunn, Caroline, 'The Language of Ravishment in Medieval England', *Speculum* 86 (2011), 79–116.

Earenfight, Theresa, *The King's Other Body: María of Castile and the Crown of Aragon* (Philadelphia, 2010).

——, 'Where Do We Go From Here? Some Thoughts on Power and Gender in the Middle Ages', *Medieval Feminist Forum: A Journal of Gender and Sexuality* 51 (2016), 116–31.

Erler, Mary, and Maryanne Kowaleski, eds, *Gendering the Master Narrative: Women and Power in the Middle Ages* (Ithaca, 2003).

Fletcher, Christopher D., 'Narrative and Political Strategies at the Deposition of Richard II', *Journal of Medieval History* 30 (2004), 323–41.

——, 'Manhood and Politics in the Reign of Richard II', *Past & Present* 189 (2005), 3–39.

——, *Richard II: Manhood, Youth, and Politics, 1377–99* (Oxford, 2008).

——, 'The Whig Interpretation of Masculinity? Honour and Sexuality in Late Medieval Manhood', in *What Is Masculinity?*, ed. John H. Arnold and Sean Brady (Basingstoke, 2011), pp. 57–75.

——, 'Langue et nation en Angleterre à la fin du moyen âge', *Revue Francaise d'histoire des idées politiques* 2 (2012), 233–52.

Fletcher, Christopher, Sean Brady, Rachel E. Moss and Lucy Riall, eds, *The Palgrave Handbook of Masculinity and Political Culture in Europe* (London, 2018).

Forde, Simon, Lesley Johnson and Alan V. Murray, eds, *Concepts of National Identity in the Middle Ages* (Leeds, 1995).

Forrest, Ian, *The Detection of Heresy in Late Medieval England* (Oxford, 2005).

——, 'Lollardy and Late Medieval History', in *Wycliffite Controversies*, ed. Bose and Hornbeck, pp. 121–34.

——, *Trustworthy Men: How Inequality and Faith Made the Medieval Church* (Princeton, 2018).

Galbraith, Vivian H., 'Thomas Walsingham and the Saint Albans Chronicle, 1272–1422', *The English Historical Review* 47 (1932), 12–30.

Gellner, Ernest, *Nations and Nationalism* (Ithaca, 1983).

Genêt, Jean-Philippe, *La genèse de l'État moderne: Culture et société politique en Angleterre* (Paris, 2003).

Giancarlo, Matthew, 'Murder, Lies, and Storytelling: The Manipulation of Justice(s) in the Parliaments of 1397 and 1399', *Speculum* 77 (2002), 76–112.

Gillingham, John, 'Killing and Mutilating Political Enemies in the British Isles from the Late Twelfth to the Early Fourteenth Century: A Comparative Study', in *Britain and Ireland, 900–1300: Insular Responses to Medieval European Change*, ed. Brendan Smith (Cambridge, 1999), pp. 114–34.

Given-Wilson, Chris, *The Royal Household and the King's Affinity: Service, Politics, and Finance in England, 1360–1413* (New Haven, 1986).

——, 'The Manner of King Richard's Renunciation: A "Lancastrian Narrative"?', *The English Historical Review* 108 (1993), 365–70.

——, 'Adam Usk, the Monk of Evesham and the Parliament of 1397–8', *Historical Research* 66 (1993), 329–35.

——, 'The Rolls of Parliament, 1399–1421', *Parliamentary History* 23 (2004), 57–72.

——, 'Legitimation, Designation and Succession to the Throne in Fourteenth-Century England', in *Building Legitimacy: Political Discourses and Forms of Legitimacy in Medieval Societies*, ed. Isabel Alfonso, Hugh Kennedy and Julio Escalona (Leiden, 2004), pp. 89–105.

——, *Henry IV* (New Haven, 2016).

Goldberg, P. J. P., 'Masters and Men in Later Medieval England', in *Masculinity in Medieval Europe*, ed. Hadley, pp. 56–70.

Goodich, Michael, *The Unmentionable Vice: Homosexuality in the Later Medieval Period* (Santa Barbara, 1979).

——, ed. *Voices from the Bench: The Narratives of Lesser Folk in Medieval Trials* (New York, 2006).

Goodman, Anthony, *The Loyal Conspiracy: The Lords Appellant under Richard II* (Coral Gables, 1971).

——, *John of Gaunt: The Exercise of Princely Power in Fourteenth-Century Europe* (New York, 1992).

Goodman, Anthony, and James L. Gillespie, eds, *Richard II: The Art of Kingship* (Oxford, 1999).

Green, Richard Firth, *A Crisis of Truth: Literature and Law in Ricardian England* (Philadelphia, 1999).

Green, Thomas A., 'Societal Concepts of Criminal Liability for Homicide in Mediaeval England', *Speculum* 47 (1972), 669–94.

——, *Verdict According to Conscience: Perspectives on the English Criminal Trial Jury, 1200–1800* (Chicago, 1985).

Griffiths, Ralph A., ed., *Patronage, the Crown and the Provinces in Later Medieval England* (Gloucester, 1981).

——, *'This Royal Throne of Kings, This Scept'red Isle': The English Realm and Nation in the Later Middle Ages* (Swansea, 1983).

Guenée, Bernard, *States and Rulers in Later Medieval Europe*, trans. Juliet Vale (Oxford, 1985).

Hadley, D. M., ed., *Masculinity in Medieval Europe* (London, 1999).

Haemers, Jelle, 'Filthy and Indecent Words. Insults, Defamation, and Urban Politics in the Southern Low Countries, 1300–1550', in *The Voices of the People*, ed. Dumolyn, Haemers, Herrer and Challet, pp. 247–67.

Hall, Dianne, 'Words as Weapons: Speech, Violence, and Gender in Late Medieval Ireland', *Éire-Ireland* 41 (2006), 122–41.

Hanawalt, Barbara A., *Of Good and Ill Repute: Gender and Social Control in Medieval England* (New York, 1998).

Hanrahan, Michael, 'Seduction and Betrayal: Treason in the *Prologue* to the *Legend of Good Women*', *The Chaucer Review* 30 (1996), 229–40.

——, 'Speaking of Sodomy: Gower's Advice to Princes in the *Confessio Amantis*', *Exemplaria* 14 (2002), 423–46.

Harris, E. Kay, 'Censoring Disobedient Subjects: Narratives of Treason and Royal Authority in Fifteenth-Century England', in *Reputation and Representation in Fifteenth-Century Europe*, ed. Douglas L. Biggs, Sharon D. Michalove and A. Compton Reeves (Leiden, 2004), pp. 211–33.

Harriss, G. L., ed., *Henry V: The Practice of Kingship* (New York, 1985).

——, 'The Dimensions of Politics', in *The McFarlane Legacy*, ed. Britnell and Pollard, pp. 1–20.

——, *Shaping the Nation: England 1360–1461* (New York, 2005).

Harvey, I. M. W., 'Was There Popular Politics in Fifteenth-Century England?', in *The McFarlane Legacy*, ed. Britnell and Pollard, pp. 155–74.

Harvey, Karen, and Alexandra Shepard, 'What Have Historians Done with Masculinity? Reflections on Five Centuries of British History, circa 1500–1950', *Journal of British Studies* 44 (2005), 274–80.

Havens, Jill C. '"As Englishe Is Comoun Langage to Oure Puple": The Lollards and Their Imagined "English" Community', in *Imagining a Medieval English Nation*, ed. Kathy Lavezzo (Minneapolis, 2004), pp. 96–128.

Hicks, Michael A., *Bastard Feudalism* (London, 1995).

——, *English Political Culture in the Fifteenth Century* (London, 2002).

——, 'The Yorkshire Perjuries of Henry Bolingbroke in 1399 Revisited', *Northern History* 46 (2009), 31–41.

Hoppenbrouwers, Peter, Antheun Janse and Robert Stein, eds, *Power and Persuasion: Essays on the Art of State Building in Honour of W. P. Blockmans* (Turnhout, 2010).

Horrox, Rosemary, 'Service', in *Fifteenth-Century Attitudes: Perceptions of Society in Late Medieval England*, ed. Rosemary Horrox (Cambridge, 1994), pp. 61–78.

Hudson, Anne, 'The Examination of Lollards', *Historical Research* 46 (1973), 145–59.

——, *Lollards and Their Books* (London, 1985).

——, *The Premature Reformation: Wycliffite Texts and Lollard History* (New York, 1988).

Hunnisett, R. F., and J. B. Post, eds, *Medieval Legal Records: Edited in Memory of C. A. F. Meekings* (London, 1978).

Jefferson, Judith Anne, and Ad Putter, eds, *Multilingualism in Medieval Britain (c. 1066–1520): Sources and Analysis* (Turnhout, 2013).

Johnson, Tom, 'The Preconstruction of Witness Testimony: Law and Social Discourse in England before the Reformation', *Law and History Review* 32 (2014), 127–47.

Jones, Richard H., *The Royal Policy of Richard II: Absolutism in the Later Middle Ages* (Oxford, 1968).

Jordan, Mark D., *The Invention of Sodomy in Christian Theology* (Chicago, 1998).

Jurkowski, Maureen, 'New Light on John Purvey', *The English Historical Review* 110 (1995), 1180–90.

——, 'Heresy and Factionalism at Merton College in the Early Fifteenth Century', *The Journal of Ecclesiastical History* 48 (1997), 658–81.

——, 'Lawyers and Lollardy in the Early Fifteenth Century', in *Lollardy and the Gentry*, ed. Aston and Richmond, pp. 155–82.

——, 'The Arrest of William Thorpe in Shrewsbury and the Anti-Lollard Statute of 1406', *Historical Research* 75 (2002), 273–95.

——, 'Lollard Book Producers in London in 1414', in *Text and Controversy from Wyclif to Bale*, ed. Barr and Hutchison, pp. 201–26.

——, 'Lollard Networks', in *Wycliffite Controversies*, ed. Bose and Hornbeck, pp. 261–78.

——, 'Henry V's Suppression of the Oldcastle Revolt', in *Henry V: New Interpretations*, ed. Dodd, pp. 103–29.

Justice, Steven, 'Inquisition, Speech, and Writing: A Case from Late-Medieval Norwich', *Representations* 48 (1994), 1–29.

——, *Writing and Rebellion: England in 1381* (Los Angeles, 1996).

——, 'Lollardy', in *The Cambridge History of Medieval English Literature*, ed. Wallace, pp. 662–89.

Kaeuper, Richard W., *War, Justice, and Public Order: England and France in the Later Middle Ages* (Oxford, 1988).

——, *Chivalry and Violence in Medieval Europe* (Oxford, 1999).

——, ed., *Law, Governance, and Justice: New Views on Medieval Constitutionalism* (Leiden, 2013).

Kane, Bronach C., 'Defamation, Gender and Hierarchy in Late Medieval Yorkshire', *Social History* 43 (2018), 356–74.

Kantorowicz, Ernst H., *The King's Two Bodies: A Study in Mediaeval Political Theology* (Princeton, 1957).

Karras, Ruth Mazo, *From Boys to Men: Formations of Masculinity in Late Medieval Europe* (Philadelphia, 2003).

——, *Sexuality in Medieval Europe: Doing Unto Others* (New York, 2005).

——, 'The Lechery That Dare Not Speak Its Name: Sodomy and the Vices in Medieval England', in *In the Garden of Evil: The Vices and Culture in the Middle Ages*, ed. Richard Newhauser (Toronto, 2005), pp. 193–205.

Keen, Maurice H., 'Treason Trials under the Law of Arms: The Alexander Prize Essay', *Transactions of the Royal Historical Society*, Fifth Series, 12 (1962), 85–103.

——, *Chivalry* (New Haven, 1984).

——, *England in the Later Middle Ages: A Political History*, 2nd ed. (London, 2003).

King, Andy, '"They Have the Hertes of the People by North": Northumberland, the Percies and Henry IV, 1399–1408', in *Henry IV: The Establishment of the Regime*, ed. Dodd and Biggs, pp. 139–59.

——, 'False Traitors or Worthy Knights? Treason and Rebellion against Edward II in the *Scalacronica* and the Anglo-Norman Prose *Brut* Chronicles', *Historical Research* 88 (2015), 34–47.

Kingsford, C. L., 'A Legend of Sigismund's Visit to England', *The English Historical Review* 26 (1911), 750–1.

——, 'The First Version of Hardyng's Chronicle', *The English Historical Review* 27 (1912), 462–82.

Kirby, John L., *Henry IV of England* (London, 1970).

Kruger, Steven F., 'Conversion and Medieval Sexual, Religious, and Racial Categories', in *Constructing Medieval Sexuality*, ed. Karma Lochrie, Peggy McCracken and James A. Schultz (Minneapolis, 1998), pp. 158–79.

Kuefler, Mathew, 'Male Friendship and the Suspicion of Sodomy in Twelfth-Century France', in *Gender and Difference in the Middle Ages*, ed. Sharon A. Farmer and Carol Braun Pasternack (Minneapolis, 2003), pp. 145–81.

Lacey, Helen, *The Royal Pardon: Access to Mercy in Fourteenth-Century England* (York, 2009).

Langbein, John H., *Torture and the Law of Proof: Europe and England in the Ancien Régime* (Chicago, 1977).

Lecuppre-Desjardin, Élodie, 'Des portes qui parlent: Placards, feuilles volantes et communication politique dans les villes des Pays-Bas à la fin du moyen âge', *Bibliothèque de l'école des chartes* 168 (2010), 151–72.

Lees, Clare A., Thelma S. Fenster and Jo Ann McNamara, eds, *Medieval Masculinities: Regarding Men in the Middle Ages* (Minneapolis, 1994).

Leitch, Megan, *Romancing Treason: The Literature of the Wars of the Roses* (Oxford, 2015).

Lemon, Rebecca, *Treason by Words: Literature, Law, and Rebellion in Shakespeare's England* (Ithaca, 2006).

Levy, Leonard W., *Treason against God: A History of the Offense of Blasphemy* (New York, 1981).

Lewis, Katherine J., 'Becoming a Virgin King: Richard II and Edward the Confessor', in *Gender and Holiness: Men, Women, and Saints in Late Medieval Europe*, ed. Sam Riches and Sarah Salih (London, 2002), pp. 86–100.

——, *Kingship and Masculinity in Late Medieval England* (New York, 2013).

Liddle, Mark, 'State, Masculinities and Law: Some Comments on Gender and English State-Formation', *British Journal of Criminology* 36 (1996), 361–80.

Liddy, Christian D., '"Sir Ye Be Not Kyng": Citizenship and Speech in Late Medieval and Early Modern England', *The Historical Journal* 60 (2017), 571–96.

Lindenbaum, Sheila, 'London Texts and Literate Practice', in *The Cambridge History of Medieval English Literature*, ed. Wallace, pp. 284–309.

Maddern, Philippa, 'Honour among the Pastons: Gender and Integrity in Fifteenth-Century English Provincial Society', *Journal of Medieval History* 14 (1988), 357–71.

Manning, Roger B., 'The Origins of the Doctrine of Sedition', *Albion* 12 (1980), 99–121.

Masschaele, James, *Jury, State, and Society in Medieval England* (New York, 2008).

McClintock, Anne, '"No Longer in a Future Heaven": Gender, Race and Nationalism', in *Dangerous Liaisons: Gender, Nation, and Postcolonial Perspectives*, ed. Anne McClintock, Aamir Mufti and Ella Shohat (Minneapolis, 1997), pp. 89–112.

McFarlane, K. B., *Lancastrian Kings and Lollard Knights* (Oxford, 1972).

McHardy, A. K., '*De Heretico Comburendo*, 1401', in *Lollardy and the Gentry*, ed. Aston and Richmond, pp. 112–26.

McKisack, May, *The Fourteenth Century: 1307–1399* (Oxford, 1959).

McNiven, Peter, 'The Scottish Policy of the Percies and the Strategy of the Rebellion of 1403', *Bulletin of the John Rylands Library* 62 (1980), 498–530.

——, 'Legitimacy and Consent: Henry IV and the Lancastrian Title, 1399–1406', *Mediaeval Studies* 44 (1982), 470–88.

——, 'The Problem of Henry IV's Health, 1405–1413', *The English Historical Review* 100 (1985), 747–72.

——, *Heresy and Politics in the Reign of Henry IV: The Burning of John Badby* (Woodbridge, 1987).

——, 'Rebellion, Sedition and the Legend of Richard II's Survival in the Reigns of Henry IV and Henry IV', *Bulletin of the John Rylands Library* 76 (1994), 93–117.

McSheffrey, Shannon, *Gender and Heresy: Women and Men in Lollard Communities, 1420–1530* (Philadelphia, 1995).

——, 'Men and Masculinity in Late Medieval London Civic Culture: Governance,

Patriarchy, and Reputation', *Conflicted Identities and Multiple Masculinities*, ed. Murray, pp. 243–78.

——, 'Sanctuary and the Legal Topography of Pre-Reformation London', *Law and History Review* 27 (2009), 483–514.

——, *Seeking Sanctuary: Crime, Mercy, and Politics in English Courts, 1400–1550* (Oxford, 2017).

McSheffrey, Shannon, and Julia Pope, 'Ravishment, Legal Narratives, and Chivalric Culture in Fifteenth-Century England', *Journal of British Studies* 48 (2009), 818–36.

McVitty, E. Amanda, 'False Knights and True Men: Contesting Chivalric Masculinity in English Treason Trials, 1388–1415', *Journal of Medieval History* 40 (2014), 458–77.

——, '"My Name of a Trewe Nan": Gender, Vernacularity, and Treasonous Speech in Late Medieval England', *Parergon* 33 (2016), 91–111.

——, 'Prosecuting Treason in Lancastrian London: The Language and Landscape of Political Dissent', in *Medieval Urban Culture*, ed. Andrew Brown and Jan Dumolyn, Studies in European Urban History 43 (Turnhout, 2017), pp. 93–109.

Meekings, C. A. F., 'Thomas Kerver's Case, 1444', *The English Historical Review* 90 (1975), 331–46.

Moffat, Ralph, '"Armed and Redy to Come to the Felde": Arming for the Judicial Duel in Fifteenth-Century England', in *Courts of Chivalry and Admiralty*, ed. Musson and Ramsay, pp. 121–33

Morgan, Philip, 'Henry IV and the Shadow of Richard II', in *Crown, Government and People in the Fifteenth Century*, ed. Rowena E. Archer (New York, 1995), pp. 1–31.

Mortimer, Ian, 'Sermons of Sodomy: A Reconsideration of Edward II's Sodomitical Reputation', in *The Reign of Edward II*, ed. Dodd and Musson, pp. 48–60.

Moss, Rachel E., 'Ready to Disport with You: Homosocial Culture amongst the Wool Merchants of Fifteenth-Century Calais', *History Workshop Journal* 86 (2018), 1–21.

Muir, Edward, and Guido Ruggiero, eds, *History from Crime* (Baltimore, 1994).

Murray, Jacqueline, ed. *Conflicted Identities and Multiple Masculinities: Men in the Medieval West* (New York, 1999).

Musson, Anthony, 'Turning King's Evidence: The Prosecution of Crime in Late Medieval England', *Oxford Journal of Legal Studies* 19 (1999), 467–79.

——, *Medieval Law in Context: The Growth of Legal Consciousness from Magna Carta to the Peasants' Revolt* (Manchester, 2001).

Musson, Anthony, and W. M. Ormrod, *The Evolution of English Justice: Law, Politics, and Society in the Fourteenth Century* (New York, 1999).

Musson, Anthony, and Nigel Ramsay, eds, *Courts of Chivalry and Admiralty in Late Medieval Europe* (Woodbridge, 2018).

Nagel, Joane, 'Masculinity and Nationalism – Gender and Sexuality in the Making of Nations', in *Nations and Nationalism: A Reader*, ed. Philip Spencer and Howard Wollman (Edinburgh, 2005), pp. 110–30.

Neal, Derek G., *The Masculine Self in Late Medieval England* (Chicago, 2008).

——, 'What Can Historians Do with Clerical Masculinity? Lessons from Medieval Europe', in *Negotiating Clerical Identities*, ed. Thibodeaux, pp. 16–36.

Neville, Cynthia J., 'The Law of Treason in the English Border Counties in the Later Middle Ages', *Law and History Review* 9 (1991), 1–30.

——, 'Common Knowledge of the Common Law in Later Medieval England', *Canadian Journal of History* 29 (1994), 462–78.

——, 'Scotland, the Percies and the Law in 1400', in *Henry IV: The Establishment of the Regime*, ed. Dodd and Biggs, pp. 73–93.

Oliver, Clementine, *Parliament and Political Pamphleteering in Fourteenth-Century England* (York, 2010).

Ormrod, W. Mark, *Political Life in Medieval England, 1300–1450* (New York, 1995).

——, 'The Use of English: Language, Law, and Political Culture in Fourteenth-Century England', *Speculum* 78 (2003), 750–87.

——, 'Knights of Venus', *Medium Aevum* 73 (2004), 290–305.

——, 'The Sexualities of Edward II', in *The Reign of Edward II*, ed. Dodd and Musson, pp. 22–47.

——, 'The Language of Complaint: Multilingualism and Petitioning in Later Medieval England', in *Language and Culture in Medieval Britain. The French of England c.1100–c.1500*, ed. Jocelyn Wogan-Browne (York, 2009), pp. 31–43.

Orr, D. Alan, *Treason and the State: Law, Politics and Ideology in the English Civil War* (Cambridge, 2002).

Oschema, Klaus, 'The Cruel End of the Favourite. Clandestine Death and Public Retaliation at Late Medieval Courts in England and France', in *Death at Court*, ed. Karl-Heinz Spiess and Immo Warntjes (Wiesbaden, 2012), pp. 171–95.

Phillips, Kim M., 'Masculinities and the Medieval English Sumptuary Laws', *Gender & History* 19 (2007), 22–42.

Pilbrow, Fionn, 'The Knights of the Bath: Dubbing to Knighthood in Lancastrian and Yorkist England', in *Heraldry, Pageantry and Social Display in Medieval England*, ed. Peter R. Coss and Maurice Keen (Woodbridge, 2002), pp. 195–218.

Plucknett, Theodore F. T., 'Presidential Address: State Trials under Richard II', *Transactions of the Royal Historical Society* 2 (1952), 159–71.

——, 'Presidential Address: Impeachment and Attainder', *Transactions of the Royal Historical Society* 3 (1953), 145–58.

Pollard, A. J., 'The Lancastrian Constitutional Experiment Revisited: Henry IV, Sir John Tiptoft and the Parliament of 1406', *Parliamentary History* 14 (1995), 103–19.

Pollard, Anthony J., 'The People, Politics and the Constitution in the Fifteenth Century', in *Law, Governance, and Justice*, ed. Kaeuper, pp. 311–29.

Pollock, F., and F. W. Maitland, *The History of English Law before the Time of Edward I*, 2 vols. (Cambridge, 1895–8).

Post, J. B., 'Jury Lists and Juries in the Late Fourteenth Century', in *Twelve Good Men and True: The Criminal Trial Jury in England, 1200–1800*, ed. J. S. Cockburn and Thomas Andrew Green, (Princeton, 1988), pp. 65–77.

Powell, Edward, *Kingship, Law, and Society: Criminal Justice in the Reign of Henry V* (Oxford, 1989).

——, 'The Strange Death of Sir John Mortimer: Politics and the Law of Treason in Lancastrian England', in *Rulers and Ruled in Late Medieval England*, ed. Archer and Walker, pp. 83–97.

——, 'The Restoration of Law and Order', in *Henry V: The Practice of Kingship*, ed. Harriss, pp. 53–74.

Pugh, T. B., *Henry V and the Southampton Plot of 1415* (Gloucester, 1988).

Pugh, Tison, '"For to Be Sworne Bretheren Til They Deye": Satirizing Queer Brotherhood in the Chaucerian Corpus', *The Chaucer Review* 43 (2009), 282–310.

Rex, Richard, *The Lollards* (New York, 2002).

Rexroth, Frank, *Deviance and Power in Late Medieval London* (Cambridge, 2007).

Rezneck, Samuel, 'Constructive Treason by Words in the Fifteenth Century', *The American Historical Review* 33 (1928), 544–52.

Richards, Jeffrey, *Sex, Dissidence, and Damnation: Minority Groups in the Middle Ages* (London, 1991).

Rogers, Alan, 'Parliamentary Appeals of Treason in the Reign of Richard II', *The American Journal of Legal History* 8 (1964), 95–124.

Roper, Michael, and John Tosh, eds, *Manful Assertions: Masculinities in Britain since 1800* (London, 1991).

Rose, Jonathan, 'Medieval Attitudes towards the Legal Profession: The Past as Prologue', *Stetson Law Review* 27 (1998), 345–69.

——, *Maintenance in Medieval England* (Cambridge, 2017).

Rosenthal, Joel T., 'The King's "Wicked Advisers" and Medieval Baronial Rebellions', *Political Science Quarterly* 82 (1967), 595–618.

Ross, Charles D., 'Forfeiture for Treason in the Reign of Richard II', *The English Historical Review* 71 (1956), 560–75.

Ross, James, 'Seditious Activities: The Conspiracy of Maud de Vere, Countess of Oxford, 1403–4', in *The Fifteenth Century III*, ed. Clark, pp. 25–41.

Rosser, Gervase, *Medieval Westminster, 1200–1540* (Oxford, 1989).

Rothwell, W., 'English and French in England after 1362', *English Studies* 82 (2001), 539–59.

Royer, Katherine, 'The Body in Parts: Reading the Execution Ritual in Late Medieval England', *Historical Reflections / Réflexions Historiques* 29 (2003), 319–39.

Ruddick, Andrea, 'Ethnic Identity and Political Language in the King of England's Dominions: A Fourteenth-Century Perspective', in *The Fifteenth Century VI*, ed. Clark, pp. 15–32.

——, *English Identity and Political Culture in the Fourteenth Century* (Cambridge, 2013).

Russell, Frederick H., *The Just War in the Middle Ages* (Cambridge, 1975).

Russell, M. J., 'Trial by Battle in the Court of Chivalry', *Journal of Legal History* 29 (2008), 335–57.

Salter, Elizabeth, and Helen Wicker, eds, *Vernacularity in England and Wales, c. 1300–1500* (Turnhout, 2011).

Saul, Nigel, 'Richard II and the Vocabulary of Kingship', *The English Historical Review* 110 (1995), 854–77.

——, *Richard II* (New Haven, 1997).

——, 'The Kingship of Richard II', in *Richard II: The Art of Kingship*, ed. Goodman and Gillespie, pp. 37–57.

Sayles, G. O., 'The Deposition of Richard II: Three Lancastrian Narratives', *Historical Research* 54 (1981), 257–70.

Scase, Wendy, '"Strange and Wonderful Bills": Bill-Casting and Political Discourse in Late Medieval England', *New Medieval Literatures* 2 (1998), 225–47.

——, 'The Audience and Framers of the Twelve Conclusions', in *Text and Controversy from Wyclif to Bale*, ed. Barr and Hutchison, pp. 283–301.

——, *Literature and Complaint in England, 1272–1553* (Oxford, 2007.

Schirmer, Elizabeth, '"Trewe Men": Pastoral Masculinity in Lollard Polemic', in *Masculinities and Femininities in the Middle Ages and Renaissance*, ed. Frederick Kiefer (Turnhout, 2009), pp. 117–29.

Schofield, John, *Medieval London Houses* (New Haven, 1994).

Scott, Joan W., 'Gender: A Useful Category of Historical Analysis', *The American Historical Review* 91 (1986), 1053–75.

Sherborne, James, 'Perjury and the Lancastrian Revolution of 1399', *Welsh History Review* 14 (1988), 217–41.

Simms, Norman, 'The Visit of King Sigismund to England, 1416', *Hungarian Studies Review* 17 (1990), 21–9.

Soergel, Philip M., ed., *Nation, Ethnicity, and Identity in Medieval and Renaissance Europe* (New York, 2006).

Somerset, Fiona, Jill C. Havens and Derrick G. Pitard, eds, *Lollards and Their Influence in Late Medieval England* (Woodbridge, 2003).

Squibb, G. D., *The High Court of Chivalry: A Study of the Civil Law in England* (New York, 1959).

Stamp, A. E., 'Richard II and the Death of the Duke of Gloucester', *The English Historical Review* 38 (1923), 249–51.

Steffen, Lisa, *Defining a British State: Treason and National Identity, 1608–1820* (New York, 2001).

Stone, Rachel, *Morality and Masculinity in the Carolingian Empire* (Cambridge, 2012).

Storey, Robert L., 'Clergy and Common Law in the Reign of Henry IV', in *Medieval Legal Records: Edited in Memory of C. A. F. Meekings*, ed. R. F. Hunnisett and J. B. Post (London, 1978), pp. 342–408.

Stow, George B., 'The Continuation of the *Eulogium Historiarum*: Some Revisionist Perspectives', *The English Historical Review* 119 (2004), 667–81.

——, 'Richard II in Thomas Walsingham's Chronicles', *Speculum* 59 (1984), 68–102.

Strickland, Matthew, 'A Law of Arms or a Law of Treason? Conduct in War in Edward I's Campaigns, 1296–1307', in *Violence in Medieval Society*, ed. Richard W. Kaeuper (Woodbridge, 2000), pp. 39–77.

Strohm, Paul, *Hochon's Arrow: The Social Imagination of Fourteenth-Century Texts* (Princeton, 1992).

——, 'The Trouble with Richard: The Reburial of Richard II and Lancastrian Symbolic Strategy', *Speculum* 71 (1996), 87–111.

——, *England's Empty Throne: Usurpation and the Language of Legitimation, 1399–1422* (New Haven, 1998).

Tait, James, 'Did Richard II Murder the Duke of Gloucester?', in *Historical Essays by Members of the Owens College, Manchester*, ed. T. F. Tout and James Tait (London, 1902), pp. 193–216.

Tarbin, Stephanie, 'Civic Manliness in London, c. 1380–1550', *Governing Masculinities*, ed. Broomhall and Van Gent, pp. 23–46.

Taylor, Craig David, 'Henry V, Flower of Chivalry', in *Henry V: New Interpretations*, ed. Dodd, pp. 217–47.

Taylor, John, 'Richard II in the Chronicles', in *Richard II: The Art of Kingship*, ed. Goodman and Gillespie, pp. 15–35.

Theilmann, John M., 'Political Canonization and Political Symbolism in Medieval England', *The Journal of British Studies* 29 (1990), 241–66.

——, 'Caught Between Political Theory and Political Practice: "The Record and Process of the Deposition of Richard II"', *History of Political Thought* 25 (2004), 599–619.

Thibodeaux, Jennifer D., ed. *Negotiating Clerical Identities: Priests, Monks and Masculinity in the Middle Ages* (New York, 2010).

Thiranagama, Sharika, and Tobias Kelly, eds, *Traitors: Suspicion, Intimacy, and the Ethics of State-Building* (Philadelphia, 2011).

Thornley, Isobel D., 'Treason by Words in the Fifteenth Century', *The English Historical Review* 32 (1917), 556–61.

——, 'The Act of Treasons, 1352', *History* 6 (1921), 106–8.

——, 'Sanctuary in Medieval London', *Journal of the British Archaeological Association* 38 (1932), 293–315.

Tosh, John, 'Hegemonic Masculinity and the History of Gender', in *Masculinities in Politics and War: Gendering Modern History*, ed. Stefan Dudink, Karen Hagemann and John Tosh (Manchester, 2004), pp. 41–58.

Tuck, Anthony, *Richard II and the English Nobility* (London, 1973).

——, 'Henry IV and Europe: A Dynasty's Search for Recognition', in *The McFarlane Legacy*, ed. Britnell and Pollard, pp. 107–25.

——, 'Henry IV and Chivalry', in *Henry IV: The Establishment of the Regime*, ed. Dodd and Biggs, pp. 55–72.

Valente, Claire, *The Theory and Practice of Revolt in Medieval England* (Burlington, 2003).

Van Dussen, Michael, *From England to Bohemia: Heresy and Communication in the Later Middle Ages* (Cambridge, 2012).

Van Eickels, Klaus, 'Gendered Violence: Castration and Blinding as Punishment for Treason in Normandy and Anglo-Norman England', *Gender & History* 16 (2004), 588–602.

Waldron, Ronald, 'Usk, Thomas (c.1354–1388)', *Oxford Dictionary of National Biography* (Oxford, 2008).

Walker, Simon, 'Political Saints in Later Medieval England', in *The McFarlane Legacy*, ed. Britnell and Pollard, pp. 77–106.

——, 'Janico Dartasso: Chivalry, Nationality and the Man-at-Arms', *History* 84 (1999), 31–51.

——, 'Rumour, Sedition and Popular Protest in the Reign of Henry IV', *Past & Present* 166 (2000), 31–65.

——, 'The Yorkshire Risings of 1405: Texts and Contexts', in *Henry IV: The Establishment of the Regime*, ed. Dodd and Biggs, pp. 161–84.

Wallace, David, ed., *The Cambridge History of Medieval English Literature* (Cambridge, 1999).

Watson, Nicholas, 'Censorship and Cultural Change in Late-Medieval England: Vernacular Theology, the Oxford Translation Debate, and Arundel's Constitutions of 1409', *Speculum* 70 (1995), 822–64.

Watts, John L., *Henry VI and the Politics of Kingship* (Cambridge, 1996).

——, 'The Pressure of the Public on Later Medieval Politics', in *The Fifteenth Century IV*, ed. Clark and Carpenter, pp. 159–80.

——, 'Public or Plebs: The Changing Meaning of "The Commons", 1381–1549', in *Power and Identity in the Middle Ages: Essays in Memory of Rees Davies*, ed. Huw Pryce and John Watts (Oxford, 2007), pp. 242–60.

——, *The Making of Polities: Europe, 1300–1500* (Cambridge, 2009).

Waugh, W. T., 'Sir John Oldcastle', *The English Historical Review* 20 (1905), 434–56.

——, 'Sir John Oldcastle (Continued)', *The English Historical Review* 20 (1905), 637–58.

Westerhof, Danielle, 'Deconstructing Identities on the Scaffold: The Execution of Hugh Despenser the Younger, 1326', *Journal of Medieval History* 33 (2007), 87–106.

——, *Death and the Noble Body in Medieval England* (Woodbridge, 2008).

Wicker, Helen, 'The Politics of Vernacular Speech: Cases of Treasonable Language, c. 1440–1453', in *Vernacularity in England and Wales*, ed. Salter and Wicker, pp. 171–97.

White, Stephen D., 'The Problem of Treason: The Trial of Daire Le Roux', in *Law, Laity, and Solidarities: Essays in Honour of Susan Reynolds*, ed. Pauline Stafford, Janet L. Nelson and Jane Martindale (Manchester, 2001), pp. 95–115.

Wilkinson, B., 'The Deposition of Richard II and the Accession of Henry IV', *The English Historical Review* 54 (1939), 215–39.

Wright, Edmund, 'Henry IV, the Commons and the Recovery of Royal Finance

in 1407', in *Rulers and Ruled in Late Medieval England*, ed. Archer and Walker, pp. 65–81.
Wright, H. G., 'Richard II and the Death of the Duke of Gloucester', *The English Historical Review* 47 (1932), 276–80.
Wylie, James Hamilton, *History of England under Henry the Fourth*, 4 vols. (London, 1884–98).
Wylie, James Hamilton, and W. T. Waugh, *The Reign of Henry V*, 3 vols. (Cambridge, 1914–29).

DIGITAL SOURCES

Anglo-Norman Dictionary, 7 vols., ed. Louise W. Stone, T. B. W. Reid and William Rothwell (London, 1977–1992). Accessed at the *Anglo-Norman Online Hub* http://www.anglo-norman.net/gate/index.shtml?session=S3160571301181156.
British History Online (2010). Accessed at https://www.british-history.ac.uk/
Jenks, Susanne, 'General Pardons'. Accessed at http://www.uh.edu/waalt/index.php/General_Pardons.
Kurath H. et al., *Middle English Dictionary* (Ann Arbor, 1954–2001). Accessed at https://quod.lib.umich.edu/m/middle-english-dictionary/dictionary

INDEX

GENDER IN THE MIDDLE AGES

I *Gender and Medieval Drama*, Katie Normington, 2004

II *Gender and Petty Crime in Late Medieval England: The Local Courts in Kent, 1460–1560*, Karen Jones, 2006

III *The Pastoral Care of Women in Late Medieval England*, Beth Allison Barr, 2008

IV *Gender, Nation and Conquest in the Works of William of Malmesbury*, Kirsten A. Fenton, 2008

V *Monsters, Gender and Sexuality in Medieval English Literature*, Dana M. Oswald, 2010

VI *Medieval Anchoritisms: Gender, Space and the Solitary Life*, Liz Herbert McAvoy, 2011

VII *Middle-Aged Women in the Middle Ages*, edited by Sue Niebrzydowski, 2011

VIII *Married Women and the Law in Premodern Northwest Europe*, edited by Cordelia Beattie and Matthew Frank Stevens, 2013

IX *Religious Men and Masculine Identity in the Middle Ages*, edited by P. H. Cullum and Katherine J. Lewis, 2013

X *Reconsidering Gender, Time and Memory in Medieval Culture*, edited by Elizabeth Cox, Liz Herbert McAvoy and Roberta Magnani, 2015

XI *Medicine, Religion and Gender in Medieval Culture*, edited by Naoë Kukita Yoshikawa, 2015

XII *The Unspeakable, Gender and Sexuality in Medieval Literature, 1000–1400*, Victoria Blud, 2017

XIII *Popular Memory and Gender in Medieval England: Men, Women, and Testimony in the Church Courts, c.1200–1500*, Bronach C. Kane, 2019

XIV *Authority, Gender and Space in the Anglo-Norman World, 900–1200*, Katherine Weikert, 2020

XV *Female Desire in Chaucer's* Legend of Good Women *and Middle English Romance*, Lucy M. Allen-Goss, 2020

Printed and bound by CPI Group (UK) Ltd, Croydon, CR0 4YY

15/09/2026

14962417-0002